TOP **10**
BARCELONA

ANNALISE SORENSEN
RYAN CHANDLER

EYEWITNESS TRAVEL

Left **Interior, Casa Lleó Morera** Right **La Rambla**

LONDON, NEW YORK,
MELBOURNE, MUNICH AND DELHI
www.dk.com

Produced by Departure Lounge, London

Reproduced by Colourscan, Singapore
Printed and bound in China by Leo Paper
Products Ltd

First published in Great Britain in 2002
by Dorling Kindersley Limited
80 Strand, London WC2R 0RL
A Penguin Company

A CIP catalogue record is available from the
British Library.

ISBN 978 1 40533 371 9

Within each Top 10 list in this book,
no hierarchy of quality or popularity is
implied. All 10 are, in the editor's opinion,
of roughly equal merit.

Contents

Barcelona's Top 10

Sagrada Família   8
La Rambla   12
Barcelona Cathedral   14
Parc de la Ciutadella   16
Museu Nacional d'Art de
Catalunya   18
La Pedrera   20
Fundació Joan Miró   22
Museu Picasso   24
Palau de la Música
Catalana   26
Museu d'Art Contemporani
& Centre de Cultura
Contemporánia   28
Stages in History   30
Modernista Buildings   32
Perfect Squares   36
Charming Churches &
Chapels   38
Museums   40
Cafés & Light Bites   42
Best Restaurants & Tapas
Bars   44
Night-time Hot Spots   46

Left **Jardins Mossèn Jacint Verdaguer** Centre **Bar, Pachito** Right **Terrace café, Barri Gòtic**

Gay & Lesbian Hang-outs   48
Best Shopping Areas   50
Most Fascinating Markets   52
City Views   54
Parks & Beaches   56
Walks & Bike Rides   58
Activities in Barcelona   60
Attractions for Children   62
Catalan Folk Festivals
& Traditions   64
Performing Arts & Music
Venues   66

Around Town
Barri Gòtic   70
El Raval   80
Montjuïc   88
Port Vell, Barceloneta &
Port Olímpic   96
Eixample   102
Grácia, Tibidabo &
Zona Alta   110
Beyond Barcelona   118

Streetsmart
Tips on Getting to
Barcelona   130
Tips on Getting Around
Barcelona   131
Ways to Explore
Catalonia   132
Tours & Tips   133
Sources of
Information   134
Communication Tips   135
Security & Health Tips   136
Banking & Money Tips   137
Eating & Drinking Tips   138
Shopping Tips   139
Barcelona on a Budget   140
Things to Avoid   141
Accomodation Tips   142
Places to Stay   143
General Index   150
Phrase Book   158

Left **Plaça de Sant Felip Neri, Barri Gòtic** Right **Stained-glass ceiling, Palau de la Música catalana**

Key to abbreviations
Adm *admission charge payable* **DA** *disabled access*

BARCELONA'S TOP 10

Barcelona's Highlights
6–7

Sagrada Família
8–11

La Rambla
12–13

Barcelona Cathedral
14–15

Parc de la ciutadella
16–17

Museu Nacional
d'Art de Catalunya
18–19

La Pedrera
20–21

Fundació Joan Miró
22–23

Museu Picasso
24–25

Palau de la
Música Catalana
26–27

Museu d'Art
Contemporani &
Centre de Cultura
Contemporània
28–29

Top 10 of Everything
30–67

BARCELONA'S TOP 10

📷10 Barcelona's Highlights

With warm, crystal-clear waters lapping its sandy shores and mountains nuzzling up to its northern edge, this glittering jewel in the Mediterranean is blessed with desirable geographical genes. From the buoyant, revamped port area to the atmospheric medieval streets of the Barri Gòtic and the beautiful Modernista *buildings of the Eixample, Barcelona has it all. A host of treasure-filled museums, architectural wonders, lively beaches and enchanting squares provide the icing on the cake.*

Sagrada Família
The enduring symbol of the city and its *Modernista* legacy is this church, Gaudí's other-worldly *pièce de résistance*. Piercing the Barcelona skyline are eight of the twelve planned spires *(above)* that have so far been built. *See pp8–10.*

La Rambla
Barcelona's centrepiece, this 1-km-(0.6-mile) long, thriving pedestrian thoroughfare *(above)* cuts a wide swathe through the old town, from Plaça de Catalunya to the glistening Mediterranean. *See pp12–13.*

Barcelona Cathedral
Dominating the heart of the old town is this magnificent Gothic Cathedral *(above)*, with a soaring, elaborate façade and a graceful, sun-dappled cloister containing palm trees and white geese. *See pp14–15.*

Parc de la Ciutadella
A verdant oasis in the city centre, Barcelona's largest park is crisscrossed with pleasant paths. It boasts a zoo, two museums, and a lavish *Modernista* fountain *(right)*. *See pp16–17.*

5 Museu Nacional d'Art de Catalunya

The stately Palau Nacional *(right)* is home to the Museu Nacional d'Art de Catalunya (MNAC), which holds one of the most extensive collections of Romanesque art in the world. The works were rescued from churches around Catalonia in the 1920s. *See pp18–19.*

6 La Pedrera

Unmistakably Gaudí, this *Modernista* marvel *(below)* seems to grow from the very pavement itself. Fluid and eerily alive, its curving façade sprouts writhing wrought-iron balconies. A cluster of mosaic chimneys keeps watch over the rooftop like shrewd-eyed knights. *See pp20–21.*

7 Fundació Joan Miró

An incomparable blend of art and architecture, this spacious museum, awash with natural light, showcases the work of Joan Miró, one of Catalonia's greatest 20th-century artists. Paintings, sculptures, drawings and textiles represent 60 prolific years. *See pp22–3.*

8 Museu Picasso

Housed in a medieval palace complex, this museum charts Picasso's rise to fame with an extensive collection of his early works, including numerous masterful portraits painted at the age of 13. *See pp24–5.*

9 Palau de la Música Catalana

No mere concert hall, the aptly named Palace of Catalan Music *(left)* is one of the finest, and most exemplary, *Modernista* buildings in Barcelona. *See pp26–7.*

10 Museu d'Art Contemporani & Centre de Cultura Contemporània

The city's gleaming contemporary art museum *(above)* and it's cutting-edge cultural centre have sparked an urban revival in the El Raval area. *See pp28–9.*

🔟 Sagrada Família

Nothing quite prepares you for the impact of the Sagrada Família up close. A fantastical tour de force of the imagination, Antoni Gaudí's ambitious church has provoked endless controversy. After a lifetime of dedication, the church was only partially complete when Gaudí died in 1926 and, as a work in progress, it offers the unique chance to watch the eighth wonder of the world in the making. During the last 80 years and at incalculable cost, sculptors and architects have added their own touches to Gaudí's dream. Now financed by over a million visitors each year, it is estimated the project will be complete by 2030.

Passion Façade

🍷 Try sitting in a terrace bar on nearby Avinguda Gaudí and drinking in the view of Gaudi's masterpiece illuminated at night.

📷 For the best photos, get to the temple before 8am: the light on the Nativity Façade is excellent and the tour buses haven't yet arrived.

Look out for the cryptogram on the Passion Façade, where all the numbers add up to the age of Christ at the time of his death.

• Entrances: C/Marina & C/Sardenya • Map G2
• 93 207 30 31
• www.sagradafamilia.org
• Metro: Sagrada Família.
• Open: Oct–Mar: 9am–6pm daily; Apr–Sep: 9am–8pm daily
• Adm: €8 • Guided tours: May–Oct: 11am, 1pm, 3pm & 5pm daily; Nov–Apr: 11am & 1pm daily • €3.50
• Limited DA

Top 10 Features

1. Nativity Façade
2. Passion Façade
3. Spiral Staircases
4. Spires
5. Hanging Model
6. Nave
7. Rosedoor Cloister
8. Crypt Museum
9. Apse
10. Unfinished Business

1 Nativity Façade

Gaudí's love of nature is visible in this façade *(above)*. Up to a hundred plant and animal species are sculpted into the stone, and the two main columns are supported by turtles.

2 Passion Façade

Started in 1978 and completed in 2002, this façade by Josep Subirachs represents the pain and sacrifice of Jesus. The difference between the Gothic feel of Subirachs' style and the intricacy of Gaudí's original work has not been without polemic.

3 Spiral Staircases

These helicoidal stone stairways, which wind up the bell towers, look like snail shells. They allow access to the towers.

4 Spires

For a close-up look at the gargoyles and mosaic tiling on the spires *(left)*, scale the bell tower stairs – or ride up in a lift. The views are equally spectacular *(see p55)*. Not for sufferers of vertigo.

For more churches in Barcelona See pp38–9

Hanging Model
5 This bizarre contraption in the crypt museum is testimony to Gaudí's ingenuity. Gaudí created this 3D construction – made of chains and small weighted sacks of sand – as a model for the arches and vaulted ceilings of the Colonia Güell crypt. No-one, in the history of architecture, had ever designed a building like this.

Sagrada Familia Floor Plan

Nave
6 The immense central body of the temple, still in progress, is made up of leaning, tree-like columns with branches spreading out across the ceiling. Inspired by towering redwood trees, the overall effect is that of a stone forest.

Rosedoor Cloister
7 In the only cloister to be finished by Gaudí, the imagery is surprisingly modern. Thought to be inspired by the anarchist riots that began in 1909 (see pp30–31), the devil's temptation of man is represented by the sculpture of a serpent wound around a bomb-throwing rebel.

Crypt Museum
8 Gaudí now lies in the crypt (left) and his tomb is visible from the museum. Recently renovated to include a small cinema, the museum offers information about the temple's construction. The highlight is the maquette workshop, producing scale plaster and stone models for the ongoing work.

Apse
9 Adorned with lizards, serpents and two gigantic snails, the apse was the first section of the temple to be completed by Gaudí.

Unfinished Business
10 The church buzzes with activity: sculptors dangle from spires; stone masons carve huge slabs of stone; and cranes and scaffolding litter the site. Observing the construction in progress (left) enables visitors to grasp the monumental scale of the project.

Sight Guide

The entrances to the Sagrada Família are on C/Sardenya (along with the gift shop and one of the bell tower lifts) and C/Marina. On the C/Marina side, there are stairs (and another lift) to the other bell towers, and stairs to the museum below. If you don't want to pay the charge to use the lifts (€2), be warned – it's quite a climb.

Left **Spiral staircase** Right **Detail of doorway, Passion Façade**

Key Sagrada Família Dates

1 **1882**
The first stone of the Sagrada Família is officially laid, with architect Francesc del Villar heading the project. Villar soon resigns after disagreements with the church's religious founders.

2 **1883**
The young, up-and-coming Antoni Gaudí is commissioned as the principal architect. He goes on to devote the next 40 years of his life to the project: by the end he even lives on the premises.

3 **1889**
The crypt is completed, ringed by a series of chapels, one of which is later to house the tomb of Gaudí.

4 **1904**
The final touches are made to the Nativity Façade, which depicts Jesus, Mary and Joseph amid a chorus of angels.

5 **1925**
The first of 18 bell towers, 100 m (328 ft) in height, is finished.

6 **1926**
On 10 June, Gaudí is killed by a tram while crossing the street near his beloved church. No-one recognizes the city's most famous architect.

7 **1936**
The advent of the Spanish Civil War brings construction of the Sagrada Família to a halt for some 20 years. During this time, Gaudí's studio and the crypt in the Sagrada Família are burned by revolutionaries, who despise the Catholic church for siding with the nationalists.

8 **1987–1990**
Artist Josep Maria Subirachs (b 1927) takes to living in the Sagrada Família just as his famous predecessor did. Subirachs completes the statuary of the Passion Façade. His angular, severe and striking sculptures draw both criticism and praise.

9 **2000**
On 31 December, the nave is at long last declared complete.

10 **2010–2030**
The whole nave and apse is projected to be fully roofed by 2010. The completion of the entire Sagrada Família is forecast for 2030, though this depends largely on funding. The building of the Sagrada Família – as Gaudí intended – relies on donations from the public. With so many paying visitors pouring in daily, construction work is gaining momentum.

Stained-glass window

For more on Modernista *architecture* **See pp32–3**

Top 10 Gaudí Sights in Barcelona

1. Sagrada Família
2. La Pedrera (1910)
   See pp20–21
3. Parc Güell (1900)
   See p112
4. Casa Batlló (1905)
   See p33
5. Palau Güell (1890)
   See p81
6. Bellesguard (1875)
7. Finca Güell (1887)
8. Casa Calvet (1899)
9. Colegio Teresiano (1890)
10. Casa Vicens (1885)

Antoni Gaudí

A flag bearer for the late 19th-century Modernista movement, Antoni Gaudí is Barcelona's most famous architect. A devout Catholic and a strong Catalan nationalist, he led an almost monastic existence, consumed by his architectural vision and living in virtual poverty for most of his life. In 2001, he was beatified and there are currently moves within the Catalan Catholic Church to declare him a saint.

Chimneypot, Casa Vicens

Gaudí's extraordinary legacy dominates the architectural map of Barcelona. His name itself comes from the Catalan verb gaudir, "to enjoy", and an enormous sense of exuberance and playfulness pervades his work. As was characteristic of Modernisme, nature prevails, not only in the decorative motifs, but also in the very structure of Gaudí's buildings. His highly innovative style is also characterized by intricate wrought-iron gates and balconies and trencadís tiling.

Trencadís Tiling

Gaudí's revolutionary use of *trencadís* tiling, a decorative art form which consisted of smashing up ceramics and piecing them back together in mosaic patterns, is particularly prevalent at Parc Güell. Another fine example of this technique is the rooftop of La Pedrera where some of the chimneys were tiled using hundreds of broken *cava* bottles.

Antoni Gaudí (1852–1926)

Trencadís tiled lizard, Parc Güell

TOP 10 La Rambla

There may be no better place in the country to indulge in the Spanish ritual of the paseo (stroll) than on this wide, pedestrian street that is anything but pedestrian. An orgy of activity day and night, La Rambla is voyeuristic heaven. Spray-painted human statues stand motionless among the passing crowds; buskers croon crowd-pleasing classics; caricaturists deftly sketch faces; bustling stalls create an open-air market of bright bouquets and chattering parakeets; and round-the-clock kiosks sell everything from The Financial Times to porn videos.

Street performer

🅞 Kick back at the Cafè de l'Òpera at No. 74 *(see p42)* and soak up the Rambla ambience with a cool *granissat* (crushed ice drink) in hand.

🅒 Be warned: La Rambla is rife with pick-pockets.

•Map L2–L6 • Metro: Catalunya; Liceu; Drassanes. • Gran Teatre del Liceu: open 11:30am–1pm daily (€4); guided tour of the main building: 10am (€8.30); guided backstage tour of the stage, rehearsal rooms, wardrobe and make-up room: 9:30am (€10); box office: open 1:30–8pm Mon–Fri, one hour before the performance Sat–Sun • Mercat de La Boqueria: open 7am–8pm Mon–Sat • DA • Palau de la Virreina: open 11am–2pm, 4–8:30pm Tue–Sat, 11am–3pm Sun; free • DA • Centre d'Art Santa Mònica: open 11am–8pm Tue–Sat, 11am–3pm Sun; free • Església de Betlem: open 8am–1:30pm & 5:30–8pm daily

Top 10 Attractions

1. Gran Teatre del Liceu
2. Monument a Colom
3. Mercat de La Boqueria
4. Flower & Bird Stalls
5. Font de Canaletes
6. Miró Mosaic
7. Palau de la Virreina
8. Centre d'Art Santa Mònica
9. Bruno Quadras Building
10. Església de Betlem

Gran Teatre del Liceu
The city's grand opera house *(above)*, founded in 1847, brought Catalan opera stars such as Montserrat Caballé to the world. Twice gutted by fire, it has been fully restored.

Monument a Colom
Pointing resolutely out to sea, this statue *(above right)* of Christopher Columbus (1888) commemorates his return to Spain after discovering the Americas. An elevator takes visitors to the top for sensational views *(see p54)*.

Mercat de La Boqueria
A cacophonous shrine to food, this cavernous market has it all, from stacks of

fruit to suckling pigs and writhing lobsters.

For sights in the Barri Gòtic & La Ribera See pp70–73

Flower & Bird Stalls

Will the real Rambla please stand up? Amid the here-today-gone-tomorrow street performers and tourists, the true Rambla old-timers are the flower and bird stalls that flank the pedestrian walkway. Many of the stalls have been family-run for decades.

Font de Canaletes

Ensure your return to the city by drinking from this 19th-century fountain, inscribed with the legend that all who drink from it "will fall in love with Barcelona and always return".

La Rambla

Miró Mosaic

Splashed on the walkway on La Rambla is a colourful pavement mosaic *(above)* by Catalan artist Joan Miró. His signature abstract shapes and primary colours unfold at your feet.

Palau de la Virreina

Constructed by the viceroy of Peru in 1778 – the name means "Palace of the Viceroy's Wife" – this Neo-Classical palace hosts a range of temporary exhibitions, from sculpture to photography to video.

Centre d'Art Santa Mònica

Once the hallowed haunt of rosary beads and murmured prayers, this former 17th-century monastery was reborn in the 1980s. Thanks to a massive government-funded facelift, it is now a cutting-edge contemporary art centre. Temporary exhibitions run the gamut from large-scale video installations to sculpture and photography.

Bruno Quadras Building

Once an umbrella factory, this playful, late 19th-century building *(left)* is festooned with umbrellas.

Església de Betlem

A relic from a time when the Catholic Church was rolling in pesetas (and power), this hulking 17th-century church is a seminal reminder of when La Rambla was more religious than risqué.

For sights in El Raval See pp80–83

Barcelona Cathedral

From its Gothic cloister and Baroque chapels to its splendid, 19th-century façade, the Cathedral, dating from 1298, is an amalgam of architectural styles, each one paying homage to a period in Spain's religious history. Records show that an early Christian baptistry was established here in the 6th century, later replaced by a Romanesque basilica in the 11th century, which gave way to the current Gothic Cathedral. This living monument still functions as the Barri Gòtic's spiritual hub.

Main entrance

● Bask in the Cathedral's Gothic glory at the outdoor terrace of Estruch café on Plaça de la Seu.

◐ Organ and choral concerts are usually held monthly; enquire at the Pia Almoina. Watch *sardanes* – Catalonia's regional dance – in Plaça de la Seu (6pm Sat, noon Sun).

• Plaça de la Seu
• Map M3 • 93 315 15 54 • Metro: Liceu, Jaume I • Cathedral: open 8am–7:30pm daily (8pm Sun); numerous services daily; €5; free access: 8am–12:45pm (1:45pm Sun) & 5:15–7:30pm • Casa de L'Ardiaca: open Sep–Jul: 9am–8:45pm Mon–Fri, 9am–1pm Sat; Aug: 9am–7:30pm Mon–Fri; free • Museu Diocesà: open Jun–Sep: 10am–8pm daily; Oct–May: 10am–2pm & 5–8pm Tue–Sat, 11am–3pm Sun; C0 • DA

Top 10 Features

1. Main Façade
2. Choir Stalls
3. Cloister
4. Crypt of Santa Eulàlia
5. Capella del Santíssim Sacrament i Crist de Lepant
6. Capella de Sant Benet
7. Capella de Santa Llúcia
8. Nave & Organ
9. Pia Almoina & Museu Diocesà
10. Casa de L'Ardiaca

Main Façade

The 19th-century façade *(right)* – reaching up to 70 m (230 ft) – draws your gaze up. Flanking the eye-catching entrance are twin towers, *Modernista* stained-glass windows and 100 carved angels.

Choir Stalls

The lavish choir stalls (1340), crowned with wooden spires, are decorated with colourful coats of arms *(left)* by artist Joan de Borgonya.

Cloister

Graced with a fountain, palm trees and roaming geese, the cloister dates back to the 14th century. The mossy fountain is presided over by a small, iron statue *(right)* of Sant Jordi (St George).

For more churches in Barcelona See pp38–9

4 Crypt of Santa Eulàlia

In the crypt's centre lies the graceful alabaster sarcophagus (1327) of Santa Eulàlia, Barcelona's first patron saint. Reliefs depict her martyrdom.

5 Capella del Santíssim Sacrament i Crist de Lepant

This 15th-century *capella* (chapel) features the Christ de Lepanto, which, legend has it, guided the Christian fleet in its 16th-century battle against the Ottoman Turks.

Cathedral Floor Plan

6 Capella de Sant Benet

Honouring Sant Benet, the patron saint of Europe, this chapel showcases the 15th-century altarpiece *Transfiguration of the Lord (below)* by illustrious Catalan artist Bernat Martorell.

7 Capella de Santa Llúcia

This lovely Romanesque chapel is dedicated to Santa Llúcia, the saint of sight and vision. On her saint's day (13 December), the blind (*els cecs*) arrive in droves to pray at her chapel.

8 Nave & Organ

The immense nave *(below)* is supported by soaring Gothic buttresses, which arch over 16 chapels. The 16th-century organ looming over the interior fills the Cathedral with music during services.

Cathedral Guide

The most impressive entrance to the Cathedral is its main portal on Plaça de la Seu. As you enter, to the left lie a series of chapels, the organ and elevators that take you to the terrace for phenomenal views of the Barri Gòtic *(see p55)*. The Casa de L'Ardiaca lies to the right of the Cathedral's main entrance (at Carrer Santa Llúcia 1); the Museu Diocesà is to the left (at Avinguda de la Catedral 4).

9 Pia Almoina & Museu Diocesà

The 11th-century Pia Almoina, once a rest house for pilgrims and the poor, houses the Museu Diocesà, with Romanesque and Gothic works of art from around Catalonia.

10 Casa de L'Ardiaca

Originally built in the 12th century, the Archdeacon's House sits near what was once the Bishop's Gate in the city's Roman walls. Expanded over the centuries, it now includes a leafy patio with a fountain.

➡ *For more sights in the Barri Gòtic & La Ribera* **See pp70–73**

Parc de la Ciutadella

Unfolding languidly just to the east of the old town, this green, tranquil oasis provides a welcome respite from the city centre. Built in the late 1860s on the site of a former military fortress (ciutadella), the park was artfully designed to offer Barcelona's citizens an experience of nature (shady corners, paths and greenhouses), recreation (rowing boats on the lake) and culture (two museums). The 1888 Universal Exhibition was held here and in preparation

Statuary on the Cascade Fountain

the city's great Modernista architects were brought in to work their magic. Lluís Domènech i Montaner created the eye-catching Castell dels Tres Dragons (today the Zoological Museum) and a young Antoni Gaudí helped design the flamboyant Cascade Fountain.

🍴 Pick up a picnic at the bustling Santa Caterina food market (northwest of the park), or have a drink and a snack within the colonial elegance of the Hivernacle café. If it's a hot day, cool down with a bowl of *gazpacho*.

• Main entrance: Pg Pujades • Map R4
• Park: open 8am–10:30pm daily; free; DA
• Zoo: open Nov–Feb: 10am–5pm daily; Mar–May & Oct: 10am–6pm daily; Jun–Sep: 10am–7pm daily; €16, children €10; DA
• Museu de Zoologia & Museu de Geologia: open 10am–6:30pm Tue–Sat, 10am–2:30pm Sun; €3.50 joint ticket; DA

Top 10 Sights

1. Cascade Fountain
2. Arc de Triomf
3. Parc Zoològic
4. Llac
5. Antic Mercat del Born
6. Museu de Zoologia
7. Museu de Geologia
8. Hivernacle & Umbracle
9. Parlament de Catalunya
10. *Homenatge a Picasso*

Cascade Fountain
One glimpse of this fanciful, Baroque-style fountain *(right)* and you'll probably guess Gaudí had a hand in its creation. Winged horses with serpent tails rear over a mossy waterfall and chubby cherubs giggle at play amid jets of water.

Arc de Triomf
The grandest entrance to the park is the Arc de Triomf *(above)*, designed for the 1888 Exhibition by Josep Vilaseca i Casanoves. Topping the arch are angels tooting horns and offering wreaths.

Parc Zoològic
These colourful flamingos are just some of the stars at this child-friendly zoo, which also has pony rides, electric cars and a train *(see p62)*.

For sights in the Barri Gòtic & La Ribera See p70–73

4 Llac
In the centre of the park is a placid, man-made lake *(above)*, where you can rent a boat for half an hour or more.

5 Antic Mercat del Born
The outline of Barcelona's medieval streets, houses, shops and palaces are revealed below this old market. The foundations date from 1714, the year Felipe V and his French allies entered the city.

Park Plan

6 Museu de Zoologia
The Zoological Museum is housed in Domènech i Montaner's striking building. The centrepiece is a colossal whale skeleton, which hangs amid scores of stuffed animals, including a sabre-toothed tiger.

7 Museu de Geologia
Roam to your heart's content among 15,000 minerals, 14,000 rocks and over 100,000 palaeontological pieces, including a collection of Catalonian fossils.

9 Parlament de Catalunya
Housed in the lovely Palau de la Ciutadella *(below)*, 1891, is the Catalonian Parliament, where Pascual Maragall (the President of Catalonia) and other political groups meet. In front is the Plaça d'Armes and a graceful water-lily pond with a sculpture (1907) by Josep Llimona.

10 Homenatge a Picasso
Antoni Tàpies toasts Picasso's cubist legacy with an abstract creation of his own. Tàpies' *Homage to Picasso* – a large glass cube filled with furnishings and abstract objects – requires some mental gymnastics to decipher its meaning.

8 Hivernacle & Umbracle
Palm trees and other tropical vegetation exude humidity inside the late 19th-century Hivernacle and Umbracle greenhouses *(above)*. The latter was designed by architect Josep Fontseré, the former by Josep Amargós.

Park Guide
Two metro stops provide access to the park: to approach through the grand Arc de Triomf, disembark at the metro station of the same name. If you're heading to the zoo, get off at Barceloneta metro stop, which is within easy walking distance.

🔟 Museu Nacional d'Art de Catalunya

Incorporating one of the most important medieval art collections in the world, the Museu Nacional d'Art de Catalunya (MNAC) is housed in the majestic Palau Nacional, built in 1929. The high point of the museum is the Romanesque art section, consisting of the painted interiors of churches from the Pyrenees dating from the 11th and 12th centuries. There is also the Thyssen-Bornemisza Collection, with works from the Gothic period to the Rococo; the Cambó Bequest, with works by the likes of Goya and Zurbarán; and a collection of works by Catalan artists from the early 19th century to the 1940s.

Palau Nacional façade

🍽 On the first floor there is a top-notch restaurant in impressively elegant surroundings. There's also a great café in the Oval Room.

👁 There are spectacular city views from the entrance to the huge glass foyer.

• Palau Nacional, Parc de Montjuïc
• Map B4
• Metro: Espanya
• 93 622 03 76
• www.mnac.cat
• Open 10am–7pm Tue–Sat, 10am–2:30pm Sun
• Adm: €8.50; con €6 (valid for two days within one month; free first Sun of the month)
• Guided tours by appointment • DA

Top 10 Exhibits

1. Interior: Sant Joan de Boí
2. Frescoes: Sant Climent de Taüll
3. Virgin: Ger
4. Crucifix of Batlló Majesty
5. Murals: Santa Maria de Taüll
6. Apse: Santa Maria d'Aneu
7. Madonna of Humility
8. The Madonna of the Councillors
9. Retaule de Sant Agustí
10. Cambó Bequest

(Floor plan labels: Toilets, Café, Book Shop, Gift shop)

1 Interior: Sant Joan de Boí

Painted in French Romanesque style, this is one of the museum's most complete church interiors (c.1100). The boldly kinetic *Stoning of St Stephen* is set beside a dramatic depiction of heaven and hell. Other scenes depict saints in heaven, animals and minstels.

2 Frescoes: Sant Climent de Taüll

Among the most important examples of European Romanesque is the Taüll interior *(left)*, a melange of Byzantine, French and Italian influences. The apse is dominated by *Christ in Majesty* and the symbols of the four Evangelists and the Virgin, with the apostles beneath.

3 Virgin: Ger
This outstanding 12th-century sculpture *(left)* came from a series that evolved in Catalonia and the Pyrenees. Mary sits rigid in flowing robes, acting as a human throne for the young Christ, who raises his hand in blessing.

4 Crucifix of Batlló Majesty
This splendid, mid-12th-century wooden carving *(left)* depicts Christ on the cross with open eyes and no signs of suffring, because he has defeated death. He is clothed in royal robes.

5 Murals: Santa Maria de Taüll
The well-preserved interior of Santa Maria de Taüll (c.1123) gives an idea of how incredibly colourful the Romanesque churches must have been. The symbolism concentrates on Jesus's early life, with scenes of the Wise Men and John the Baptist.

6 Apse: Santa Maria d'Aneu
This late 11th-century apse *(right)* is dominated by a seraph, its six wings disconcertingly covered in eyes. The Latin inscription reads "Holy, holy, holy" as the angel reaches out with burning hot coals to purify the words of the prophets Isaiah and Elijah.

7 Madonna of Humility
This magnificent panel *(right)* was probably part of a triptych. The Virgin, with the Child on her lap, sits on a throne surrounded by angels.

8 The Madonna of the Councillors
Commissioned by Barcelona's city council in 1443, this work by Lluís Dalmau is rich in political symbolism. It reveals the head councillors, supported by saints and martyrs, kneeling before a regally enthroned Virgin.

9 Retaule de Sant Agustí
This altarpiece (1463–85), by master painter Jaume Huguet, is a dramatic illustration of the wealth of the medieval Church.

10 Cambó Bequest
A collection of mostly Renaissance and Baroque art, donated by Francesc Cambó. Work by Flemish artists such as Rubens reveal the transformation from Gothic to Rennaissance, while the darker visions of Goya and Zurbarán represent Spain's 18th-century Golden Age.

Key
- Romanesque Art Gallery
- Sala Oval
- Gothic Art Gallery
- Renaissance and Baroque Art
- Thyssen-Bornemisza Collection

Gallery Guide
The Cambó Bequest and the Thyssen-Bornemisza Collection are on the main floor. On the first floor are the Baroque and Modern art galleries, along with the photography and numismatics collections.

Map labels: Toilets · Ticket office · Cloakroom · Stairs down to temporary exhibitions · Main Entrance · Toilets

For information on the Font Màgica, located at the bottom of the steps that lead up to the Palau Nacional, **See p89**

La Pedrera

Completed in 1910, this fantastic, undulating apartment block, with its out-of-this-world roof and delicate wrought ironwork, is one of the most emblematic of all Gaudí's works. La Pedrera (the Stone Quarry), also known as Casa Milà, was Gaudí's last great civic work before he dedicated the rest of his life to the Sagrada Família (see pp8–10). Restored to its former glory in 1996 after years of decay, La Pedrera now contains a museum dedicated to the architect, the exhibition centre of the Caixa de Catalunya, a furnished museum apartment, as well as private residences. What makes La Pedrera so magical is that every last detail, from door knobs to light fittings, bears the hallmark of Gaudí's visionary genius.

Façade, La Pedrera

🍷 During the summer months, a terrace bar on the roof (9pm–midnight Fri & Sat) allows visitors to enjoy a drink and live music amid the spectacular surroundings. Reservations essential *(see p47)*.

✪ For more information on temporary exhibitions held here, check the website of the Caixa de Catalunya (http://obrasocial. caixacatalunya.es)

• Passeig de Gracia 92
• Map E2
• 90 240 09 73
• Metro: Diagonal
• Open: 9am–8pm daily (Nov–Feb: 9am–6:30pm; mid-Jun–late Jul: 9am–midnight Fri & Sat with reservation – 90 210 12 12)
• Adm: €8; con €4.50 (Free admission to the temporary exhibition space.)

Top 10 Features

1. Façade & Balconies
2. Roof
3. Espai Gaudí
4. El Pis de La Pedrera
5. Interior Courtyard: C/Provença
6. Gates
7. Temporary Exhibition Room
8. Interior Courtyard: Pg de Gràcia
9. Auditorium
10. La Pedrera Shop

Façade & Balconies
Defying the laws of gravity, La Pedrera's irreverent curved walls are held in place by undulating horizontal beams attached to invisible girders. Intricate wrought-iron balconies *(above)* are a perfect example of the artisan skill so integral to *Modernisme*.

Espai Gaudí
A series of drawings, photos, maquettes and multimedia displays helps visitors grasp Gaudí's architectural wizardry. The museum is housed in the breathtaking, vaulted attic with its 270 brick arches forming skeletal corridors.

Roof
The strikingly surreal rooftop sculpture park *(above)* has chimneys resembling medieval warriors and huge ventilator ducts twisted into bizarre organic forms *(below)*; not to mention good views over the Eixample.

➤ *For more on* Modernista *architecture* **See pp32–3**

4 El Pis de La Pedrera

This furnished *Modernista* flat *(right)*, set up with period furniture, reconstructs a typical bourgeois flat of late 19th-century Barcelona. It provides an engaging contrast between the staid middle-class conservatism of the era and the undeniable wackiness of the building itself.

5 Interior Courtyard: C/Provença

A brigade of guides take hordes of visitors through here each day. A closer inspection of this first courtyard reveals beautiful mosaics and wall paintings lining a swirling fairytale staircase.

6 Gates

The mastery involved in these huge, wrought-iron gates reveals the influence of Gaudí's predecessors – four generations of artisan metal-workers. The use of iron is integral to many of Gaudí's buildings.

7 Temporary Exhibition Room

This gallery space, run by the Caixa de Catalunya, holds regular free art exhibitions. It has shown work by Marc Chagall, Salvador Dalí, Francis Bacon and others. The ceiling *(above)* looks as if it has been coated with whisked egg whites.

8 Interior Courtyard: Pg de Gràcia

Like the first courtyard, here, too, is a grand, ornate staircase (left). This one is adorned with a stunning, floral ceiling painting.

9 Auditorium

The basement auditorium (currently closed for renovation) hosts regular conferences and concerts. The adjacent garden offers a glimpse of greenery.

10 La Pedrera Shop

A wide range of Gaudí-related memorabilia includes replicas of the warrior chimneys in ceramic and bronze.

Sight Guide

The Espai Gaudí (attic), El Pis (fourth floor) and the rooftop are all accessible by lift. The Temporary Exhibition Room is located up the staircase from the Pg de Gràcia courtyard. The courtyards, staircases and shops are also accessible from the main entrance on C/Provença.

For more on Antoni Gaudí **See p11**

Fundació Joan Miró

This superb tribute to a man whose legacy as an artist and as a Catalan is visible city-wide was founded in 1975 by Joan Miró himself, who wanted it to be a contemporary arts centre. The museum holds more than 11,000 examples of the artist's colourful paintings, sketches and sculptures. The 400 or so on display trace Miró's development from an innovative Surrealist phase in the 1920s to his place as one of the world's most challenging masters in the 1960s.

Façade, Fundació Joan Miró

○ The elegant restaurant here is one of the best dining options in the area *(see p93)*.

○ In summer, live experimental music is showcased in the Fundació auditorium, usually on Thursday nights.

The gift shop has an original range of Miróesque curiosities, from tablecloths to champagne glasses.

• Av Miramar,
Parc de Montjuïc
• Map B4
• 93 443 94 70
• www.bcn.fjmiro.es
• Metro to Paral·lel, then funicular; or metro to Pl. Espanya, then bus 61; or buses 50 or 55 from the city centre
• Open: 10am–7pm Tue, Wed, Fri & Sat (until 8pm Jul–Sep) 10am–9:30pm Thu, 10am–2:30pm Sun
• Adm: €8 (complete collection); €4 (temporary exhibitions) • DA

Top 10 Works of Art

1. *Tapis de la Fundació* (1979)
2. *L'Estel Matinal* (1940)
3. *Pagès Català al Cla de Lluna* (1968)
4. *Home i Dona Davant un Munt d'Excrement* (1935)
5. *Sèrie Barcelona* (1944)
6. *Font de Mercuri* (1937)
7. Sculpture Room
8. Terrace Garden
9. Visiting Exhibitions
10. Espai 13

Tapis de la Fundació
This immense, richly-coloured tapestry *(right)* represents the culmination of Miró's work with textiles, which began in the 1970s.

L'Estel Matinal
This is the only one of 23 paintings on paper known as the *Constellation Series* held by the Fundació. The *Morning Star's* introspective quality reflects Miró's state of mind at the outbreak of World War II, when he was living in hiding in Normandy. Spindly shapes of birds, women and heavenly bodies are suspended in front of an empty space.

Pagès Català al Cla de Lluna
The figurative painting *Catalan Peasant by Moonlight (left)* dates from the late 1960s and depicts two of Miró's favourite themes: earth and night. The figure of the peasant, a simple collage of colour, is barely decipherable, as the crescent moon merges with his sickle and the night sky takes on the rich green tones of earth.

For more on contemporary Catalan art, visit MACBA See pp28–9

4 Home i Dona Davant un Munt d'Excrement

Tortured, misshapened and lurid semi-abstract figures attempt to embrace against a black sky. Miró's pessimism at the time of *Man and Woman in Front of a Pile of Excrement (right)* would soon be confirmed by the outbreak of Spain's Civil War.

5 Sèrie Barcelona

The Fundació holds the only complete set of prints of this series of more than 50 black-and-white lithographs. This important collection is only occasionally on display.

6 Font de Mercuri

Alexander Calder donated the *Mercury Fountain* to the Fundació as a mark of his friendship with Miró. The work was an anti-fascist tribute, conceived in memory of the attack on the town of Almadén.

7 Sculpture Room

This room *(above)* focuses on Miró's sculptures from the mid-1940s to the late-1950s when he experimented first with ceramic, then bronze and finally with painted media and found objects. Outstanding works include *Sun Bird* (1946–9) and *Moon Bird* (1946–9).

8 Terrace Garden

More of Miró's vibrantly colourful and playful sculptures are randomly scattered on a spacious terrace *(right)*, from which you can appreciate city views and the rationalist architecture of Josep Lluís Sert's geometric building. The 3-m (10-ft) tall *Caress of a Bird* (1967) dominates the terrace.

10 Espai 13

This space showcases the experimental work of new artists from around the world. The exhibitions, which are based on a single theme each year, are usually radical and often make full use of new technologies.

9 Visiting Exhibitions

Over the years, these temporary exhibitions (usually held in the west wing) have included retrospectives of high-profile artists such as Rothko, Warhol and Magritte.

The New Gallery Extension

The Fundació celebrated its 25th anniversary in 2001 by opening a new extension (known as Sala K) to house 25 Miró paintings on long-term loan from a private collection.

The Fundació's collection is vast; only a portion of it is on show at any one time.

Museu Picasso

Pay homage to the 20th-century's most acclaimed artist at this treasure-filled museum. Highlighting Pablo Picasso's (1881–1973) formative years, the museum boasts the world's largest collection of the artist's early works. At the tender age of 10, Picasso was already revealing remarkable artistic tendencies. In 1895, aged 14, he and his family moved from the town of La Coruña to Barcelona, where Picasso blossomed as an artist. From precocious schoolbook sketches and powerful family portraits to selected works from his Blue and Rose periods, the Museu Picasso offers visitors the rare chance to discover the artist as he was discovering himself.

Entrance, Carrer Montcada

🍴 After you've had your fill of art, duck into the café *(see p42)* at the nearby Museu Tèxtil, where you can enjoy a drink or light meal on a graceful outdoor patio.

🕐 The Museu Picasso is housed in a Gothic palace complex, replete with leafy courtyards, all of which can be explored.

• C/Montcada 15–23
• Map P4 • 93 256 30 00
• www.museupicasso. bcn.cat • Metro: Jaume I
• Open 10am–8pm Tue–Sun • Guided tours: 4–6:15pm Thu, 10am–12:15pm Sat (reservations are essential, email museupicasso_ reserves@bcn.cat)
• Adm: €9 (permanent collection); €6 (temporary shows); free first Sun of month (permanent collection only) • DA

Top 10 Exhibits

1. *Hombre con boina* (1895)
2. *Autoretrato con peluca* (1896)
3. *Ciencia y Caridad* (1897)
4. Menu de Els Quatre Gats (1899–1900)
5. *Margot* & *La Nana* (1901)
6. *El Loco* (1904)
7. *Arlequín* (1917)
8. *Caballo corneado* (1917)
9. *Hombre sentado* (1917)
10. *Las Meninas* Series (1957)

Hombre con boina
This insightful portrait *(below)* reveals brush strokes – and a subject matter – that are far beyond a child who has just turned 13. No puppies or racing cars for the young Picasso; instead, he searched for the oldest men in the village and painted their portraits. The artist signed this portrait P Ruiz, because at this time he was still using his father's last name.

Autoretrato con peluca
At 14, Picasso painted a series of self-portraits, including *Self-portrait with Wig*, a whimsical depiction of how he might have looked during the time of his artistic hero, Velázquez.

Ciencia y Caridad
One of Picasso's first publicly exhibited paintings was *Science and Charity*. Picasso's father posed as the doctor.

For more museums See pp40–41

4 Menu de Els Quatre Gats

Picasso's premier Barcelona exhibition was in 1900, held at the Barri Gòtic café, Els Quatre Gats *(see p45)*. The artist's first commission was the pen-and-ink drawing of himself and a group of artist friends in top hats, which graced the menu of this bohemian hang-out.

5 Margot & La Nana

Picasso's *Margot (centre)* is an evocative painting of a call-girl waiting for her next customer, while *La Nana* captures the defiant gaze and stance of a heavily rouged dwarf dancer.

6 El Loco

The Madman (left) is a fine example of Picasso's Blue period. This artistic phase, which lasted from 1901 to 1904, was characterized by melancholic themes and sombre colours.

7 Arlequín

A lifting of spirits led to Picasso's Neo-Classical period, typified by paintings like *Arlequín*, celebrating the light-hearted liberty of circus performers.

8 Caballo corneado

The anguished horse in this painting later appears in *Guernica*, which reveals the horrors of war. This work gives viewers the chance to observe the process that went into the creation of Picasso's most famous painting.

9 Hombre sentado

Works such as *Man Sitting (right)* confirmed Picasso's status as the greatest Analytic Cubist painter of the 20th century.

10 Las Meninas Series

Picasso's reverence for Velázquez culminated in this remarkable series of paintings *(below)*, based on the Velázquez painting *Las Meninas*.

Gallery Guide

The museum is made up of five inter-connected medieval palaces. The permanent collection is arranged chronologically on the first and second floors of the first three palaces. Temporary exhibitions – usually showcasing one modern artist – are housed on the first and second floors of the last two palaces.

For more sights in the Barri Gòtic & La Ribera **See pp70–73**

Palau de la Música Catalana

Barcelona's Modernista movement reached its aesthetic culmination in this magnificent concert hall (1905–1908), designed by renowned architect Lluís Domènech i Montaner. The lavish façade, ringed by mosaic pillars and brick arches, just hints at what awaits within. Domènech's "garden of music" (as he called it) unfolds beyond the front doors, with each surface of the ornate foyer, from pillars to banisters, emblazoned with a flower motif. The concert hall – designed so that its height is the same as its breadth – is a celebration of natural light and forms, climaxing in a stained-glass, golden orb skylight that showers the hall with sunlight.

Façade, Palau de la Música Catalana

For a pre-concert, cocktail, settle in at the *Modernista* stained-glass bar just beyond the foyer.

Enjoy bargain early concerts, which usually happen twice monthly around 6 or 7pm on Saturday (Sep–Jun) and Sunday (Feb–May).

Buy tickets for the shows and guided tours from the ticket office round the corner at C/Sant Francesc de Paula 2: (90 244 28 82), open 10am–9pm daily.

• Sant Pere Mes Alt
• Map N2 • 90 244 28 82 • www.palaumusica.org • Metro: Urquinaona
• Guided tours every half hour: Sep–Jul: 10am–3:30pm; Aug & Easter: 10am–6pm (book a week in advance, call 90 247 54 85) • Adm: €10 • Limited DA

Top 10 Features

1. Stained-Glass Ceiling
2. Stage
3. Stained-Glass Windows
4. Busts
5. Horse Sculptures
6. Chamber Music Room
7. Lluís Millet Hall
8. Foyer & Bar
9. Façade
10. Concert & Dance Series

1 Stained-Glass Ceiling

Topping the concert hall is a breathtaking, stained-glass inverted dome ceiling *(right)*, surrounded by 40 angels. By day, light streams through the fiery red and orange stained glass, illuminating the hall.

3 Stained-Glass Windows

Blurring the boundaries between the outdoors and the interior, Domènech encircled the concert hall with vast stained-glass windows to let in sunlight and reveal the changing times of day.

2 Stage

The main, semicircular stage *(above)* swarms with activity – even when no one's performing. Eighteen mosaic and terracotta muses spring from the backdrop, playing everything from the harp to the castanets.

 For more on Modernista architecture **See pp32–3**

Busts
A bust of Catalan composer Josep Anselm Clavé (1824–74) celebrates the Palau's commitment to Catalan music. Facing him across the concert hall, a stern-faced, unruly-haired Beethoven *(above)* represents the hall's classical and international repertoire.

Horse Sculptures
Charging forth from the ceiling are winged horses (designed by architect Eusebi Arnau), infusing the concert hall with movement and verve. Also depicted is a representation of Wagner's chariot ride of the Valkyries, led by galloping horses that leap toward the stage.

Chamber Music Room
Designed as a rehearsal space, the semicircular, accoustically-sound Chamber Music Room is a smaller version of the massive concert hall one floor above. In its centre is an inlaid foundation stone commemorating the construction of the Palau.

Lluís Millet Hall
Named after Catalan composer Lluís Millet, this immaculately preserved lounge boasts gorgeous stained-glass windows. On the main balcony outside are rows of stunning mosaic pillars *(right)*.

Foyer & Bar
Modernista architects worked with ceramic, stone, wood, marble and glass, all of which Domènech used liberally, most notably in the opulent foyer and bar

Façade
(below) reveals *Modernista* delights on every level. An elaborate mosaic represents the Orfeò Català choral society, founded in 1891.

Concert & Dance Series
Over 300 concerts and dance shows are staged each year, and seeing a show here is an experience not to be missed. For traditional Catalan dance and choral singing, look out for the *Cobla, Cor, i Dansa* series (usually begins February).

Orfeó Catalá

Perhaps the most famous choral group to perform here is the Orfeó Catalá, for whom the concert hall was originally built. This 90-person chorus performs regularly and holds a concert on 26 December every year. Book in advance.

For more sights in the Barri Gòtic & La Ribera **See pp70–73**

🔟 Museu d'Art Contemporani & Centre de Cultura Contemporània

Barcelona's sleek contemporary art museum looms in bold contrast to the surrounding area. Together with the nearby Centre de Cultura Contemporània (CCCB), the Museu d'Art Contemporani (MACBA) has provided a focal point for modern Barcelona since its opening in 1995, and, has played an integral part in the rejuvenation of El Raval. MACBA's permanent collection includes a slew of big-name Spanish and international contemporary artists, while excellent temporary exhibits feature everything from painting to video installations. The CCCB serves as a crossroads of contemporary culture with cutting-edge art exhibits, lectures and film screenings.

Gallery space, MACBA

🍴 Snack at the nearby restaurant Pla dels Àngels (on Carrer Ferlandina), which offers budget-priced nouvelle/Catalan food to a hip crowd.

- *MACBA*
- *Plaça dels Àngels*
- *Map K2*
- *Metro: Catalunya*
- *93 412 08 10*
- *www.macba.es*
- *Open Oct–Jun: 11am–7:30pm Mon & Wed–Fri, 10am–8pm Sat, 10am–3pm Sun; Jul–Sep: 11am–8pm Mon, Wed, Fri, 11am–midnight Thu, 10am–8pm Sat, 10am–3pm Sun*
- *Adm: €7.50 (all floors); €6 (2 floors); €4 (1 floor) Thu–Tue; €3.50 (all floors) Wed • DA*

- *CCCB*
- *Montalegre 5 • Map K1 • Metro: Catalunya*
- *93 306 41 00 • www. cccb.org • Open: 11am–8pm Tue–Sun (to 10pm Thu) • Adm: €4.40; free first Wed of month and 8–10pm Thu*

Top 10 Features

1. Interior Corridors
2. Visiting Artist's Space
3. Revolving Permanent Collection
4. Façade
5. Puzzle Area
6. *A Sudden Awakening*
7. Thinking & Reading Spaces
8. El Patio de les Donnes/CCCB
9. Temporary Exhibitions/CCCB
10. Plaça Joan Coromines

1 Interior Corridors
Space and light are omnipresent in the walkways between floors. Look through the glass panels onto the Plaça dels Àngels for myriad images before you even enter the gallery spaces.

2 Visiting Artist's Space
The *raison d'etre* of MACBA is this flexible area showing the best in contemporary art. Past exhibitions have included Zush and acclaimed painter Dieter Roth.

3 Revolving Permanent Collection
The permanent collection comprises over 2000 – mostly European – modern artworks, 10 per cent of which are on show at any one time. All major contemporary artistic trends are represented. This work *(right)* by Eduardo Arranz Bravo is titled *Homea* (1974).

Façade
American architect Richard Meier's stark, white, geometrical façade makes a startling impression against the backdrop of this dilapidated working-class neighbourhood. Hundreds of panes of glass reflect the skateboarders who gather here daily.

Puzzle Area
On the ground floor, several tables are set out with jigsaw puzzles *(left)*. The puzzles, which feature photos taken in neighbouring flats, give an intriguing glimpse of life in the nearby tenement buildings.

A Sudden Awakening
One of the only pieces of art on permanent display is Antoni Tàpies' deconstructed bed (1992–3), with its bedding flung across the wall in disarray *(above)*. Its presence to the right of the main entrance underlines Tàpies' importance as a key player in the world of Catalan modern art.

Thinking & Reading Spaces
Pleasant and unusual features of MACBA are the white leather sofas between the galleries. Usually next to a shelf of relevant books and a set of headphones, these spaces provide the perfect resting spot to contemplate – and learn more about – the art.

El Patio de les Donnes/CCCB
This courtyard *(left)* off Carrer Montalegre forms part of the neighbouring CCCB. An ultra-modern prismatic screen provides a mirror reflecting the 18th-century patio – a magical juxtaposition of different architectural styles.

Temporary Exhibitions/CCCB
Unlike MACBA, exhibitions at the CCCB tend to be more theme based than artist specific. Home to both a festival of cinema shorts (Sep) and the Sònar techno festival (Jun), the CCCB always manages to be at the forefront of the latest cultural trend.

Plaça Joan Coromines
The contrast between the modern MACBA, the new University building, the Tuscan-style CCCB and the 19th-century mock-Romanesque church make this square one of the most enchanting in the city. It is home to the terrace restaurants of MACBA and CCCB.

Sights Guide
The MACBA and CCCB have separate entrances, though they share the Plaça Joan Coromines courtyard. The CCCB is accessible from C/Montalegre and MACBA from the Plaça dels Àngels. Both multi-level galleries have flexible display spaces.

For more sights in El Raval **See pp80–83**

Left **La Setmana Tràgica, 1909** Right **Olympic Games, 1992**

🔟 Stages in Barcelona's History

1 BC: The Founding of a City

Barcino, as the city was first known, was founded in the 3rd century BC by Carthaginian Hamilcar Barca. It was taken by the Romans in 218 BC, but played second fiddle in the region to the provincial capital of Tarragona.

2 4th–11th Centuries: Early Invasions

As the Roman Empire began to fall apart in the 5th century, the Visigoths took over the city, followed by the Moors in the 8th century. Around AD 800, Charlemagne conquered the area with the help of the Pyrenean counts.

Poster, 1929 International Exhibition

3 12th–16th Centuries: The Middle Ages

During this period, Barcelona was the capital of a Catalan empire that included much of modern Spain and parts of the Mediterranean. The city's fortune was built on commerce, but as neighbouring Castile expanded into the New World, trading patterns shifted and the Catalan dynasty faltered. Barcelona fell into decline and came under Castilian domination.

4 1638–1652: Catalan Revolt

In reaction to the oppressive policies set out in Madrid, now ruled by the Austrian Habsburgs, various local factions, known as *Els Segadors*, revolted. Fighting began in 1640 and dragged on until 1652, when the Catalans and their French allies were defeated.

5 19th Century: Industry & Prosperity

Booming industry and trade with the Americas brought activity to the city. Immigrants poured in from the countryside, laying the foundations of prosperity but also the seeds of unrest. The old city walls came down, broad Eixample avenues were laid out and workers crowded the old city neighbourhoods left behind by the middle classes.

6 1888–1929: The Renaixença

This new wealth, showcased in the International Exhibitions of 1888 and 1929, sparked a Catalan renaissance. *Modernista* mansions sprouted up, and the nationalist bourgeoisie sparked a revival of Catalan culture, particularly of literature, theatre and art.

7 1909–1931: The Revolutionary Years

But discontent brewed among workers, Catalan nationalists, communists, Spanish fascists, royalists, anarchists and republicans. In 1909, protests against the Moroccan war sparked a brutal riot, the *Setmana Tràgica* (Tragic Week). Lurching towards Civil War, Catalonia passed under a dictatorship before being declared a Republic in 1931.

8 1936–1975: Civil War & Franco

At the outbreak of war in 1936, Barcelona's workers and militants managed to fend off Franco's troops for a while. The city was taken by Fascist forces in 1939, prompting a wave of repression, particularly of the Catalan language which was banned in schools.

9 1975–1980s: Transition to Democracy

Franco's death in 1975 paved the way for democracy. The Catalan language was rehabilitated and, following the introduction of a new democratic constitution in Spain, Catalonia was granted regional autonomy. The first Catalan government was elected in 1980.

10 1992–Present Day: The Olympics & Beyond

Barcelona was catapulted onto the world stage in 1992 with the highly successful Olympics. Today, the city remains socialist in politics and ready to perceive itself as both Spanish and Catalan.

Civil War, 1936

Top 10 Historical Figures

1 Guifré the Hairy
The first Count of Barcelona (d. 897) is regarded as the founding father of Catalonia.

2 Ramon Berenguer IV
He united Catalonia and joined it with Aragon by marrying Princess Petronila in 1137.

3 Jaume I the Conqueror
This 13th-century warrior-king (d. 1276) conquered the Balearics and Valencia, laying the foundations for the empire.

4 Ramon Llull
Mallorcan philosopher and missionary, Llull (d. 1316) is the greatest figure in medieval Catalan literature.

5 Ferdinand the Catholic
King of Aragon and Catalonia (d.1516), he married Isabel of Castile, paving the way for the Kingdom of Spain's formation and the end of Catalan independence.

6 Idlefons Cerdà
19th-century urban planner who designed the Eixample.

7 Antoni Gaudí
An idiosyncratic and devout *Modernista* architect, Gaudí was responsible for Barcelona's most famous monuments.

8 Francesc Macià
This socialist nationalist politician proclaimed the birth of the Catalan Republic (1931) and Catalan autonomy (1932).

9 Lluís Companys
Catalan president during the Civil War. Exiled in France, he was arrested by the Gestapo in 1940 and returned to Franco, who had him executed.

10 Jordi Pujol
A centre-right regionalist politician, Pujol's Convergència i Unió coalition ruled Catalonia from 1980 to 2003.

Stained-glass windows, Casa Lleò Morera

🔟 Modernista Buildings

1 Sagrada Família
Dizzying spires and intricate sculptures adorn Gaudí's magical masterpiece. Construction began at the height of *Modernisme*, but is still in progress more than a century later. *See pp8–10.*

2 La Pedrera
This amazing apartment block, with its curving façade and bizarre rooftop, has all of Gaudí's architectural trademarks. Especially characteristic are the wrought-iron balconies and the ceramic mosaics decorating the entrance halls. *See pp20–21.*

3 Palau de la Música Catalana
Domènech i Montaner's magnificent concert hall is a joyous celebration of Catalan music. Ablaze with mosaic friezes, stained glass, ceramics and sculptures, it displays the full glory of

Chimneys and rooftop, Casa Batlló

the *Modernista* style. The work of Miquel Blay on the façade is rated as one of the best examples of *Modernista* sculpture in Barcelona. *See pp26–7.*

4 Hospital de la Santa Creu i de Sant Pau
In defiant contrast to the Eixample's symmetrical grid-like pattern, this ambitious project was planned around two avenues running at 45-degree angles to the Eixample streets. Started by Domènech i Montaner in 1905 and later completed by his son in 1930, the hospital pavilions are lavishly embellished with mosaics, stained glass and sculptures by Eusebi Arnau. The octagonal columns with floral capitals are inspired by those in the Monestir de Santes Creus *(see p124)*, to the south of Barcelona. *See p103.*

5 Fundaciò Tàpies
With a rationally plain façade alleviated only by its *Mudéjar*-style brick work, this austere building, dating to 1886, was originally home to the publishing house Montaner i Simon. It bears the distinction of being the first *Modernista* work to be designed by Domènech i Montaner, which explains why it has so few of the ornate decorative touches that distinguish his later works. Home to the Fundaciò Tàpies, it is now dominated by an enormous sculpture by the contemporary Catalan artist, Antoni Tàpies. *See p104.*

➜ *A ticket for* La Ruta Modernista *includes discounted entry to all* Modernista *buildings and a map/guide* **See p133**

6 Casa Batlló

Illustrating Gaudí's nationalist sentiments, Casa Batlló, on La Mansana de la Discòrdia *(see p103)*, represents an allegory of the legend of Sant Jordi *(see p39)*. The roof is the dragon's back and the balconies, sculpted in the form of carnival masks, are the skulls of the dragon's victims. The polychrome façade reveals Gaudí's remarkable use of colour and texture. ◈ Pg de Gràcia 43 • Map E2 • Open 9am–8pm daily • Adm €16.50 • DA

7 Casa Amatller

The top of Casa Amatller's ochre-white façade bursts into a brilliant display of blue, cream and pink ceramics with burgundy florets. Architect Puig i Cadafalch's exaggerated decorative use of ceramics is typical of *Modernisme*. This Mansana de la Discòrdia *(see p103)* is a private house, but it is possible to access the ground and first floors, which house the Amatller Foundation. ◈ Pg de Gràcia 41 • Map E2 • Open 10am–8pm Mon–Sat, 10am–3pm Sun • Free • DA

8 Palau Güell

This palace is a fine example of Gaudí's experiments with structure, especially the use of parabolic arches to orchestrate space. Also remarkable is the use of unusual building materials, such as ebony and rare South American woods. *See p81.*

9 Casa de les Punxes (Casa Terrades)

Taking *Modernisme's* Gothic and medieval obsessions to extremes that others seldom dared, Puig i Cadafalch created this imposing, castle-like structure between 1903 and 1905. Nicknamed the "House of Spines" because of its sharp, needle-like spires rising up from conical turrets, its true name is Casa Terrades. The flamboyant spires contrast with a façade that is, by *Modernista* standards, sparsely decorated. ◈ Diagonal 416 • Map F2 • Closed to public

Casa de les Punxes

10 Casa Lleó Morera

Ironwork, ceramics, sculpture and stained glass come together here in a synthesis of the decorative and fine arts. The interior of this house, by Domènech i Montaner, has some superb sculptures by Eusebi Arnau and some of the finest *Modernista* furniture in existence. ◈ Pg de Gràcia 35 • Map E3 • Closed to public

Left **Plaça de Catalunya** Right **Plaça Reial, Barri Gòtic**

🔟 Perfect Squares

Plaça Reial

The arcaded Plaça Reial, in the heart of the Barri Gòtic, is unique among Barcelona's squares, with its old-world charm, gritty urbanization and Neo-Classical flair. It is home to majestic, mid-19th-century build-ings, Gaudí lampposts, a slew of happening bars and clubs, and an entertaining and colourful crowd of inner-city denizens. *See p72.*

Plaça de Catalunya

Barcelona's nerve centre is the huge Plaça de Catalunya, a lively hub from which all the city's activity seems to radiate. This square is most visitors first real glimpse of Barcelona. The airport bus stops here, as do RENFE trains and countless metro and bus lines. The square's commercial swagger is evident all around, headed by Spain's omnipresent department store, El Corte Inglés *(see p139)*. Pigeons flutter chaotically in the square's centre, lively Peruvian

bands play to booming sound systems and hordes of travellers – from backpackers to tour groups – meander about. To add to the melting pot, the square is allegedly home to 25 people (mostly homeless immigrants). ◈ *Map M1*

Plaça del Rei

One of the city's best pre-served medieval squares, the Barri Gòtic's Plaça del Rei is ringed by grand buildings. Among them is the 14th-century Palau Reial *(see p71)*, which houses the Saló del Tinell, a spacious Catalan Gothic banqueting hall. ◈ *Map N4*

Plaça de Sant Jaume

Weighty with power and history, this is the administrative heart of modern-day Barcelona. The *plaça* is flanked by the city's two key government buildings, the stately Palau de la Generalitat and the 15th-century Ajuntament. *See p71.*

Café, Plaça Sant Josep Oriol, Barri Gòtic

Sign up for DK's email newsletter on traveldk.com

Plaça de Rius i Taulet

The progressive, bohemian area of Gràcia, a former village annexed by Barcelona in 1897, still exudes a small-town ambience, where socializing with the neighbours means heading for the nearest *plaça*. Topping the list is this atmospheric square, with an impressive clock tower rising out of its centre. Bustling outdoor cafés draw buskers and a sociable crowd. ◈ *Map F1*

Façade, Plaça del Pi

Plaça de Sant Josep Oriol & Plaça del Pi

Old-world charm meets café culture in the Barri Gòtic's leafy Plaça de Sant Josep Oriol and Plaça del Pi, named after the pine trees (*pi*, in Catalan) that shade its nooks and crannies. The lovely Gothic church of Santa Maria del Pi *(see p38)* rises between the two squares. ◈ *Map M3 & M4*

Plaça Comercial

The buzzy Passeig del Born culminates in Plaça Comercial, an inviting square dotted with cafés and bars. It faces the 19th-century Born Market *(see p72)*, which will re-open in 2008 as a cultural centre and exhibition space. ◈ *Map P4*

Plaça del Sol

Tucked within the cosy grid of Gràcia, this square is surrounded by handsome 19th-century buildings. As evening descends, it becomes one of the most lively spots to start your night-time festivities, along with all the *Barcelonins* who mingle on the outdoor terraces. ◈ *Map F1*

Plaça de Santa Maria

The magnificent Església de Santa Maria del Mar *(see p76)* imbues its namesake *plaça*, in the El Born district, with a certain spiritual calm. Bask in its Gothic ambience, people watch, and soak up the sun at one of the outdoor terrace cafés. ◈ *Map N5*

Plaça de la Vila de Madrid

Mere steps from La Rambla *(see pp12–13)* is this spacious *plaça*, graced with the remains of a Roman necropolis. A remnant of Roman Barcino, the square sat just beyond the boundaries of the walled Roman city. A row of unadorned 2nd–4th-century AD tombs were discovered here in 1957. The complete remains are open to the public. ◈ *Map M2*

For parks & beaches See pp56–7

37

Left **Església del Betlem** Right **Temple Expiatori del Sagrat Cor**

Charming Churches & Chapels

1 Barcelona Cathedral
Barcelona's magnificent Gothic cathedral boasts an eye-catching façade and a peaceful cloister. *See pp14–15.*

2 Església de Santa Maria del Mar
The elegant church of Santa Maria del Mar (1329–83) is one of the finest examples of Catalan Gothic, a style characterized by measured simplicity. A spectacular stained-glass rose window illuminates the lofty interior. *See p76.*

3 Capella de Sant Miquel & Església al Monestir de Pedralbes
Inside the Monestir de Pedralbes *(see p111)* is a Gothic cloister and the Capella de Sant Miquel, decorated with murals by Catalan artist Ferrer Bassa in 1346. The adjoining Gothic church contains the alabaster tomb of Queen Elisenda, the monastery's founder. ✪ *C/Baixada del Monestir 14 • Map A1 • Open Oct–Mar: 10am–2pm Tue–Sat, 10am–3pm Sun; Apr–Sep: 10am–5pm Tue–Sat, 10am–3pm Sun (church also open 7–8:30pm)*

4 Església de Sant Pau del Camp
Founded as a Benedictine monastery in the 9th century by Guifre II, a count of Barcelona, this church was rebuilt the following century. Its sculpted façade

and intimate cloister with rounded arches bear all the trademarks of the Romanesque style. *See p83.*

5 Església de Sant Pere de les Puelles
Built in 801 as a chapel for troops stationed in Barcelona, this *església* later became a spiritual retreat for young noble women. The church was rebuilt in the 1100s and is notable today for its Romanesque central cupola and a series of capitals topped with carved leaves. Look out for two stone tablets depicting a Greek cross, which are from the original chapel. ✪ *Pl de Sant Pere • Map P2 • Open 8:45am–1pm, 5–7:30pm Mon–Fri; 8:45am–1pm, 4:30–6:30pm Sat; 10am–2pm Sun*

Santa Eulàlia, Barcelona Cathedral

6 Església de Santa Maria del Pi
This lovely Gothic church with its ornate stained-glass windows graces Plaça del Pi *(see p37)* with its elegant presence. ✪ *Pl del Pi • Map L3 • Open 9am–1:30pm & 4:30–9pm daily • DA*

7 Capella de Santa Àgata
Within the grand walls of the Palau Reial *(see p71)* is the medieval Capella de Santa Àgata, with its lovely stained glass windows and 15th-century altarpiece. ✪ *Pl del Rei • Map N3 • Open 10am–8pm Tue–Sat (Oct–May: 10am–2pm, 4–7pm Tue–Sat), 10am–3pm Sun • Adm*

8 Temple Expiatori del Sagrat Cor

Mount Tibidabo is an appropriate perch for this huge, over-the-top Neo-Gothic church, topped with a gold Christ with outstretched arms. The name Tibidabo takes its meaning from the words, "I shall give you" (*tibi dabo*), uttered by the Devil in his temptation of Christ. Zealously serving the devoted, the priest here performs the Eucharist throughout the day. ◈ *Tibidabo • Map B1 • Open 10:30am–7:30pm daily*

9 Capella de Sant Jordi

Inside the Palau de la Generalitat *(see p71)* is this fine 15th-century chapel, dedicated to Catalonia's patron saint. ◈ *Pl Sant Jaume • Map M4 • Guided tours 10:30am–1:30pm 2nd & 4th Sun of month*

10 Església de Betlem

La Rambla was once dotted with religious buildings, most built in the 17th and 18th centuries when the Catholic Church was flush with money. This *església* remains one of the most important functioning churches from this period. ◈ *C/ Xuclà 2 • Map L3 • Open 8am–1:30pm & 5:30–8pm daily • DA*

Gothic nave, Capella de Santa Àgata

Top 10 Catalan Saints & Virgins

1 Sant Jordi
Catalonia's patron saint is Saint George, whose dragon-slaying prowess is depicted all over the city.

2 Virgin Mercè
She became the female patron saint ob Barcelona in 1637. The most raucous festival in town is the Festes de La Mercè *(see p64)*.

3 Virgin of Montserrat
Catalonia's famous "Black Virgin" is the city's patron virgin.

4 Santa Eulàlia
Santa Eulàlia, Barcelona's first female patron saint, was martyred by the Romans when they took the city.

5 Santa Elena
Legend has it that Saint Helena converted to Christianity after discovering Christ's cross in Jerusalem in 346 AD.

6 Santa Llúcia
The saint of eyes and vision is celebrated on 13 December, when the blind come to worship at the Santa Llúcia chapel in the cathedral *(see pp14–15)*.

7 Sant Cristòfol
Though officially stripped of his sainthood as there was little evidence he existed, Saint Christopher was once the patron saint of travellers.

8 Sant Antoni de Padua
On 13 June, those seeking a husband or wife pray to the patron saint of love.

9 Santa Rita
Deliverer of the impossible, Santa Rita is prayed to by those searching for miracles.

10 Sant Joan
The night of Saint John *(see p64)* is celebrated with giant bonfires and fireworks.

Left **Frank Gehry's *Peix*** *Right* **Camp Nou Stadium**

🔟 Museums

1 Museu Nacional d'Art de Catalunya

Discover Catalonia's rich Romanesque and Gothic heritage at this impressive museum, housed in the 1929 Palau Nacional. Striking medieval frescoes – many culled from ancient Pyrenean churches – are the highlight. *See pp18–19.*

2 Fundació Joan Miró

The airy, high-ceilinged galleries of this splendid museum are a fitting resting place for the bold, abstract works of Joan Miró, one of Catalonia's most acclaimed 20th-century artists. *See pp22–3.*

3 Museu Picasso

Witness the budding – and meteoric rise – of Picasso's artistic genius at this unique museum. One of the world's largest collections of the painter's early works. *See pp24–5.*

4 Museu d'Art Contemporani & Centre de Cultura Contemporània

Inaugurated in 1995, MACBA is Barcelona's centre for modern art. Combined with the neighbouring CCCB, the two buildings form an artistic and cultural hub in the heart of El Raval. Both regularly host temporary exhibitions: the MACBA showcases contemporary artists; the CCCB is more theme-based. *See pp28–9.*

5 Fundació Tàpies

Works by Catalan artist Antoni Tàpies are showcased in this graceful *Modernista* building. Venture inside to discover Tàpies' rich repertoire, from early collage works to large, abstract paintings, many alluding to political and social themes. *See p104.*

Terrace, Fundació Tàpies

6 Conjunt Monumental de la Plaça del Rei

Explore the medieval Palau Reial and wander among the splendid remains of Barcelona's Roman walls and waterways at the city's history museum. The museum is partly housed in the 15th-century Casa Padellàs on the impressive medieval Plaça del Rei. *See p71.*

Badge, FC Barcelona

7 Museu del FC Barcelona

This shrine to the city's football club draws a mind-boggling number of fans paying homage to their team. Trophies, posters and other memorabilia celebrate the club's 100-year history. Also visit the adjacent Camp Nou Stadium. *See p111.*

Museu Marítim

Barcelona's formidable sea-faring history is showcased in the cavernous, 13th-century Drassanes Reials (Royal Ship-yards). The collection, which spans from the Middle Ages to the 19th century, includes a full-scale replica of the *Real*, the flagship galley of Don Juan of Austria, who led the Christians to victory against the Turks during the Battle of Lepanto in 1571. Also on display are model ships, maps and navigational instruments. *See p81.*

Museu Frederic Marès

Catalan sculptor Frederic Marès (1893–1991) was a passionate and eclectic collector. Housed here, under one roof,

are many remarkable finds amassed during his travels. Among the vast array of historical objects on display are Romanesque and Gothic religious art and sculptures, plus everything from dolls and fans to pipes and walking sticks.

Virgin, Museu Frederic Marès *See p72.*

CosmoCaixa Museu de la Ciencia

Exhibits covering the whole history of science, from the Big Bang to the computer age, are housed in this modern museum. Highlights include an interactive tour of the geological history of our planet, an area of real Amazonian rain forest, and a planetarium. ✪ *Teodor Roviralta 47–51* • *Map B1* • *Open 10am–8pm Tue–Sun* • *Adm (free first Sun of month)* • *DA* • *www.cosmocaixa.com*

Top 10 Quirky Museums/Monuments

1 Museu de Carrosses Fúnebres

Late 19th-century hearses reveal how *Barcelonins* of the past met their maker. ✪ *C/Sancho d'Àvila 2* • *Map G3*

2 Museu de l'Eròtica

A historical overview of sex from Kama Sutra drawings to salacious posters. ✪ *La Rambla 96* • *Map L3*

3 Museu de la Màgia

A museum devoted to magic, with a collection dating from the 18th century. ✪ *Carrer Oli 6* • *Map N4*

4 Museu dels Autòmates

A colourful museum of human and animal automatons. ✪ *Parc d'Atraccions del Tibidabo* • *Map B1*

5 Museu de la Xocolata

A celebration of chocolate, with interactive exhibits, edible city models and tastings. ✪ *Pl Pons i Clerch* • *Map P4*

6 Museu de Cera

Over 350 wax figures, from Marilyn Monroe to Franco and Gaudí. ✪ *Ptge de la Banca 7* • *Map L5*

7 Museu del Calçat

Footwear from all ages, including shoes worn by famous folks. ✪ *Pl de Sant Felip Neri 5* • *Map M3*

8 Museu del Perfum

Hundreds of perfume bottles from Roman times to the present. ✪ *Pg de Gràcia 39* • *Map E2*

9 Cap de Barcelona

Pop artist, Roy Lichtenstein's "Barcelona Head" (1992). ✪ *Pg de Colom* • *Map N5*

10 Peix

Frank Gehry's huge shimmering fish sculpture (1992). ✪ *Port Olímpic* • *Map G5*

Many museums are free one day a month **See p140**

Left **Cafè de l'Òpera, La Rambla** Right **Waterside dining, Port Vell**

Cafés & Light Bites

Cafè Bliss

Hidden down a tiny side street, in one of the loveliest Gothic squares in the old city, is this delightful café. There is a bright terrace, comfy sofas and a range of international magazines and newspapers to browse through. It is perfect for coffee, cakes, light meals or a romantic drink in the evening. *See p78.*

Cafè de l'Òpera

Kick back at this elegant, late 19th-century café while being tended to by vested *cambrers* (waiters). This former *xocolateria* (confectionary café) – named after the Liceu opera house opposite – still serves fine gooey delights such as *xurros amb xocolata* (strips of fried dough with thick chocolate). It's perfect for people-watching on La Rambla.
🅢 *La Rambla 74 • Map L4*

Tèxtil Cafè

Tèxtil Cafè

Nestled in a sun-splashed medieval courtyard, this soothing café offers a cheery respite from the outside world. Tuck into the *amanida tèxtil*, with goat's cheese, artichokes and leafy greens, or international fusion favourites, from *baba ganoush* to couscous.
🅢 *C/Montcada 12 • Map P4 • Closed Mon*

Bar Lobo

This chic café is a popular brunch spot during the day, but it really comes alive in the evenings. From Thursday to Saturday, the second floor becomes a hip club, with guest DJs and a chill-out space 🅢 *Pintor Fortuny, 3 • Map Q4 • 93 481 53 46 • Closed Sun eve and for occasional events • DA*

Madame Jasmine

This relaxed, arty café is furnished with flea market finds, and the mismatched tables and chairs give it a boho-chic feel. There are delicious croissants at breakfast, huge salads at lunchtime and killer cocktails in the evenings. 🅢 *Rambla de Raval 22 • Map K4 • 60 788 04 43*

Bar Kasparo

This laid-back, outdoor café serves a sprightly menu of fresh, international fare with an Asiatic twist, including chicken curry and Greek salad. After the sun dips beneath the horizon, a bar-like vibe takes over, fuelled by beer and cider. 🅢 *Pl Vicenç Martorell 4 • Map L2 • Closed Jan*

All food and drink names are given in Catalan, but in many cases the Castilian variant is used just as commonly.

Cafè Salambó

7 Stylish evidence of Gràcia's intellectual and literary character, this airy, lofty café draws arty locals. While away the afternoon over a steaming *cafè amb llet* or munching on fresh salads and *entrepans* (sandwiches). *See p115.*

Cafè Salambó

Laie Llibreria Cafè

8 Tuck into a generous buffet of rice, pasta, greens, chicken and more at this charming, long-running Eixample café-bookshop. You can also opt for the well-priced vegetarian menu, including soup, salad and a main dish. *See p108.*

Granja Dulcinea

9 The *xocolateries* and *granjes* along Carrer Petritxol *(see p74)* have been satiating sugar cravings for decades. Among them is this old-fashioned café with to-die-for delights, from *xurros amb xocolata* to strawberries and whipped cream. In the summer, delicious *orxates* and *granissats* are on the menu. ◈ *C/ Petritxol 2 • Map L3 • Closes at 9pm*

El Jardí

10 This outdoor café-bar occupies a corner of the Gothic courtyard in front of the medieval hospital of Santa Creu. It is a great spot for a quiet drink, and there is live jazz in the summer. During the winter gas heaters are brought outside. *See p87.*

Top 10 Café Drinks

1 Cafè amb llet
Traditionally enjoyed in the morning, *cafè amb llet* is an ample cup of milky coffee.

2 Tallat & Cafè Sol
Need a fortifying caffeine fix? Try a *tallat*, a small cup of coffee with a dash of milk. A *cafè sol* is just plain coffee. In the summer, opt for either one *amb gel* (with ice).

3 Cigaló
For coffee with a bite, try a *cigaló (carajillo)*, which has a shot of alcohol, usually *conyac* (cognac), *whisky* or *rom* (rum).

4 Orxata
This sweet, milky-white drink made from a tuber (tiger nut) is a summertime favourite.

5 Granissat
Slake your thirst with a cool *granissat*, a crushed-ice drink, usually lemon flavoured.

6 Aigua
Stay hydrated with *aigua mineral* (mineral water) – *amb gas* is sparkling, *sense gas*, still.

7 Cacaolat
Chocolate lovers swoon over this chocolate-milk concoction, one of Spain's most popular sweet drink exports.

8 Una Canya & Una Clara
Una canya is roughly a quarter of a litre of *cervesa de barril* (draft beer). *Una clara* is the same, but with fizzy lemonade mixed in.

9 Cava
Catalonia's answer to champagne is its home-grown *cava*, of which Freixenet and Codorníu are the most famous brands.

10 Sangría
This ever-popular concoction of red wine, fruit juices, and liquors is ordered at cafés throughout the city.

Left **Cinc Sentits** Right **Comerç 24**

🔟 Best Restaurants & Tapas Bars

1 Cal Pep

The line-up at this traditional, boisterous tapas bar includes top-notch cured hams and sausages, *truita de patates* (potato omelette), fresh *mariscs* (shellfish) and an array of daily tapas specials. *See p79.*

Wall tile advertising Barcelona restaurant

2 Noti

In a city where style often triumphs over substance, Noti stands out as a glorious exception. The decor is as stylish and glamorous as the crowd, but doesn't draw focus away from the main event – the exceptional Mediterranean and French cuisine, prepared with flair and originality. *See p109.*

3 El Asador d'Aranda

This palatial restaurant, perched high above the city on Tibidabo, dishes up the best in Castilian cuisine. Sizeable starters include *pica pica*, a tasty array of sausages, peppers and hams. The signature main dish is *lechazo* (young lamb) roasted in a wood-fired oven. *See p117.*

Paella

4 Kaiku

This unassuming, beachfront restaurant makes possibly the best paella in the city. It is on the menu as *arròs del xef*, and is prepared with smoked rice and succulent shellfish. The desserts are great too. In the summer book a table on the terrace and enjoy the views and sea breeze. *See p101.*

5 Inopia

It may be off the beaten track, but this bar is a must for dedicated foodies. The menu has gone back to basics, offering classic tapas such as *croquetas* and *patatas bravas,* prepared with the finest local ingredients. The tuna and tomato salad and anchovy-wrapped artichoke are both excellent. *See p109.*

6 Bar Ra

A funky, flower-filled oasis in El Raval, this juice-bar-café-restaurant is the place for organic, multi-cultural cuisine. Start your day with muesli or muffins and a fresh papaya or pear juice. The lunch and dinner menu might include Japanese tofu, Peruvian *ceviche* (raw seafood marinated in lemon) or a Cuban chicken and mango chutney dish. *See p87.*

7 Cinc Sentits

This elegant restaurant is known for its innovative cuisine. The tasting menu, created by

All food and drink names are given in Catalan, but in many cases the Castilian variant is used just as commonly.

chef Jordi Aretal, can be paired with specially chosen wines. The set-price lunch menu, available from Monday to Friday, is a bargain. *See p109.*

Casa Leopoldo

This comfortable, family-run restaurant serves some of the finest Catalan cuisine in the city. Fresh seafood is the highlight, with innovative platters of *bacallà* (salt cod), *llenguado* (sole) and *gambes* (prawns). *See p87.*

Bar-Restaurante Can Tomàs

A cheap, no-nonsense tapas bar in the uptown area of Sarrià. Every tapas-lover knows that the city's best *patates braves* and *patates amb alioli* are found here. Ask for the *doble mixta* to sample both. *See p117.*

Outdoor terrace, Bar Ra

Comerç 24

Perhaps one of the most adventurous restaurants in the city, Comerç 24 has an innovative head chef, Carlos Abellan. The constantly changing menu consists of a series of *platillos* (small dishes), which fuse an extraordinary variety of flavours and textures. Try the quail lollipops, sea urchins with foie gras ice cream, or gold-wrapped macadamia nuts. *See p79.*

Top 10 Tapas

1 Patates Braves
This traditional tapas favourite consists of fried potatoes topped with a spicy sauce. Equally tasty are *patates* heaped with *alioli* (garlic mayonnaise).

2 Calamars
A savoury seafood option is *calamars* (squid) *a la romana* (deep-fried in batter) or *a la planxa* (grilled).

3 Pa amb Tomàquet
A key part of any tapas spread is this bread topped with tomato and olive oil.

4 Croquetes
A perennial favourite are croquettes; tasty fried morsels of bechamel, usually with ham, chicken or tuna.

5 Musclos o Escopinyes
Sample Barcelona's fruits of the sea with tapas of tasty mussels or cockles.

6 Truita de Patates
The most common tapas dish is this thick potato ome-lette, often topped with *alioli.*

7 Ensaladilla Russa
This "Russian salad" in-cludes potatoes, onions, tuna (and often peas, carrots and other vegetables), all generous-ly enveloped in mayonnaise.

8 Gambes al'allet
An appetizing dish of fried prawns (shrimp) coated in garlic and olive oil.

9 Pernil Serrà
Cured ham is a Spanish obsession. The best, and most expensive, is Extremadura's speciality, Jabugo.

10 Fuet
Embotits (Catalan sausa-ges) include the ever-popular *fuet*, a dry, flavourful variety, most famously produced in the Catalonian town of Vic.

 For price categories **See p79**
For tips on dining and standard opening hours **See p138 & p140**

Elephant

🔟 Night-time Hot Spots

1 Elephant
Housed in a Modernista villa, filled with candles and Moroccan lamps, this swish nightclub attracts a fashionable young crowd. But the real highlight is the garden, where lounge beds with diaphanous white drapes, fountains and giant elephant statues add an exotic touch. In winter, the outdoor dance floor is transformed into a spectacular tent. *See p116.*

Decoration, Elephant Club

2 Marsella
Founded in 1820, this atmospheric throwback, run by the fifth generation of the Lamiel family, sits in the heart of the Barri Xinès *(see p82)*. Marsella is one of the few places in town where you can enjoy the potent drink absinthe (*absenta*). Settle in at one of the wrought-iron *Modernista* tables, surrounded by ancient mirrors and old religious statues, and test your mettle with the potent yellow liquor that is specially bottled for the bar. *See p86.*

3 Otto Zutz
A swanky Barcelona nightlife institution, this three-storey disco is on the itinerary for well-heeled media types. The music verges on the mainstream, with big-name DJs spinning everything from techno to contemporary favourites. *See p116.*

4 Mond Bar
This tiny, trendy bar in the heart of Gràcia is a magnet for mellow barflies who come to mingle, smoke and listen to DJ-spun tunes, including techno, pop, soul and 1970s classics. *See p116.*

5 Arena Madre
This gay disco, located in a basement, has an unpretentious atmosphere. Well-known for its dark room, Arena Madre also hosts leather shows, stripteases and comic performances. Music is mainly handbag house and Latin, while Sunday is 80s night.
Ⓝ *Balmes, 32 • 93 487 83 42*
• Open 12:30pm–6am daily • DA

6 La Terrrazza
Located inside the Poble Espanyol *(see p91)*, La Terrrazza is one of the most popular summer nightclubs in Barcelona. The patio becomes the dance-floor, the porches are bars and the garden provides a refreshing chill-out area. Ⓝ *Poble Espanyol, Av Marquès de Comillas • Map A3 • Open Thu–Sun (May–Sep) • Adm*

Sala BeCool

For tips on drinking and standard opening hours See p138 & p140

Sala BeCool

7 This stylish club has become a staple on Barcelona's busy party scene. Situated in the chic, uptown Sant Gervasi neighbourhood, the multi-functional space has everything from live music, to club nights and theme parties. Downstairs there are hugely popular DJ sessions offering electro, techno and minimal music from Friday to Saturday; upstairs plays the latest indie hits. The website has a complete listing of the full weekly programme. *See p116.*

Inside Razzmatazz

La Pedrera de Nit

8 If Gaudí's undulating Pedrera rooftop *(see pp20–21)* looks surreal by day, experience it at night for full effect. On Friday and Saturday evenings between mid June and late July, La Pedrera opens up its magical rooftop for a night of live music and *cava* drinking. Wander among Gaudí's mosaic chimneys, illuminated against the night sky, while enjoying jazz, flamenco fusion or tango. ◐ *C/Provença 261–265 • Map E2 • Reservations essential: call 90 210 12 12 • Adm • DA*

Jamboree

9 Venture underground – quite literally – to this popular, hopping jazz club-cum-nightclub in a vaulted space beneath Plaça Reial. Nightly live jazz sessions kick off around 11pm. DJs take over later with dance-inducing sounds. *See p77.*

Jamboree

Razzmatazz

10 Part of the Port Olímpic party strip, this is nothing less than the city's best all-round nightlife venue. Music bands from around the world have played at Razzmatazz, and recent concerts have included Antony and the Johnsons, the Arctic Monkeys and Róisín Murphy. On Friday and Saturday nights (1am–6am), the venue is divided into five clubs, each with its own individual theme. The club regularly hosts international guest DJs, including Jarvis Cocker, Shaun Rider and Peter Smith among others. *See p100.*

For more bars & clubs in the old town **See pp76–7 & p86**

Left **Club scene, Sitges** Right **Restaurante Castro**

Gay & Lesbian Hang-outs

1 Antinous Llibreria-Cafè
Antinous is a popular, gay meeting point just off the southern end of La Rambla. The café incorporates a spacious shop, stocking gifts, books and videos, and has a small bar area with exhibitions. Pick up a copy of *Nois*, a free magazine available in most gay venues, which gives the lowdown on the gay scene. ⊗ *C/Josep Anselm Clavé 6 • Map L6 • Closed Sun • DA*

Party-goers, Free Girls

2 Dietrich Gay Teatro Café
A gay venue with a mixed door policy, Dietrich is a trendy club with attractive golden walls and an internal garden. As well as playing house and garage music, it features performances by drag artists, dancers and acrobats. ⊗ *Consell de Cent 255 • Map D3*

3 Restaurante Castro
This ultra-chic restaurant offers hefty portions of Mediterranean cuisine with an exotic twist. The heavy duty decor of industrial-style black chains and metal is toned down by soft lighting and relaxing music. Make a reservation, as this is

one of the most popular gay restaurants in town. ⊗ *C/Casanova 85 • Map D2 • 93 323 67 84 • Closed Sat lunch & Sun • €€€€ • DA*

4 Sauna Galilea
Barcelona's newest gay sauna (for men only) is ultra-clean, with four floors offering Turkish baths, Jacuzzis and saunas, as well as a bar and internet service. There are also private cabins, some with video players. ⊗ *C/Calàbria 59 • Map C3 • Adm*

5 Zeltas
One of the hottest club-bars in town, Zeltas has trendy decor, in the style of a loft apartment, and really pulls in the crowds. A heady mix of testosterone, potent drinks and pumping house makes this a prime spot to mingle with some Barcelona beauties. ⊗ *C/Casanova 75 • Map D3 • Occasional adm*

Books, Antinous Llibería-Cafè

b-guided **(see p134)** is available from selected stores and venues; it gives more information on gay-friendly restaurants, bars and shops.

6 Martin's

This exclusively gay club (only men are admitted) is at the top of the Passeig de Gràcia. Spread over three floors, there is a big dance floor, several bars, a pool area and a dark room. The atmosphere is hard-core without being sleazy. ◎ *Passeig de Gràcia 130 • Map E1 • Adm*

7 Metro

Metro has two dance floors, one playing house, while the other has a free-and-easy music policy and a pool table. The club only livens up around 2am. You can sometimes pick up free tickets at nearby Dietrich restaurant, another gay haunt. ◎ *C/Sepúlveda 185 • Map J1 • Adm • DA*

8 Free Girls

This classic, lesbian hangout is a booming club with beautiful bodies and fantastic dance music. Ultra-chilled surroundings mean it's easy to make acquaintances and relax the night away. The door policy is strictly female only. ◎ *C/Marià Cubí 4 • Map E1 • Occasional adm • Closed Mon–Wed*

9 Punto BCN

For over 10 years, this relaxed, friendly bar has stayed in vogue on a fickle gay scene. It gets impossibly busy around midnight at weekends and the music is loud, but it's a good place to get fired up for a night out and get the latest on what else is happening in town. ◎ *C/Muntaner 63 • Map D3 • DA*

10 Beaches

In summer, gay men gather for some sun, fun and plenty of posing in front of the Club de Natació Barcelona on Barceloneta beach near Plaça del Mar. ◎ *Map E6*

Top 10 Gay Hot Spots in Sitges

1 XXL

Popular with the in-crowd, with nice decor, a good drinks selection and techno music. ◎ *C/Joan Tarrida 7*

2 Parrots

A classic Sitges meeting point, this bar has drag queen waiters and a lovely outdoor terrace. ◎ *Plaça Industrial 2*

3 El Mediterráneo

A visit to this multi-space bar is a must for its original design. ◎ *C/St Bonaventura 6*

4 Trailer

Sitges' oldest gay disco is always packed with friendly faces. ◎ *C/Àngel Vidal 36 • Adm*

5 Organic

Organic is a new disco on the gay scene, frequented by a fashion-industry crowd. ◎ *C/Bonaire 15 • Adm*

6 Beaches

The beach in front of the Hotel Calípolis in Sitges' centre is a gay magnet, as is the nudist one on the way to the town of Vilanova.

7 Night-time Cruising

The pier just past Hotel Calípolis is one of the busiest cruising spots. Prime time is between 3am and dawn.

8 Miami

Keen prices and a friendly atmosphere make this restaurant a Sitges favourite. ◎ *C/St Pau 11 • 93 894 02 06*

9 Privilege

One of the newest gay music bars in town, Privilege has a different theme every night. ◎ *Carrer de Bonaire 24*

10 El Hotel Romàntic

A simple, gay-friendly hotel, with a pretty garden. ◎ *C/St Isidre 33 • 93 894 83 75 • www.hotel romantic.com*

The "Gayxample" around the intersection of C/Casanova and C/Diputació, is the heart of Barcelona's gay scene.

Left **Handbags, Avinguda Diagonal** Right **Shop front, Passeig de Gràcia**

🔟 Best Shopping Areas

1 Passeig de Gràcia
Barcelona's grand avenue of lavish *Modernista* buildings is fittingly home to the city's premier fashion and design stores. From the international big league (Chanel, Gucci, Swatch) to Spain's heavy hitters (Loewe, Camper, Zara, Mango; *see p139*), it's all here. And topping the interior design list is the perennially popular Vinçon *(see p106)*. Side streets reveal more sublime shopping, notably Carrer Consell de Cent, which is dotted with art galleries, and carrers Mallorca, València and Roselló. 🖲 *Map E3*

2 Bulevard Rosa & Bulevard dels Antiquaris
Opened in 1978, Barcelona's first fashion mall, Bulevard Rosa, is still one of its classiest, with over 100 shops showcasing clothes, shoes and accessories by Spanish and international designers. The adjoining Bulevard dels Antiquaris is a spacious mall, with over 60 antiques and

arts shops. 🖲 *Bulevard Rosa: Pg de Gràcia 53 • Map E2 • Open 10:30am– 9pm Mon–Sat* 🖲 *Bulevard dels Antiquaris: Pg de Gràcia 55–57 • Map E2 • Open 10:30am–8:30pm Mon–Sat*

3 Plaça de Catalunya & Carrer Pelai
The city's booming centrepiece is also its commercial crossroads, flanked by the department store El Corte Inglés and the shopping mall El Triangle, which includes FNAC (books, CDs, videos) and Séphora (perfumes and cosmetics). Lined with shoe and clothing shops, the nearby Carrer Pelai is said to have more pedestrian traffic than any other shopping street in Spain. 🖲 *El Corte Inglés: Pl de Catalunya 14 • Map M1 • Open 10am– 10pm Mon–Sat* 🖲 *El Triangle: C/Pelai 39 • Map L1 • Open 10am–10pm Mon–Sat*

4 Portal de l'Àngel
Once a Roman thoroughfare leading into the walled city of Barcino, today the pedestrian street of Portal de l'Àngel is traversed by hordes of shoppers toting bulging bags. The street is chock-full of shoe, clothing, jewellery and accessory shops. 🖲 *Map M2*

5 Rambla de Catalunya
The genteel, classier extension of La Rambla, this well-maintained

Shopping crowds, Portal de l'Àngel

street offers a refreshing change from its cousin's more down-at-heel carnival atmosphere. Chic shops and cafés, as well as their moneyed customers, pepper the street's length, from Plaça de Catalunya to Diagonal. You'll find everything from fine footwear and leather bags to linens and lamps. ◈ Map E2

Storefront, Carrer Portaferrisa

Gràcia

Old bookstores, family-run *botigues de comestibles* (grocery stores) and bohemian shops selling Indian clothing and accessories cluster along Carrer Astúries (and its side streets) and along Travessera de Gràcia. A string of contemporary clothing and shoe shops also lines Gran de Gràcia. ◈ Map F1

Avinguda Diagonal

Big and brash, traffic-choked Diagonal is hard to miss, a cacophonous avenue that cuts, yes, diagonally across the entire city. It is a premier shopping street, particularly west of Passeig de Gràcia to its culmination in L'Illa mall and the large El Corte Inglés department store near Plaça Maria Cristina. Lining this long stretch is a host of high-end clothing and shoe stores (Armani, Loewe and Hugo Boss among them), interior design shops, jewellery and watch purveyors, and more. ◈ Map D1

Carrer Portaferrissa

From zebra platform shoes to bellybutton rings and pastel baby T-shirts, this street's other name could well be Carrer "Trendy". Along this strip you'll find El Mercadillo (see p75) mini-mall, crammed with hip little shops selling spiked belts, frameless sunglasses, surf wear and the like. Just off this street is Galeries Maldà, Barcelona's first shopping gallery, with a range of shops and a cinema showing original-version independent and Bollywood films (see p67).
◈ Galeries Maldà: Pl del Pi 1 • Map M3
• Open 10am–1:30pm & 4–8pm Mon–Sat

El Born

Amid El Born's web of streets are all sorts of art and design shops. Passeig del Born and Carrer Rec are dotted with innovative little galleries (from sculpture to interior design), plus clothing and shoe boutiques. ◈ Map P4

La Maquinista

Housed in a converted locomotive factory in the Barri de Sant Andreu is Barcelona's gleaming new shopping complex. The mall offers everything under one roof, with over 200 shops, a multiplex cinema, a bowling alley and fast-food eateries galore. ◈ Pg de Potosí 2, 4 km E city centre • Off map • Open 10am–10pm Mon–Sat

Produce, Mercat de Santa Caterina

Most Fascinating Markets

Mercat de La Boqueria
Barcelona's most famous food market is conveniently located on La Rambla *(see pp12–13)*. Freshness reigns supreme and shoppers are spoiled for choice, with hundreds of stalls selling everything from vine-ripened tomatoes to haunches of beef and moist wedges of Manchego cheese. The city's seaside status is in full evidence at the fish stalls. ◈ *La Rambla 91 • Map L3 • Open 7am–8pm Mon–Sat*

Els Encants
Barcelona's best flea market, Els Encants (east of the city) is where you'll find everything you want, from second-hand clothes, electrical appliances and toys to home-made pottery and used books. Discerning browsers can fit out an entire kitchen from an array of pots and pans. Bargain-hunters should come early. The market may move to a different location in 2010. ◈ *Pl de les Glòries Catalanes • Map H3 • Open 7am–5:30pm Mon, Wed, Fri & Sat*

Fira de Santa Llúcia
The Christmas season is officially under way when local artisans set up shop outside the Cathedral for the annual Christmas fair. Well worth a visit if only to peruse the row upon row of *caganers*, miniature figures squatting to *fer caca* (take a poop). Uniquely Catalan, the *caganers* are usually hidden in the back of nativity scenes. This unusual celebration of the scatological also appears in other Christmas traditions. ◈ *Pl de la Seu • Map N3 • Open 1–23 Dec: 10am–8pm (times may vary) daily*

Book & Coin Market at Mercat de Sant Antoni
For book lovers, there's no better way to spend Sunday morning than browsing at this market (west of the city). You'll find a mind-boggling assortment of weathered paperbacks, ancient tomes, stacks of old magazines, comics, postcards and lots more, from coins to videos. ◈ *C/Comte d'Urgell • Map D2 • Open 8am–3pm Sun*

Fira de Santa Llúcia, Plaça de la Seu

Fira Artesana, Plaça del Pi

The Plaça del Pi *(see p37)* brims with natural and organic foods during the Fira Artesana, when producers bring their goods to this corner of the Barri Gòtic. The market specializes in home-made cheeses

Cheeses, Fira Artesana, Plaça del Pi

and honey – from clear clover honey from the Pyrenees to nutty concoctions from Morella. ® *Pl del Pi • Map M3 • Open 10am–2pm & 5–9pm 1st & 3rd Fri, Sat & Sun of month*

Fira de Numismàtica

Spread out in the elegant Plaça Reial *(see p72)*, this popular stamp and coin market draws avid collectors from all over the city. The newest collectors' items are phone cards and old *xapes de cava* (cava bottle cork foils). When the market ends (and the local police go to lunch), a makeshift flea market takes over. Old folks from the barrio and immigrants haul out their belongings – old lamps, clothing, junk – and lay it all out on cloths on the ground. ® *Pl Reial • Map L4 • Open 9:30am–2:30pm Sun*

Mercat de la Concepció

In the heart of the Eixample is this large market, renowned for its flower stalls, which are open continuously from Monday to Saturday. Blooming bouquets at the entrance offer a fragrant welcome to the market. ® *C/ València at C/Bruc • Map F2 • Open 8am–3pm Mon & Sat, 8am–8:30pm Tue–Fri*

Mercat de Santa Caterina

Each barrio has its own food market with tempting displays but this one boasts a spectacular setting. Opened in 2005, the new building was designed by Catalan architect Enric Miralles (1955–2000). ® *Av Francesc Cambó 16 • Map N3 • Open 8am–2pm Mon, 8am–3:30pm Tue, Wed & Sat, 8am–8:30pm Thu & Fri*

Mercat del Art de la Plaça de Sant Josep Oriol

At weekends, local artists flock to this Barri Gòtic square to sell their art and set up their easels. You'll find everything from watercolours of Catalan landscapes to oil paintings of churches and castles. ® *Pl de Sant Josep Oriol • Map M4 • Open 11am–8:30pm Sat, 10am–2pm Sun*

Mercat dels Antiquaris

Antiques aficionados and collectors contentedly rummage through jewellery, watches, candelabras, silver trays, embroidery and assorted bric-a-brac at this long-running antiques market in front of the Cathedral. ® *Pl de la Seu • Map N3 • Open 10am–9pm Thu*

For more on shopping **See pp50–51**

53

Left **City vista**, Mirador de Colom Right **Gargoyles and view, Sagrada Família**

🔟 City Views

1 Tibidabo
The mountain of Tibidabo is the best vantage point for a bird's-eye view of Barcelona. Thrill-seekers opt for a spin on the Tibidabo fairground attraction *(see p111)* called La Atalaya, a rickety basket attached to an ancient crane-like contraption which gives a 360-degree view of Barcelona, the sea and the Pyrenees. A less giddy option is the Torre de Collserola *(see p111)* with its transparent lift rising up 288 m (945 ft). And for those who wish to keep their feet firmly on solid ground – cocktail in hand – settle in at the Mirablau bar. *See p116.*

2 Castell de Montjuïc
Montjuïc offers myriad viewpoints. The best is from the castle and gardens with their superb panoramas over the port and the city. Take the cable car up to the castle and walk down through ever-changing vistas to the Bar Miramar *(see p95)* for a refreshing drink. *See p89.*

Barcelona from Castell de Montjuïc

3 Les Golondrines & Orsom Catamaran
The sea offers a less vertiginous view of the cityscape. Glide out of the harbour on the pleasure boats known as *golondrines* or try the exhilarating trip under sail on an enormous catamaran. Both trips offer ample views of the city and of the new Port Olímpic area *(see p133).* ◊ Les Golondrines, Portal de la Pau • Map L6 • Call 93 442 31 06 for times • www.lasgolondrinas. com ◊ Orsom Catamaran, Portal de la Pau • Map L6 • Call 93 441 05 37 for times • www.barcelona-orsom.com

4 Cable Cars
The swaying cable cars that glide slowly between the Port and Montjuïc are something of a Barcelona landmark. To those not afraid of heights, they reveal hidden aspects of the city and provide a pleasurable way to get to the top of Montjuïc *(see p133).* ◊ Miramar, Montjuïc/Port de Barcelona • Map C5, D6 & E6 • Open daily Apr–May, Oct: 10am–7pm; Jun–Sep: 10am–9pm; Nov–Mar: 10am–6pm • Adm

5 Mirador de Colom
At the end of La Rambla, the statue of Christopher Columbus offers a good vantage point for viewing the city. The column, rising 80 m (262 ft), was built in 1888. The elevator that whisks visitors to the top has, fortunately, been renovated since then! ◊ La Rambla/Drassanes • Map L6 • Open May–Oct: 9am–8:30pm daily; Nov–Apr: 10am–6:30pm daily • Adm

Sagrada Família

When work first began, Gaudí's magical church lay on the outskirts of the city and Barcelona would have been just a shadow in the distance. A hundred years on, the church is located in the heart of the Eixample and the bell towers offer dizzying vistas of the entire city. An added bonus are the wonderful close-ups of the extraordinary Sagrada Família itself. *See pp8–11.*

View of the city and Casa-Museu Gaudí, Parc Güell

El Corte Inglés

The top floor of this department store has a glass-fronted cafeteria and restaurant with a terrace – an excellent place to lunch or just have a coffee. From here there are views of the nearby Plaça de Catalunya, the old town and the Eixample. The enormous store below stocks just about anything you might need to buy. ✆ *Pl de Catalunya 14 • Map M1 • Free • DA*

Parc Güell

In the north of the city, Gaudí's monumental *Modernista* park presents spectacular views across Barcelona and out to the Mediterranean from its various terraced levels. Trees and patches of woodland act as welcome shade from the fierce summer sun. *See p112.*

Barcelona Cathedral

From the heart of the Barri Gòtic, the Cathedral rooftop offers one of the least changed vistas in the city. Look out over the ramshackle rooftops – some dating to the 12th century – and the narrow alleys that spill out in all directions. There is a small charge for the elevator to the top. *See pp14–15.*

Helicopter Rides

For a bird's-eye view of Barcelona, consider a helicopter ride over the city. Helipistas SL will take a minimum of 2 people on a 30-minute ride over Montjuïc, the port and the southern part of the city. Transport to and from the out-of-town airport is included in the price. ✆ *Pick up from any city centre location • Call 93 730 49 11 or check www.helipistas.com for more information • Adm • DA*

Barcelona's Top 10

Left **Barceloneta beach** Right **Parc de Joan Miró**

🔟 Parks & Beaches

1 Parc de la Ciutadella
Barcelona's largest land-scaped park offers a serene antidote to city life. Once the location of the 18th-century military citadel, this lovely 19th-century park is now home to the zoo, the Catalan parliament, two museums and a boating lake. There is an inviting café in the Hivernacle (winter green-house), which hosts occasional live music. *See pp16–17.*

2 Parc Güell
Originally conceived as a suburban estate to the north of the city, Parc Güell is like a sur-real, Asian terraced farm. Twisting pathways and avenues of col-umned arches blend in with the hillside, playfully fusing nature and fantasy. The esplanade, with its stunning, curved, mosaic bench, is the park's centrepiece. From here

Cascade Fountain, Parc de la Ciutadella

there are spectacular views *(see p55)* of the entire city and of the fairy-tale gatehouses below. Gaudí's former home is now the Casa-Museu Gaudí. *See p112.*

3 Jardins del Laberint d'Horta
These enchanting Neo-Classical gardens date back to 1791, making this elegant park one of the oldest in the city. Situated up above the city, where the air is cooler and cleaner, the park includes themed gardens, waterfalls and a small canal. The highlight is the enor-mous maze, which has a statue of Eros at its centre. *See p113.*

4 Parc de Cervantes
Built in 1964 to celebrate 25 years of Franco rule, this beautiful park on the outskirts of town would have been more appropriately named Park of the Roses. There are over 11,000 rose bushes of 245 varieties; when in bloom, their aroma pervades the park. People pour in at weekends, but the park is blissfully deserted during the week. ⊗ *Av Diagonal • Off map*

5 Jardins de Pedralbes
These picturesque gardens lie just in front of the former Palau Reial (royal palace) of Pedralbes – now home to the Museu de Ceràmica and Museu de les Arts Decoratives *(see p112)*. Under the shade of an enormous eucalyptus tree and near a small bamboo forest is a fountain by Gaudí,

All the city parks are officially open from around 10am until dusk.

which was only discovered in 1983. ◈ *Av Diagonal 686* • *Off map*

6 Parc de Joan Miró

Also know as Parc de l'Escorxador, this park was built on the site of a 19th-century slaughter-house (*excorxador*). Dominating the paved upper level of the park is Miró's striking 22-m (72-ft)

Parc de l'Espanya Industrial

sculpture, *Dona i Ocell (Woman and Bird*; 1983). Elsewhere there are three children's play areas set around a café. ◈ *C/Tarragona* • *Map B2*

7 Parc de l'Espanya Industrial

Built on the site of a former textiles factory, this modern park, by Basque architect Luis Peña Ganchegui, has deteriorated somewhat since its inauguration in 1985. It still has a certain appeal, including ten strange lighthouse-style towers that line the boating lake and an enormous cast-iron dragon, which doubles as a slide. There's a good terrace bar with a playground for the kids. ◈ *Pl de Joan Peiró* • *Off map*

8 City Beaches

The beaches of Barcelona were once insalubrious areas to be avoided. With the 1992 Olympics they underwent a radical face-lift and today the stretches of Barceloneta and the Port Olímpic are a major people magnet. Just a short hop on the metro from the city centre, they provide the perfect opportunity for a refreshing Mediterranean dip. The beaches are regularly

cleaned and the many facilities include showers, toilets, childrens' play areas, volleyball nets and an open-air gym. There are boats and surfboards for rent. Be warned: bag snatching is endemic. *See p97*.

9 Castelldefels

Just 20 km (12 miles) south of Barcelona are 5 km (3 miles) of wide, sandy beaches with shallow waters. Beach bars entice week-end sun worshippers out of the afternoon sun for long, lazy sea-food lunches and jugs of sangria aplenty. Windsurfers and pedalos are for hire. ◈ *Off map* • *Train to Platja de Castelldefels from Estació de Sants or Passeig de Gràcia*

10 Premià/El Masnou

By far the best beaches within easy reach of Barcelona, just 20 km (12 miles) to the north, these two adjoining beaches lure locals with gorgeous golden sand and clear, blue waters. ◈ *Train to Premià or El Masnou from Plaça de Catalunya or Estació de Sants*

Explore Barcelona's parks by bike
For details on bicycle hire **See p131 & p133**

Left **La Rambla** Right **Cyclist, Passeig Marítim**

🔟 Walks & Bike Rides

La Rambla & The Port
From Plaça de Catalunya, stroll the length of Barcelona's most famous street, La Rambla *(see pp12–13)*, stopping en route to enjoy the street performances. Turn left at the port and admire the luxury yachts as you follow the water round to Barceloneta. Continue along Pg Joan de Borbó and turn left down any of the side streets that lead to the sand and sea. ◈ *Map M1*

Barri Gòtic
Wandering this network of atmospheric, ancient streets is the best way to experience the old town. Take a short stretch of the busy C/Portaferrisa *(see p51)* from La Rambla and turn right down tiny C/Petritxol *(see p74)*, with its confectionery shops and jewellers, to the Església de Santa Maria del Pi. Continue down C/Rauric, left onto C/Ferran and up to Plaça de Sant Jaume *(see p71)*. Turn left onto C/Bisbe leading to Plaça de la Seu and the Cathedral *(see pp14–15)*. ◈ *Map L3*

Eixample
For some of the city's most breathtaking *Modernista* gems, walk the length of Pg de Gràcia south to north, past the Mansana de la Discòrdia *(see p103)* and La Pedrera *(see pp20–21)*. Turn right onto C/Mallorca, which leads to Gaudí's Sagrada Família *(see pp 8–11)*. Take a left along C/Marina, past the church's awe-inspiring Nativity Façade, and head up Av Gaudí to Hospital de la Santa Creu i de Sant Pau *(see p103)*. ◈ *Map E3*

Tibidabo
Get high above the city by following the gently climbing Av del Tibidabo from the FGC station. Then follow signposts to the right through the steep wooded park, Font del Racó, and continue until you arrive at Plaça Doctor Andreu with its terrace bars and panoramic city views. ◈ *Map B1*

Montjuïc
Take in the city's green scene with an amble around Montjuïc's verdant slopes. The initial climb

Parc de Collserola

> The CCCB *(see pp28–9)* offers occasional guided walks in English during the year. For more on walking tours **See p133.**

to the grandiose Palau Nacional *(see pp18– 19)* from Plaça d'Espanya is eased by a series of escalators. From the palace, veer left and continue along the main road, stopping off at Jardí Mossèn Jacint Verdaguer *(see p94)* before continuing round to Miramar for a spectacular view. 🅢 *Map B3*

Backstreet, Barri Gòtic

Parc de Collserola

It's difficult to believe that this serene nature reserve lies just 10 minutes drive from the metropolis. Explore its delightful hiking, biking and nature trails on foot or by mountain bike. Take the funicular train to the top of Tibidabo and head towards the Torre de Collserola *(see p111)*, turning off on any one of the colour-coded woodland paths. A tourist information point provides maps and further information. 🅢 *Tourist Info: Carretera de Vallvidrera a Sant Cugat, km 4.7 • Map E3 • Open 9:30am–3pm daily*

Coastal Bike Ride

Breeze along the city's coastal cycle path and take in seaside Barcelona. Pick up the path from the bottom of La Rambla and follow it north to Barceloneta, where it runs along the beachfront, past the shiny new Port Olímpic as far as Platja de la Mar Bella. 🅢 *Map B3*

Diagonal Bike Ride

From Pedralbes to the sea, this route along the city's most elegant boulevard gives you a clear idea of Barcelona's size. The tree-lined cycle path follows Diagonal; start at the top (Zona Universitària) and continuing through the new city of Diagonal Mar until you arrive on the other side of the city just a stone's throw from the Besòs River. 🅢 *Map A1*

Les Planes

Just a 15-minute *ferrocarril* ride from Plaça de Catalunya (in the direction of Sant Cugat) is the picturesque spot of Baixador de Valvidrera. Perfect for an out-of-town stroll, there is a steep path through the woods, which opens up into a beautiful, green valley. In summer, there are barbecue facilities where you can throw on your own steaks. 🅢 *4 km N of Barcelona*

Costa Brava Coastal Path

At the end of the Platja de Sant Pol in Sant Feliu de Guíxols is the start of a beautiful, coastal path that winds north through shady tamarind trees with views of rocky coves and the Mediterranean. Around the headland and down a stairway, you will find the fabulous beach of Sa Conca, voted the sixth best in Spain. 🅢 *75 km NE of Barcelona*

Bike rental is available from Barcelona Bici, Mirador de Colom (tel: 93 285 38 32). For more on bike rental See p131 & p133.

59

Left **Bernat Picornell outdoor pool** Right **Sunbathers, Platja de la Barceloneta**

🔟 Activities in Barcelona

1 Sunbathing & Swimming
Head to the city beaches (see p57) to cool down and escape the stifling heat. Barcelona boasts a wide range of fabulous beaches, from Barceloneta, lined with bars and restaurants, to the reclaimed beaches of Vila Olímpica, Bogatell and Mar Bella. ◈ *Map F6–H6*

2 Watersports
A wide variety of activities is on offer in the jet-set surroundings of Port Olímpic and neighbouring beaches, including dinghy sailing and windsurfing. For the experienced, boats are available for hire from the Escola Municipal de Vela; for the beginner, there are classes. Night-time kayaking tours of the city's beaches are available from Desconnecta. ◈ *Escola Municipal de vela • Moll de Gregal • Map G6 • 93 225 79 40 • Open 9:30am–8pm daily* ◈ *Desconnecta • C/Ticia 42 • 93 417 93 62 • www.desconnecta.com*

Volleyball, Platja de Nova Icària

3 Swimming
Set in the green environs of Montjuïc, the outstanding outdoor pool of Bernat Picornell is surprisingly uncrowded, especially in summer. Renovated for the Olympics, it has sun loungers, an ice-cream stall and a huge electronic timer for swimmers to time their sprints. During the summer, there's a film programme known as "watch and swim". ◈ *Av del Estadi • Map A4 • Open 7am–midnight Mon–Fri, 7am–9pm Sat, 7am–8:30pm (4pm winter) Sun • Adm • DA*

4 Pitch-&-Putt Golf
The Costa Brava is emerging as one of Spain's top golf destinations but if you're looking to tee off in town, your best bets are the nearby pitch-and-putt courses in Badalona and Castelldefells. ◈ *Castell de Godmar, Badalona, 5km NE Barcelona • 93 395 27 79 • Open 8:30am–dusk daily* ◈ *Canal Olímpic • Castelldefels, 20 km S Barcelona • 93 636 28 96 • Open 9am–9pm Tue–Sat (to 8pm Sun)*

5 Beach Volleyball
On weekend mornings year-round you can pick up a volleyball game at Platja de la Nova Icària. It is best to go with enough people to form a team, but you are usually welcome to join in an ongoing game. ◈ *Map H5*

6 Weight Lifting
The sports centre in the Parc de l'Espanya Industrial (see p57) has excellent weight-lifting facilities, a sauna, Turkish bath, Jacuzzi, badminton courts and a swimming pool. One-day membership is available. ◈ *C/ Muntadas • Off map • 93 426 10 70 • Open 6am–11pm Mon–Fri, 8am–9pm Sat, 8am–2:30pm Sun • Adm*

For more on Barcelona's parks & beaches See pp56–7

7 Biking

Hire a city bike from Barcelona Biking and breeze around Barcelona. Mountain bikes are also available for rent here. *Barcelona Biking • Baixada de Sant Miquel, 6 • 65 635 63 00*

8 Pool & Billiards

Shoot some pool at Gràcia's lovely Cafè Salambó, where there are pool and billard tables for rent upstairs, not to mention good drinks, tasty food, a friendly ambience and a lively, arty crowd *(see p115)*.

9 Sardanes

These traditional Catalan dances *(see p65)* take place regularly all over the city and at most local festas. Far from being exclusive, they often involve up to 200 people and there's no reason why you can't be one of them. The tourist office *(see p134)* can provide information on these events.

10 Frontó

Egalitarian tennis or poor man's squash, all you need is a tennis racket and ball to beat against the wall to enjoy this popular pastime. The city's parks are full of free *frontó* courts; one of the best is next to the Casa del Mig in the Parc de l'Espanya Industrial *(see p57)*.

Biking in Barcelona

Top 10 Spectator Sports & Events

1 FC Barcelona Football
Tickets to see this first-division side are rare; 4,000 are sold a week before matches – call to find out when to queue. *Sep–Jun • 93 496 36 00*

2 RCD Espanyol
It's easier to get tickets for this first-division football side; they play at Estadi Olímpic *(see p90)*. *Sep–Jun • 90 219 62 59*

3 FC Barcelona Basketball
The team of the city's second favourite sport play at the Palau Blaugrana. *Sep–May • 90 218 99 00*

4 FC Barcelona Hockey
Roller hockey (played on skates) is popular in Barcelona. *Oct–Apr • 90 218 99 00*

5 Torneo Conde de Godo
This tennis tournament attracts some big names. *mid–late Apr • 93 203 78 52*

6 Cursa El Corte Inglés
A 11-km (7-mile) run with thousands of participants. *May or Jun • 90 112 21 22*

7 La Volta Ciclista de Catalunya
Cyclists warm up for the more serious European events with this testing route. *late May–Jun • 93 431 82 98*

8 Montmeló
Motor racing, including Formula 1, regularly comes to this circuit. *Apr–May • 93 571 97 71 • www.circuitcat.com*

9 Cursa La Mercè
A 10-km (6-mile) run through Barcelona's centre. *Late Sep • 010*

10 Catalunya Rally
Top-class rally-driving in spectacular surroundings. *Oct • ww.rallyracc.com*

Left **Children at play, Port Olímpic beach** Right **Penguins, Parc Zoològic**

Attractions for Children

1 Parc d'Atraccions del Tibidabo

With its old-fashioned rides, the only surviving funfair in the city is a delight for children of all ages. The attractions include a House of Horrors, bumper cars, a ferris wheel and the Museu dels Autò-mates *(see p41)*, with animatron-ics of all shapes and sizes. There's also a puppet show, picnic areas, playgrounds and plenty of bars and restaurants. *See p111.*

2 Parc Zoològic

The zoo has an enormous adventure playground where chil-dren can run wild. There are also dolphin and whale shows in one of the aquariums. Other activities for children include guided tours and workshops. The "farm" area has goats and rabbits that younger children can stroke. *See p16.*

3 Museu Marítim

The fantastic Maritime Museum brings the seafaring world to life with the hollering

of pirates, the report of cannons and the underwater gurgling of submarines. Well worth a look is the full-size Spanish galleon com-plete with sound and light effects. Set in the vast former medieval shipyards, the Drassanes, this is an absolute must for any budding sea captain. *See p81.*

4 L'Aquàrium

One of Europe's biggest aquariums, this underwater king-dom is made up of 21 enormous tanks brimming with nearly 400 marine species. The highlight of a visit is the Oceanari, where a walk-through glass tunnel will bring you face to face with three huge grey sharks – named Drake, Morgan and Maverick – lurking in 4.5 million litres (990,000 gallons) of water. *See p97.*

5 Jardins del Laberint d'Horta

The main feature of this excep-tional park is the huge, hedged maze where children can live

Children, Parc Zoològic

out their *Alice in Wonderland* fantasies. Unfulfilled expectations of mad hatters are made up for by an enormous play area with a bar and terrace. The park is particularly busy on Sundays. See p113.

Montjuïc Cable Cars

Unlike the nerve-jangling cable-car ride across the port, these smaller, lower-altitude cable car trips are a better option if you have children with you. The ride to the Montjuïc summit also has the added appeal of the castle (see p89) at the top, with cannons for the kids to clamber on. Ⓢ *Parc de Montjuïc • Map C5 • Open Nov–Mar: 10am–6pm daily; Apr, May, Oct: 10am–7pm daily; Jun–Sep: 10am–9pm daily • Adm*

Human statue, La Rambla

La Rambla

Your shoulders will be aching from carrying the kids high above the crowds by the time you reach the end of Barcelona's main boulevard. Fire eaters, buskers, human statues decked out as Greek goddesses – you name it and it's likely to be keeping the hordes entertained on La Rambla. Put a coin in the human statue's hat and be rewarded with a sudden move, or, if you're a child, the gift of a tiny lollipop. See pp12–13.

City Beaches

For kids, there's more to going to the beach in Barcelona than just splashing in warm waters and

frolicking in the sand. The Port Vell and Port Olímpic *platges* (beaches) offer a good choice of well-equipped play areas to keep the little ones entertained. Numerous bars and restaurants make finding refreshment easy, too. See p97.

Boat Trips

Barcelona's *golondrines* (see p133) make regular trips out of the port, providing a fun excursion for older children. Younger kids, however, will probably prefer paddling around in a rowing boat on the lake at the Parc de la Ciutadella. See pp16–17.

Museu d'Història de Catalunya

This child-friendly museum traces Catalonia's history through a range of dynamic, interactive exhibits. The best of these allows visitors to get dressed up as medieval knights and gallop around on wooden horses. Very popular with Catalan school groups, it's equally enjoyable for visitors. Every Saturday, the museum hosts a story hour when Catalan legends are re-enacted for children as well as other children's activities. See p97.

Festes de la Mercè

Catalan Folk Festivals & Traditions

1 Festes de la Mercè

Barcelona's main festival is a riotous week-long celebration in honour of La Mercè *(see p39)*. The night sky lights up with fireworks, outdoor concerts are held, and there's barely a bottle of *cava* left in the city by the festival's end. Processions and parades feature *gegants* (giant wooden figures operated by people). ✿ *Week of 23 Sep*

Gegants, Festes de la Mercè

2 El Dia de Sant Jordi

On this spring day, Barcelona is transformed into a vibrant, open-air book and flower market. Men and women exchange presents of roses, to celebrate Sant Jordi *(see p39)* and books, in tribute to Cervantes and Shakespeare, who both died on 23 April 1616. ✿ *23 Apr*

3 Verbena de Sant Joan

In celebration of Saint John, and the start of summer, this is Catalonian's night to play with fire and play they do, with gusto. Fireworks streak through the night sky and bonfires are set ablaze on beaches and in towns throughout the region. ✿ *23 Jun*

4 Festa Major de Gràcia

During this week-long *festa*, (the largest party of the summer), revellers congregate in Gràcia's decorated streets. Parades, open-air concerts, fireworks and plenty of beer and cava fuel the infectious merriment. ✿ *Mid-to late-Aug*

5 Carnaval in Sitges

The buzzing beach town of Sitges *(see p121)* explodes during Carnaval, celebrated in flamboyant fashion. Over-the-top floats parade among drag queens, lip-synching contests and a fresh-off-the-beach crowd warmed by sun and plenty of beer. ✿ *3–4 days Feb–mid-Mar*

6 Festa de la Patum

The village of Berga (90 km/ 60 miles north of Barcelona) hosts one of Catalonia's liveliest festivals. The event gets its name from the folks who used to chant *pa-tum* (the sound of a drum). Streets spill over with merrymakers as fireworks crackle and dwarfs, devils and dragons dance atop parade floats. ✿ *Corpus Christi (May)*

7 Festa del Aquelarre

The small town of Cervera (100 km/62 miles west of Barcelona) erupts with parties, parades and concerts for this festival. The epicentre is C/do los Bruixes, a medieval alley that cuts through the old town. ✿ *Last weekend Aug*

The English-language website www.spain.info has a section dedicated to Spanish festivals.

Castells

8 *Castells* is one of Catalonia's most spectacular folk traditions. Trained *castellers* stand on each other's shoulders to create a human castle – the highest tower takes the prize. The crowning moment is when a child scales the human mass to make the sign of the cross. *Castells* are often performed in Plaça Sant Jaume. ◊ *Jun*

Sardanes

9 "The magnificent, moving ring" is how Catalan poet Joan Maragall described the *sardana*, Catalonia's regional dance. Subdued yet intricate, it is performed to the tunes of the *cobla*, a traditional brass and woodwind band. *Sardanes* can be seen in Plaça de la Seu and Plaça Sant Jaume year round *(see p14)*.

Catalan Christmas & Cavalcada del Reis

10 The *Nadal* (Christmas) season begins on 1 December with the arrival of the festive artisan fairs. On 5 January is the Cavalcada dels Reis, the spectacular Three Kings Parade. In Barcelona, the kings arrive by sea and are welcomed by city officials in front of transfixed children.

Castells

Top 10 Music, Theatre & Art Festivals

1 **Festival del Grec**
Barcelona's largest music, theatre and dance festival. ◊ *Late Jun–Jul • 93 316 11 11 or 90 210 12 12*

2 **Festival del Sónar**
This electronic music and multimedia festival has technology fairs and musical events. ◊ *Mid Jun • www.sonar.es*

3 **Festival Internacional de Jazz**
Big-name and experimental live jazz. ◊ *Oct–Dec • 93 481 70 40 • www.theproject.es*

4 **Sitges International Film Festival**
The foremost fantasy film festival in the world. ◊ *Early Oct • www.cinemasitges.com*

5 **Festival de Música Antiga**
Concerts of early music in the Barri Gòtic and at L'Auditori. ◊ *Apr & May • 93 247 93 00*

6 **Clàssica als Parcs**
Classical music concerts are held in the city's parks. ◊ *Jul • 010*

7 **Festival de Guitarra**
International guitar festival. ◊ *Mar–Jun • 90 210 12 12 • www.theproject.es*

8 **Festival de Músiques del Món**
Ethnic and world music acts at L'Auditori. ◊ *Oct • 93 247 93 00*

9 **Festival de Flamenco**
A week of outstanding flamenco music at the CCCB in the Raval. ◊ *Late May • 93 443 43 46*

10 **Festival de Música**
The Spanish village of Llívia, just over the French border, presents choral groups and orchestras from around the world. ◊ *Llívia • Aug & Dec • 97 289 63 13*

Left **Teatre Grec** Right **Gran Teatre del Liceu**

Performing Arts & Music Venues

1 Gran Teatre del Liceu
Phoenix-like, the Liceu has risen from the ashes of two devastating fires since its inauguration in 1847. Now one of the greatest opera houses in Europe, it has an innovative programme and is famed for performances by home-grown talent, including one of the "three tenors" José Carreras, as well as Montserrat Caballé. ◈ *La Rambla • Map L4 • 93 485 99 13 • Guided tour 10am daily • Adm • DA*

2 Palau Sant Jordi
The star of the Olympic buildings, this stadium is normally home to Barcelona's basketball team *(see p61)*. It doubles up as the city's main arena for macro-concerts, which have included Madonna and U2. *See p90.* ◈ *Box office: 93 426 20 89 • Open for visits 10am–6pm (8pm Jul & Aug) Sat & Sun • Free • DA*

3 Teatre Grec
The most magical and enigmatic of all Barcelona's venues, this open-air amphitheatre, set in thick, verdant forest, makes an incredible setting for ballet, music or theatre. Only used for shows during the summer arts Festival del Grec, the gardens are open all year to visitors. *See p90.* ◈ *Box office: 90 210 12 12 • Open for visits 10am–dusk daily • Free*

4 Palau de la Música Catalana
Domenèch i Montaner's epic *Modernista* gem regularly serves up the best in jazz and classical music. It has lost some of its prestige to the Auditori, but it still hosts the annual guitar festival and attracts many visiting world music artists. *See pp26–7.*

5 Auditori de Barcelona
Located near the Teatre Nacional, this large auditorium is home to the Orquestra Simfònica de Barcelona. Acoustics and visibility are excellent and, in addition to classical music, it hosts regular jazz concerts. ◈ *C/Lepant 150 • Map G1 • 93 247 93 00 • DA*

Concert, Palau de la Música Catalana

6 Harlem Jazz Club

This small, intimate venue is one of the longest surviving clubs for alternative and lesser-known jazz and blues troupes. Free entrance if you buy a drink. *See p77.* ◈ *93 310 07 55*

For Catalan speakers, the Teatre Nacional de Catalunya (93 306 57 00) is a fine showcase for Catalan drama.

7 Mercat de les Flors

This is the venue of choice for performance theatre groups, such as La Fura dels Baus and Comediants, whose incredible mixture of circus and drama is easily accessible to non-Catalan speakers. ◉ C/Lleida 59 • Map B4 • 93 426 18 75 • www.mercatflors.org

8 Club Apolo

An old dance hall, with velvet covered balconies and panelled bars, this place has reinvented itself as one of the city's leading nightclubs. It attracts the latest in live techno and dance music. ◉ C/Nou de la Rambla 113 • Map K4 • 93 441 40 01 • www.sala-apolo.com

Harlem Jazz Club

9 JazzSí Club – Taller de Musics

Conceived as a multi-functional space, the JazzSí Club offers music workshops, lessons and daily concerts in the auditorium. The jazz, Cuban, flamenco or rock performances start between 7:30 and 9pm, and dinner is available from Monday to Friday. ◉ Requesens, 2 • Map J2 • 93 329 00 20 • Adm

10 Club Fellini

This club offers three different spaces: the Mirrors Lounge, with chic house music, the Bad Room, with electronic sessions, and the Red Room, the perfect space for flirting. ◉ La Rambla 27 • Map L5 • 93 272 49 80 • www.clubfellini.com

Top 10 Versión Original Cinemas

1 Verdi
One of the original VO cinemas, with five different screens. ◉ C/Verdi 32 • Map B2 • 93 238 79 90

2 Icària Yelmo Cineplex
An incredible 15 screens all showing original version films. ◉ C/Salvador Espriu 61 • Map H5 • 90 222 09 22

3 Casablanca
An old style, two-screen, cinema, which has retained its character. ◉ Pg de Gràcia 115 • Map E2 • 93 218 43 45

4 Boliche
A four-screen cinema showing mainly European films. ◉ Av Diagonal 508 • Map E1 • 93 218 17 88

5 Méliès Cinemes
Two-screened repertory cinema. ◉ C/Villarroel 102 • Map J1 • 93 451 00 51

6 Renoir-Les Corts
Multi-screened cinema with lots of Spanish and English films. ◉ C/Eugeni d'Ors 12 • Map A2 • 90 288 89 02

7 Verdi Park
Four-screen version of the original Verdi. ◉ C/Torrijos 49 • Map F1 • 93 238 79 90

8 Renoir Floridablanca
A multiplex that shows films from around the world. ◉ Floridablanca 135 • Map C3 • 90 288 89 02

9 Maldà
A small new cinema showing independent and Bollywood movies. ◉ C/del Pi 5 • Map M3 • 93 481 37 04

10 Filmoteca
The Catalan government's repertory cinema runs three VO shows daily. ◉ Av Sarrià 31–33 • Map D1 • 93 410 75 90 • Closed Aug

Barcelona's many versió original (original version) cinemas provide plenty of options for non-Catalan-speaking film aficionados.

AROUND
TOWN

Barri Gòtic &
La Ribera
70–79

El Raval
80–87

Montjüic
88–95

Port Vell,
Barceloneta
& Port Olímpic
96–101

Eixample
102–109

Gràcia, Tibidabo &
Zona Alta
110–117

Beyond Barcelona
118–127

BARCELONA'S TOP 10

Left **Museu d'Història de la Ciutat** Right **Saló de Cent, Ajuntament**

Barri Gòtic & La Ribera

THOUGH HARD TO IMAGINE TODAY, *there was a time when Barcelona was just a small Roman village (named Barcino) encircled by protective stone walls. Over the centuries, the village grew, culminating in a building boom in the 14th and 15th centuries. The Barri Gòtic (Gothic Quarter), a beautifully preserved neighbourhood of Gothic buildings, medieval places (squares) and atmospheric alleys, exists today as a splendid reminder of Barcelona's medieval heyday. The web of ancient, treasure-filled streets in this compact area is best explored by aimless wandering. The barrio's centrepiece – and its religious and social heart – is the 13th–century Cathedral and surrounding complex of period buildings. Nearby, the stately Plaça del Rei (see p36) is ringed by some of the best preserved medieval buildings in the area. Extending east of the Barri Gòtic is the ancient barrio of La Ribera, which includes El Born (see p72). Here, the lovely Carrer Montcada is lined with medieval palaces – five of which house the must-see Museu Picasso.*

Roman Arch, Carrer Paradis

🔟 Sights

1. Barcelona Cathedral
2. Museu Picasso
3. Palau de la Música Catalana
4. Plaça de Sant Jaume
5. Conjunt Monumental de la Plaça del Rei
6. Plaça Reial
7. Museu Frederic Marès
8. Església de Santa Maria del Mar
9. Museu Tèxtil i d'Indumentèrla
10. Museu Barbier–Mueller d'Art Precolombí

For sights & attractions on La Rambla See pp12–13

1 Barcelona Cathedral
Soaring over the Barri Gòtic is Barcelona's mighty Cathedral dating from 1298. *See pp14–15.*

2 Museu Picasso
Discover the youthful repertoire of one of the 20th–century's most revered artists. *See pp24–5.*

3 Palau de la Música Catalana
The city's most prestigious concert hall is a monument to both *la musica Catalana* and to *Modernisme. See pp26–7.*

4 Plaça de Sant Jaume
The site of the Plaça de Sant Jaume *(see p36)* was once the nucleus of Roman Barcino. With these roots, it seems fitting that the square has become home to Barcelona's two most important government buildings: the Palau de la Generalitat (seat of the Catalan government) and the Ajuntament (city hall). Look for the detailed carved relief of Sant Jordi, Catalonia's patron saint, on the 15th-century Generalitat façade. Within is the lovely 15th-century Capella de Sant Jordi *(see p39)*, designed by architect Marc Safont. A highlight of the Gothic Ajuntament is the lavish red-and-gold Saló de Cent, where

Cathedral spire

the Council of One Hundred ruled the city from 1372 to 1714. Also of note is the Pati dels Tarongers, a graceful patio with orange trees. Ⓢ *Palau de la Generalitat • Pl de Sant Jaume • Map M4 • Open 10:30am–1:30pm 2nd & 4th Sun of month for guided tours • Free* Ⓢ *Ajuntament • Pl de Sant Jaume • Map M4 • Open 10am–1:30pm Sun for guided tours • Free*

5 Conjunt Monumental de la Plaça del Rei
In the heart of the Barri Gòtic is the beautifully preserved, medieval Plaça del Rei *(see p36)*, presided over by the 13th- to 14th-century Palau Reial (royal palace). The impressive palace complex includes the Saló del Tinell, a massive hall crowned by Gothic arches, where Ferdinand and Isabel welcomed Columbus after his 1492 voyage to the Americas. The medieval Capella de Santa Àgata has a beautiful 15th-century altarpiece by Jaume Huguet. A visit to the Museu d'Història de la Ciutat gives access to the Palau Reial and to one of the largest underground excavations of Roman ruins on display in Europe. Ⓢ *Pl del Rei • Map M4 • Open 10am–8pm Tue–Sat, 10am–3pm Sun (Oct–May: closes 2–4pm, 7pm) • Adm • DA*

Left **Italianate façade, Palau de la Generalitat** Right **Mosaic pillar, Palau de la Música Catalana**

For more on Barri Gòtic squares See pp36–7

El Born

If you're hankering for a proper martini or perhaps some alternative jazz, then look no further than El Born, a musty-turned-hip neighbourhood, which was "reborn" several years ago. Students and artists moved in, attracted by cheap rents and airy warehouses, fostering an arty vibe that now blends in with the area's old-time aura. Experimental design shops share the narrow streets with traditional, balconied buildings strung with laundry. The bustling Passeig de Born, lined with bars and cafés, leads onto the lively Plaça Comercial, where the cavernous Born Market (in operation 1870–1970) is now being converted into a cultural centre and exhibition space (to open at the end of 2009).

Plaça Reial (1850s)

Plaça Reial

Late 19th-century elegance meets sangria-swilling café society in the arcaded Plaça Reial, one of Barcelona's most emblematic and entertaining squares. The *plaça* is planted with towering palm trees and encircled by stately, 19th-century buildings. The *Modernista* lampposts were designed by a young Gaudí in 1879. At the square's centre is a wrought-iron fountain representing the Three Graces. The square is the best place to start a big night out, with a cluster of restaurants, bars and cafés that draw the hoi polloi – including all sorts of shady pickpockets. ✪ *Map L4*

Museu Frederic Marès

This fascinating museum houses the life collection of wealthy Catalan sculptor Frederic

Medieval arch, Museu Frederic Marès

Marès. No mere hobby collector, the astute (and obsessive) Marès amassed holdings that a modern museum curator would die for. Among them, an impressive array of religious icons and statues – dating from Roman times to the present – and the spectacular "Museu Sentimental", which displays anything from ancient watches to fans and dolls. Also worth a visit during the summer months is the inviting Cafè d'Estiu *(see p78)* on the museum's sun-dappled patio. ✪ *Pl de Sant Iu 5–6 • Map N3 • Open 10am–7pm Tue–Sat, 10am–3pm Sun • Adm • Free Wed eve & 1st Sun of month, free guided visits on request, call 93 256 35 00*

Església de Santa Maria del Mar

The spacious, breathtaking interior of this 14th–century church, designed by architect Berenguer de Montagut, is the city's premier example of the austere Catalan Gothic style. The church is dedicated to Saint Mary of the Sea, the patron saint of sailors, and an ancient model ship hangs near one of the statues of the Virgin. Dubbed "the people's church", this is the city's most popular spot for exchanging wedding vows. ✪ *Pl de Santa Maria 1 • Map P5 • Open 9am–1:30pm & 4:30–8pm*

9 Centre del Disseny

Housed in a pair of adjoining medieval palaces, the Centre del Disseny (Design Centre) combines activities from different areas: architecture, graphic and communications design, product design and fashion design. The small but ultra-cool museum shop sells funky clothes, accessories and design collectables, while the café beckons with outdoor tables in a shady courtyard. In 2011 the collection will be moved to a new museum currently under construction in Plaça de les Glories. ⬥ C/Montcada 12–14 • Map P4 • Open 10am–6pm Tue–Sat, 10am–3pm Sun • Adm • DA

10 Museu Barbier-Mueller d'Art Precolombè

Pre-Columbian art and artifacts, spanning 3,000 years, are exhibited in the 16th-century Palau Nadal. Sculpture, ceramics and detailed gold and silver pieces represent the rich artistic traditions of the Aztecs, Mayans and Incas. Temporary exhibits explore the diversity of these civilizations. ⬥ C/Montcada 12–14 • Map P4 • Open 11am–7pm Tue–Fri, 10am–7pm Sat, (3pm Sun) • Adm; free 1st Sun of month • DA

Interior, Església de Santa Maria del Mar

Roman Barcelona

Morning

🕐 Starting at the Jaume I metro, enter the ancient walled city of Barcino on C/Llibreteria, once the main road to and from Rome. Head right up C/Veguer to **Plaça del Rei** *(see p36)* and descend into a fascinating underground web of Roman walls and waterways via the **Museu d'Història de la Ciutat** *(see p71)*. Also visible here are the remains of a 2nd-century workshop and an ancient bodega, a source of much Roman merrymaking. Back above ground, pause for a *cafè sol* at the terrace of **Café–Bar L'Antiquari** *(see p78)* and bask in Barcelona's Gothic glory days. Stroll towards the Cathedral's spires along C/de la Pietat. Turn right onto C/Bisbe, once a Roman thoroughfare, then right again on Av de la Catedral to visit the **Pia Almoina** *(see p15)*, where you can view a section of the Roman aqueduct and ride a glass elevator past Roman wall remains. Backtrack to Plaça Nova, once the Roman gateway to Barcino, cross the *plaça* and continue along C/Arcs.

Afternoon

🍴 Stop for lunch at the **Reial Cercle Artístic**, a late 19th-century artists' society. Ignore the "members only" sign; the restaurant is open to the public, and its tranquil balcony terrace provides a welcome breather from the crowds far below. After lunch, head up Av del Portal de l'Àngel and turn left onto C/Canuda to **Plaça de la Vila de Madrid** *(see p37)*. The square is a fitting end to your Roman ramble, for here are the necropolis remains, where Romans came to rest.

Left **Carrer del Bisbe** Centre **Església de Sant Just i Sant Pastor** Right **Plaça de Sant Felip Neri**

Best of the Rest

Carrer del Bisbe
Medieval Carrer del Bisbe is flanked by the Gothic Cases dels Canonges (House of Canons) and the Palau de la Generalitat (see p71). Connecting the two is an eye-catching Neo-Gothic arched stone bridge (1928). ✎ Map M3

Carrer de Santa Llúcia
At weekends, amateur opera singers perform on this medieval street, home to the Casa de l'Ardiaca (see p15), which has a ravishing little patio. ✎ Map M3

El Call
El Call was home to one of Spain's largest Jewish communities until their expulsion in the 15th century. The dark streets of this ghetto are so narrow it is said you can tie a handkerchief across their width. ✎ Map M4

Carrer Montcada
The "palace row" of La Ribera is lined with Gothic architectural gems, including the 15th-century Palau Aguilar, home to the Museu Picasso (see pp24–5), and the 17th-century Palau Dalmases with its Gothic chapel. ✎ Map P4

Plaça de Ramon Berenguer el Gran
This square boasts one of the largest intact sections of Barcelona's Roman walls. ✎ Map N3

Carrer Regomir & Carrer del Correu Vell
You'll find splendid Roman remains on Carrer Regomir, most notably within the medieval Pati Llimona. Two Roman towers are revealed on nearby Carrer del Correu Vell, and there are Roman walls on the leafy Plaça Traginers. ✎ Map M5

Plaça de Sant Felip Neri
Sunlight filters through tall trees in this hidden oasis of calm. The plaça is home to the Museu del Calçat (see p41). ✎ Map M3

Carrer Petritxol
This well-maintained medieval street is lined with traditional granges and xocolateries (confectionary cafés). Also here is the famous Sala Parés art gallery, founded in 1877, which once exhibited Picasso, Casas and other Catalan contemporaries. ✎ Map L3

Església de Sant Just i Sant Pastor
This picturesque Gothic church (1342) has sculptures inside that date back to the 9th century. ✎ Map M4

Església de Santa Anna
Mere paces from La Rambla is the unexpected tranquillity of this Romanesque church, with a leafy, 15th-century, Gothic cloister. ✎ Map M2

Left **Escribà Confiteria i Fleca** Centre **La Manual Alpargatera** Right **Bubó**

Shops: Gifts, Garments & Goodies

Escribà Confiteria i Fleca
If the glistening pastries and towering chocolate creations aren't enough of a lure, then the *Modernista* store-front certainly is. Buy goodies to go, or enjoy them on the spot in the small café. ◈ *La Rambla 83 • Map L3*

Como Agua de Mayo
Try this tiny boutique for original fashion and footwear by Spanish designers. The style is feminine and glamorous and the prices are surprisingly affordable. ◈ *C/Argenteria • Map N4*

Cocotte
Divine women's fashions, accessories and toiletries are found in this loft-style store. Among the labels are top Spanish and French names, such as Hoss, Intropia and See by Chloé. ◈ *C/Rec 65 • Map P5*

Atalanta Manufactura
This shop's delicate, hand-painted silks are created in an on-site workshop. Unusual designs include a Klimt-inspired, gilded silk. ◈ *Pg del Born 10 • Map P5*

La Manual Alpargatera
What do the Pope, Jack Nicholson and legions of *Barcelonins* have in common? They buy their espadrilles (*alpargatas*) here. ◈ *C/Avinyó 7 • Map M4*

Casa Colomina
Sink your teeth into *torró*, the Spanish nougat-and-almond speciality. Casa Colomina, established in 1908, offers a tantalizing array. ◈ *C/Portaferrissa 8 • Map L3*

Cereria Subirà
Founded in 1761, this is Barcelona's oldest shop. Today you'll find it crammed with every kind of candle imaginable. ◈ *Baixada Llibreteria 7 • Map N4*

L'Arca de l'Àvia
Amazing antique clothing from flapper dresses to boned corsets, silk shawls, puff sleeved shirts and pin-tucked shirt fronts. There's also a selection of antique dolls and fans. ◈ *C/Banys Nous 20 • Map M3*

Guantería Alonso
This long-established shop is still the place to visit if you are looking for colourful hand-painted fans, handmade gloves, delicately embroidered shawls, ornamental combs and other traditional Spanish accessories. ◈ *C/Santa Anna 27 • Map M2*

Bubó
This ultra-modern patisserie displays its sweet treats like miniature works of art. There is an adjoining café where the products can be tasted. ◈ *C/ Caputxes 10 • Map N5*

For tips on shopping and standard opening hours See p139

Left **La Vinya del Senyor** Right **Schilling**

Cocktail & Conversation Spots

1 Schilling
Fronted by large windows overlooking the throngs on Carrer Ferran, this spacious bar draws a sociable mix of both visitors and locals. ◎ C/Ferran 23 • Map M4

2 Bar L'Ascensor
An old-fashioned, dark-wood *ascensor* (elevator) serves as the entrance to this dimly-lit, convivial bar frequented by a cocktail-swilling crowd. ◎ C/Bellafila 3 • Map M4

3 Espai Barroc
Filling the gorgeous courtyard of the 17th-century Palau Dalmases is this sumptuously decorated "Baroque Space". Live opera and classical music are often featured on Thursday evenings, but drinks are pricey. ◎ C/Montcada 20 • Map P4 • Closed Mon

4 Ginger
An elegant bar that serves fine wines, champagne, cava, cocktails and a variety of original tapas to a glamorous crowd. ◎ Palma de Sant Just 1 • Map N4 • Closed Mon, Sun

5 Glaciar
Occupying a prime corner of Plaça Reial, this atmospheric café-bar brings in all types. Grab a spot on the terrace with a front-row view of the plaça activities. ◎ Pl Reial 3 • Map L4

6 María Mulata
Intimate and inviting, this bar serves good mojitos and caipirinhas. Cinema night is on a Monday, on the weekend DJ sessions take over and Sundays are for chilling out. ◎ C/Ample 27 • Map M5

7 La Vinya del Senyor
A classy, yet cosy, bar attracting wine lovers from all over the city, who come to sample a rich array of Spanish and international varieties in the company of other wine aficionados. ◎ Pl Santa Maria 5 • Map N5

8 Cactus Bar
The main draw of this little bar is the terrace with a couple of tables underneath an elegant stone arcade, which have a perfect view of Passeig del Born. ◎ Passeig del Born 30 • Map P4

9 Gimlet
The original cocktail bar in El Born, the intimate, 1950s-style Gimlet pours nice (read: potent) cocktails to a local clientele. ◎ C/Rec 24 • Map P4

10 Mudanzas
This long-time favourite hang-out has circular marble tables, black-and-white tiled floors and an informal, "everybody's welcome" vibe. ◎ C/Vidrieria 15 • Map P5

Unless otherwise stated, bars, clubs & music venues are open daily.

Left **Sidecar Factory Club** Right **Jamboree**

🔟 Clubs & Music Venues

Jamboree
This Barri Gòtic institution has live jazz every night (11pm–1am). It then evolves into a dance club, with DJs spinning everything from hip-hop to R&B and salsa. ◐ Pl Reial 17 • Map L4 • Adm

Fellini
The interior of this bar is a homage to Baroque with plenty of red velvet and gilt. Known for its theme nights, the Nasty Monday sessions are a Barcelona classic. ◐ La Rambla 27 • Map L5 • 93 272 49 80 • Closed Tue, Wed & Sun

Club 13
One of the most glamorous places in the Old Town, Club 13 has a restaurant and terrace on the ground floor, and a nightclub in the basement, which is decorated in gold and red velvet. ◐ Plaza Reial 13 • Map L4

Harlem Jazz Club
Dark and smoky, this kickback jazz haunt features a choice line-up of jazz and blues, flamenco fusion, reggae and African music. ◐ Comtessa de Sobradiel 8 • Map M5 • Usually free • Closed Mon, concerts start 10:30pm

Fantástico Club
Pop, electro pop, and candy-coloured decor make this club a hit. ◐ Passatge Escudellers 3 • Map L5.

Karma
The hippie origins and 1970s glamour at this club are as popular as ever. ◐ Pl Reial 10 • Map L4 • Adm • Closed Mon

Magic
Live music is played here at weekends by new, up-and-coming Spanish bands. After the show, the dancing goes on until 5:30am. ◐ Pg Picasso 40 • Map P4 • Adm • Closed Sun–Wed

New York
Well-known for its 80s nights, this cosmopolitan club has a retro feel. There are occasional live concerts and reggae nights too. ◐ C/Escudellers 5 • Map L5

Al Limón Negro
The eclectic "Black Lemon" restaurant-club features ethnic and world music concerts, performance art and occasional art exhibitions. ◐ C/Escudellers Blancs 3 • Map L4 • Closed Mon

Sidecar Factory Club
Barcelona's music scene is like a motorbike to which Sidecar is inseparably bound. They say the American 6th fleet once hired the whole venue and made merry. Music, theatre, cabaret, video and good food can all be found. ◐ Pl Reial 7 • Map L4 • Adm • Closed Sun

For Barcelona's best nightlife **See pp46–7**

Left **Terrace, Cafè-Bar L'Antiquari** Centre **Ice cream, Café d'Estiu** Right **Xocoa**

Cafés & Light Eats

Cafè d'Estiu
Tucked away on the patio of the Museu Frederic Marès *(see p72)* is this alluring, sun-strewn terrace café, replete with stone pillars, climbing ivy and orange trees. ◈ *Pl de Sant Lluc 5–6 • Map N3 • Closed Mon & Oct–Mar • DA*

La Báscula
This quirky café, set in an old chocolate factory, has several vegetarian dishes and a range of tasty cakes on the menu. ◈ *C/ Flassaders 30 • Map P4 • 93 319 98 66*

Cafè-Bar L'Antiquari
In summer, bask in the old town's medieval atmosphere at the Plaça del Rei terrace. By night, sip Rioja in the intimate, rustic basement bodega.
◈ *C/Veguer 13 • Map N4*

Cafè-Bar del Pi
The Església de Santa Maria del Pi casts a shadow over this café's terrace. And if you're in that kick-back-and-donothing mode, street artists keep you entertained. ◈ *Pl Sant Josep Oriol 1 • Map M4 • Closed Tue, 7–30 Jan*

Tetería Salterio
Sit back and relax with tea and sweet Arab cakes. Do not miss the Sado, an Oriental style pizza with a variety of fillings. ◈ *Sant Domenec del Call 4 • Map M4 • Closed Mon*

Café Bliss
Take a break from exploring the Gothic Quarter at this friendly café. It serves divine cakes, light meals, and snacks. Ask for a table outside. ◈ *Plaça Sants Just i Pastor • Map N4 • 93 268 10 22*

Café del Born
Plaça Comercial is dotted with cafés, including the laid-back Café del Born, which evolves into an amiable bar as night descends. ◈ *Pl Comercial 10 • Map P4*

Caelum
Uptairs sells honey, pre-serves and other foods made in convents and monasteries all over Spain. Downstairs you can sample all the delicacies in a café on the site of a 15th century baths.
◈ *C/Palla 8 • Map M3 • Closed Mon lunch*

Venus Delicatessen
Colourful and inviting, this café-restaurant serves great cof-fee and tea as well as fresh fare, including innovative salads such as "Erotica", with asparagus, tuna and tomato. ◈ *C/Avinyó 25 • Map M5 • Closed Sun, 7–30 Jan*

Xocoa
This family-run *xocolateria* has long been serving up decadent desserts and baked goodies, such as fig ravioli with peach ice-cream. ◈ *C/Petritxol 11 • Map L3*

For more cafés in the Barri Gòtic **See pp42–3**

Cal Pep

Price Categories

For a three-course meal for one with half a bottle of wine (or equivalent meal), taxes and extra charges.

€ under 15
€€ 15–25
€€€ 25–35
€€€€ 35–45
€€€€€ over 45

🏆10 Restaurants & Tapas Bars

1 Agut d'Avignon
A French-Catalan restaurant housed in a 17th-century building. Home-style cuisine with a twist includes duck with figs and goose flavoured with pears. ⊗ C/Trinitat 3 • Map M4 • 93 302 60 34 • Closed three weeks in Jan • €€€€€

2 Cal Pep
Taste delicious tapas, including the finest cured hams, at this established eatery. ⊗ Pl de les Olles 8 • Map P5 • 93 310 79 61 • Closed Sat dinner, Sun, Mon lunch • €€€€

3 Cafè de l'Acadèmia
Superb Catalan cuisine and top-notch desserts are served at this restaurant in an 18th-century building. ⊗ C/Lledó 1 • Map N4 • 93 315 00 26 • Closed Sat & Sun • €€

4 Comerç 24
The highlight of this innovative restaurant is the constantly changing menu. Each *platillo* (little plate) blends unique flavours to create an exquisite dish. ⊗ C/ Comerç 24 • Map P4 • 93 319 21 02 • Closed Sun and Mon • €€€€

5 Senyor Parellada
Excellent Catalan cuisine, including speciality *bacalao* (cod) and *butifarra* (sausage), is the deal at this restaurant. ⊗ C/Argenteria 37 • Map N4 • 93 310 50 94 • €€€

6 Agut
For over 75 years, this friendly, family restaurant has been delighting patrons with excellent Catalan cuisine at decent prices. ⊗ C/Gignàs 16 • Map M5 • 93 315 17 09 • Closed Sun eve & Mon, one week in Jan, Aug • DA • €€€€

7 Taller De Tapas
This is part of an excellent small chain with several branches. There is a set lunch menu, or try the seafood tapas, which is particularly good. ⊗ Plaça de Sant Josep Oriol 9 • Map M3 • 93 301 80 20 • €€

8 Salero
The "Salt Cellar" has an all-white interior offset by flickering candles. An innovative menu features Mediterranean-Asian fusion cuisine. ⊗ C/Rec 60 • Map P5 • 93 319 80 22 • Closed Sun • €€€

9 El Xampanyet
A boisterous tapas bar serving champagne, pitchers of cider and generous portions of tapas. ⊗ C/Montcada 22 • Map P4 • 93 319 70 03 • Closed Sun eve, & Mon • €€

10 Govinda
This soothing eatery offers vegetarian Indian main dishes and delectable desserts, but no alcohol. ⊗ Pl Vila de Madrid 4–5 • Map M2 • 93 318 77 29 • Closed Sun eve & Mon eve • DA • €€

Unless otherwise stated, all restaurants accept credit cards.
For tips on dining and standard opening hours See p138

79

Left **Plaça de Joan Coromines** Right **Columns, Església de Sant Pau del Camp**

El Raval

THE SLEEK, SHINY, WHITE WALLS of the *Museu d'Art Contemporani (MACBA)* juxtapose the decrepit, ramshackle tenement buildings; Asian grocery stores sell herbs and spices next to what were once the most decadent brothels in Europe; and smoky, decades-old bars share dark, narrow streets with high-ceilinged art galleries showcasing video installations. The old-town barrio of El Raval is a traditional working-class neighbourhood in flux. Over the last decade it has been undergoing an enthusiastic urban renewal, led by the arrival of the MACBA. The barrio now even has its very own Rambla, a new pedestrian street called La Rambla del Raval. Not surprisingly, all of this has sparked a real-estate boom, with renovated old-fashioned flats now commanding top-tier prices and acting as a magnet to the city's young, savvy crowd.

Stained-glass window, Museu Marítim

Sights

1. Museu d'Art Contemporani
2. Centre de Cultura Contemporània & Foment de les Arts Decoratives
3. Museu Marítim
4. Palau Güell
5. La Rambla del Raval
6. Carrer Nou de la Rambla
7. Carrers Tallers & Riera Baixa
8. Barri Xinès
9. Antic Hospital de la Santa Creu
10. Església de Sant Pau del Camp

For sights & attractions on La Rambla **See pp12–13**

1 Museu d'Art Contemporani

An eclectic array of work by big-name Spanish and international contemporary artists is gathered in the city's contemporary art museum. Excellent temporary exhibitions feature everything from mixed media to sculpture and photography. *See pp28–9.*

2 Centre de Cultura Contemporània & Foment de les Arts Decoratives

Housed in the 18th-century Casa de la Caritat, the CCCB is a focal point for the city's thriving contemporary arts scene. It hosts innovative art exhibitions, lectures, film screenings and more, including multimedia and technology fairs during the popular Festival del Sònar *(see p65)*. A medieval courtyard is dazzlingly offset by a massive, angled glass wall, which has been cunningly designed to reflect the city's skyline. Nearby, Foment de les Arts Decoratives *(see p84)* is an umbrella organization of art and design groups, founded in 1903 and housed in the restored, Gothic-style, 16th-century Convent dels Àngels. Here you'll find exhibits, lectures and debates, and a smashing café-restaurant, Fad Food (open Mon–Fri). *See pp28–9.*

3 Museu Marítim

Barcelona's mighty seafaring legacy comes to life at this impressive museum housed in the vast, 13th-century Drassanes Reials (Royal Shipyards).

Central salon cupola, Palau Güell

Wander beneath looming Gothic arches and relive Barcelona's maritime history through exhibits of model ships, old maps and figureheads. A highlight is the full-scale replica of the Royal, the ship commanded by Don Juan of Austria during the Battle of Lepanto in 1571. Entrance also includes a visit to the Pailebot *Santa Eulàlia (see p98)*, a restored wooden sailing ship dating from 1918. ◎ *Av de les Drassanes • Map K6 • Open 10am–8pm daily • Adm*

4 Palau Güell

For an artist, a wealthy patron spells survival. The luck of young Gaudí turned when count Eusebi Güell recognized his talents. In 1886, Güell commissioned Gaudí to build a mansion that would set the count apart from his wealthy neighbours. The result is the Palau Güell, one of Gaudí's earliest works. An imposing façade gives way to an elaborate interior of lavish pillars and carved wooden ceilings, while the rooftop has a melange of mosaic chimneys. The building is partially open due to restoration work. ◎ *C/Nou de la Rambla 3–5 • Map L4 • Open for guided visits every 15 mins 10am–6:15pm Mon–Sat • Adm*

Puzzle table, Museu d'Art Contemporani

For more on Antoni Gaudí **See p11**

La Rambla del Raval

5 This palm tree-lined, pedestrian walkway is the latest attempt by city planners to spark a similar social environment to that of the city's famed La Rambla *(see pp12–13)*. So far it is off to a creaking start, with barely a fraction of the crowds that ply the original Rambla. Its advocates, however, are quick to point out that La Rambla del Raval is far better than the two dark, run-down streets that formerly existed here. New shops, bars and cafés mean it could well rival its cousin in years to come. ✆ *Map K4*

Carrer Nou de la Rambla

6 In the first half of the 19th century, El Raval's main street was a notorious strip of cabarets, brothels and other nocturnal dens. Today it still bustles with transactions, but of a different sort. Frayed-at-the-edge local eateries, ethnic grocery stores, and discount clothing and shoe shops dot the street. And nightspots, such as the atmospheric London Bar *(see p86)*, which have conserved their age-old identity and fixtures, lure partying visitors. ✆ *Map J5*

Carrers Tallers & Riera Baixa

7 Looking for bootleg CDs of Madonna's European tour? Or

Shoppers, Carrer Taller

vintage blue-and-white French navy tops once favoured by the likes of Picasso? Dotting Carrers Tallers and Riera Baixa, in the heart of El Raval, is a host of vintage music and clothing shops selling everything from vinyl to the latest CDs, original Hawaiian shirts and Dickies workwear. On Saturdays from 11am to 9pm, Carrer Riera Baixa hosts its own market, when the stores display their wares on the street. ✆ *Map L1 & K3*

Barri Xinès

8 The first thing locals will say when you ask about the Barri Xinès is that it no longer exists; the second is that the name has no real connection with the Chinese *(Xinès)*. Both statements are true. This barrio, unfolding south from Carrer Sant Pau towards Drassanes, was once one of Europe's most infamous neighbourhoods, inhabited by the poor and working-class and rife with prostitutes, pimps, strippers and drug dealers. Today, due to enthusiastic clean-up efforts, mere vestiges remain of the barrio's

Record shop, Carrer Tallers

previous life (though some alleys still hint at illicit activity). As for the name, the area has nothing to do with the Chinese, but was named in the barrio's early-1900s heyday as a general reference to its large immigrant population. Today you can browse in cheap thrift shops and small grocery stores by day and bar-hop your way through the area by night. ◈ Map K4

9 Antic Hospital de la Santa Creu

A rich reminder of the neighbourhoods' medieval past is this Gothic hospital complex (1401), which is today home to educational and cultural organizations. Within, you can wander a pleasant garden surrounded by Gothic pillars. ◈ Entrances on C/Carme & C/Hospital 56 • Map K3 • 9am–8pm daily • Free

Cloister, Església de Sant Pau del Camp

10 Església de Sant Pau del Camp

Deep in the heart of El Raval is this Romanesque church, one of the oldest in Barcelona. Originally founded as a Benedictine monastery in the 9th century and subsequently rebuilt, this ancient church reveals a 12th-century cloister. ◈ C/Sant Pau 101 • Map J4 • Church open for mass only: 8pm Sat, noon Sun; cloister open 10am–1:30pm Tue–Sat, 5–8pm Mon–Fri • Adm

A Ramble in El Raval

Morning

Start your ramble mid-morning by perusing the innovative temporary art exhibits at the **CCCB** (see p81). Here two world's have meshed harmoniously. The eye-catching blend of old-meets-new in this cutting-edge art space provides a fitting introduction to El Raval's new identity. Head south along C/Montalegre to the Plaça dels Àngels. Sip a coffee beneath the Gothic arches of the restored Convent dels Àngels, which houses the café-restaurant and art and design exhibition rooms of **Foment de les Arts Decoratives** (see p81). Round off your art amble with a trip down nearby C/Doctor Dou, which is speckled with commercial art galleries. If you're looking for contemporary art to jazz up your home, pop into **Ras** or **Cotthem Gallery** (see p84).

Afternoon

From here, it's a short saunter to **Mercat de La Boqueria** (see p12). Walk along C/Carme, turn left onto C/Jerusalem, and go into the back entrance of this cavernous market. Make a beeline for El Quim de La Boqueria (stall 584–585) where you can pull up a stool and dig into fresh fare from baby prawns drizzled in olive oil and garlic to steamed mussels. After, head to the medieval gardens of the **Antic Hospital de la Santa Creu**, off C/Hospital, and take in the Gothic ambience of pillared arcades and courtyards. Then, get to **Marsella** (see p86) and kick-start the evening with an absinthe before making for **London Bar** (see p86), where live music awaits.

Left **Galeria dels Àngels** Right **Window, Foment de les Arts Decoratives**

🔟 Galleries & Design Shops

1 Galeria dels Àngels
Emerging and established contemporary artists from home and abroad are shown at this cutting-edge photography, painting and sculpture gallery.
⊗ *C/Pintor Fortuny, 27 • Map L2 • Closed Sun & Mon*

2 Transformer
This store on one of the most arty streets in El Raval stocks an innovative range of lamps, furnishings, ceramics and handmade jewellery. It is a good place to find unusual gifts. ⊗ *C/Doctor Dou 16 • Map L2 • 93 301 89 05*

3 Espai Ras
Exhibits at this architecture and design gallery and bookstore include architectural models, video installations and graphic design. ⊗ *C/Doctor Dou 10 • Map L2 • Closed Sun & Mon*

4 Bagués Joieria
Iconic Barcelona jeweller since 1839 with an international reputation. Each piece is handmade using traditional methods. ⊗ *La Rambla 105 • Map L3 • Closed Sun*

5 Cotthem Gallery
This long-established gallery exhibits one of the finest line-ups of international contemporary artists in Barcelona.
⊗ *C/Doctor Dou 15 • Map L2 • Closed Sun & Mon*

6 La Capella
As well as contemporary art, this gallery boasts the R. Punt space, where you can relax and read dozens of art magazines.
⊗ *C/Hospital 56 • Map K3 • Open noon–2pm & 4–8pm Tue–Sat, 11am–2pm Sun*

7 Foment de les Arts Decoratives (FAD)
Check out the ongoing exhibitions hosted by FAD, a century-old arts, crafts and design organization. Also here is Items d'Ho, a quirky shop selling creative furnishings, bags and jewellery.
⊗ *Pl Àngels 5–6 • Map K2 • Closed Sun*

8 La Xina A.R.T.
The very latest on the contemporary art scene features at this innovative gallery, started by four local artists in the late 1990s. ⊗ *C/Doctor Dou 4 • Map L2 • Closed Sun & Mon, Tue–Fri mornings*

9 Loring Art
Multimedia and digital design are spotlighted at this trendy bookshop space. ⊗ *C/Gravina 8 • Map L1 • Closed Sat & Sun*

10 The Air Shop
A range of fun inflatable products by young designers are for sale and on display here: flower vases and accessories to furniture and all kinds of personalised items.
⊗ *C/Àngels 20 • Map K2 • Closed Sun & Mon am*

Art aficionados gather at galleries for openings once a month (Tue–Thu). Enquire at individual galleries for more information.

Left **Mies & Felj** Right **Shop window, Revólver Records**

🔟 Vintage & Second-Hand Shops

1 Mies & Felj
A labour of love for two Catalan brothers and a Dutch woman, this shop is packed with vintage fur-lined leather jackets, Chinese dresses and racks of old jeans. ◈ *C/Riera Baixa 4–5 • Map K3*

2 HoLaLa
Rummage for an outfit at this three-floor vintage store, with everything from original silk kimonos to army pants and colourful 1950s bathing suits. ◈ *C/Tallers 73 • Map L1*

3 Discos Edison's
This record shop has been attracting eclectic music hounds since 1979 with a fantastic vinyl collection, including Catalan folk, Broadway tunes and Spanish pop. ◈ *C/Riera Baixa 10 • Map K3*

4 Lailo
In this theatre-turned-vintage store, you'll find everything from glitzy 1950s cocktail dresses to 1920s costumes. ◈ *C/Riera Baixa 20 • Map K3*

5 Revólver Records
The speciality here is classic rock – as shown by the wall art depicting The Rolling Stones and Jimi Hendrix. One floor houses CDs, the other a huge selection of vinyl. ◈ *C/Tallers 11 • Map L2*

6 La Lluna de 2ª mà
Pick from a small but select array of used clothes and shoes, which may be anything from patent leather platforms to polka-dot Dr Martens. ◈ *C/Riera Baixa 18 • Map K3*

7 Le Swing
If you're looking for Chanel shoes, a Dior coat or a YSL evening gown, this chic, boudoir-style boutique is definitely the store for you. There are some wonderful accessories too. ◈ *C/Riera Baixa 13 • Map K3*

8 Smart & Clean
Hip young Barcelonians swear by this secondhand store with clothes mostly from the 60s and 70s. ◈ *C/Xucla 6 • Map L3*

9 Discos Tesla
This tiny, but well-stocked, record and CD store focuses on alternative music from decades past. It is the kind of place where you can hum a few lines of a song and the owner will track it down. ◈ *C/Tallers 3 • Map L2*

10 GI Joe Surplus
One of Spain's few army and navy surplus stores, where you can find bags, backpacks and clothing from the Russian, Israeli and US militaries. ◈ *C/Hospital 82 • Map K3*

For tips on shopping and standard opening hours **See p139**

Left **Zelig** Right **Zentraus**

Bars & Clubs

1 Bar Almirall
The *Modernista* doors swing open to a young, friendly crowd at Barcelona's oldest watering hole. Founded in 1860, the bar has many original fittings, plus eclectic music and strong cocktails. ◈ *C/Joaquin Costa 33 • Map K2*

2 Zelig
Intimate and welcoming, this gay-friendly cocktail bar is a great place to start the night. There are excellent cocktails – including a mean mojito – and light snacks. ◈ *C/Carme 116 • Map K2*

3 Bar Resolis
Formerly an old-fashioned neighbourhood bar, this is now an appealing boho-chic tavern with a small terrace. Wine and cocktails accompany delicious tapas. ◈ *C/Riera Baixa 22 • Map K3*

4 Marsella
This dimly lit *Modernista* bar serves up cocktails and absinthe to long-time regulars and first-timers. ◈ *C/Sant Pau 65 • Map K4*

5 Zentraus
One of the most stylish bars in the area, Zentraus has a trendy red-black-and-white decor and cool lighting. A restaurant until 1am, the tables are cleared once the DJ gets going. ◈ *Rambla de Raval 41 • Map K4*

6 Betty Ford's
The latest cocktail bar to arrive on lively Carrer Joaquin Costa, Betty Ford's has a relaxed, laid-back vibe. ◈ *Carrer Joaquin Costa 56 • Map K1*

7 Moog
Big-name DJs spin techno and electronica, but for a boogie to classic '80s hits head for the second floor. ◈ *C/Arc del Teatre 3 • Map L5 • Adm*

8 Boadas Cocktail Bar
This smooth little cocktail bar, founded in 1933, continues to mix the meanest martinis in town for an elbow-to-elbow crowd. ◈ *C/Tallers 1 • Map L2 • Closed Sun*

9 London Bar
This cluttered bar has long been *de rigueur*, once with the likes of Picasso, Hemingway and Miró. Sip cocktails and enjoy live music – from jazz to folk. ◈ *C/Nou de la Rambla 34 • Map K4 • Closed Mon*

10 Café Teatre Llantiol
Barcelona's cabaret tradition lives on at this theatre-bar, with its flamboyant shows and *espectacles* of mime, magic and flamenco. ◈ *C/Riereta 7 • Map J3 • 93 329 90 09 • Shows at 9pm & 11pm Mon–Thu, 9pm, 11pm & 12.30am Fri–Sat, 8pm & 9pm Sun • Adm*

Price Categories

For a three-course meal for one with half a bottle of wine (or equivalent meal), taxes and extra charges.

€	under €15
€€	€15–25
€€€	€25–35
€€€€	€35–€45
€€€€€	over €45

Bar Ra

🔟 Good-Value Eats

1 Casa Leopoldo
Dig into superb *mar i muntanya* fare (combining meat and fish) at this friendly, family-run restaurant. Try the meatballs with cuttlefish and shrimp. ◎ *C/ Sant Rafael 24 • Map K3 • 93 441 30 14 • Closed Mon, Easter, Aug • €€€€€*

2 Bar Ra
This trendy spot serves up goodies from the nearby market, from yogurt shakes to vegetarian burritos. ◎ *Pl de la Gardunya • Map L3 • 61 595 98 72 • €€€*

3 Ca L'Isidre
Picasso, Tapiès and even Woody Allen have dined on Catalan fare at this long-time artists' hang-out. ◎ *C/Flors 12 • Map J4 • 93 441 11 39 • Closed Sat (in summer), Sun, Easter, Aug, Christmas • €€€€€*

4 Silenus
Tuck into Mediterranean food in a lofty space hung with local artists' work. Try the ostrich. ◎ *C/Àngels 8 • Map K2 • 93 302 26 80 • Closed Sun • €€€€*

5 Las Fernández
This eatery has a friendly atmosphere. The original menu features dishes from the El Bierzo area in León, such as *papas don't preach* (potato salad). ◎ *C/Carretas 11 • Map J3 • 93 443 20 43 • Closed Mon, daily lunch, three weeks Aug • €€€*

6 El Jardí
Located in one of the prettiest spots in the city, El Jardí serves delicious, light cuisine, such as soups, salads and *crêpes*. ◎ *C/ de Hospital • Map K3 • Closed Mon • €*

7 Imprevist
In an old warehouse, this café-restaurant, owned (and decorated) by Catalan artists, offers a global menu. ◎ *C/Ferlandina 34 • Map J2 • 93 342 58 59 • Closed Sun lunch • €€€*

8 Mama Cafè
Organic Mediterranean dishes (many vegetarian) are served in this airy café-restaurant. Contemporary art is projected onto the wall. ◎ *C/Doctor Dou 10 • Map L2 • 93 301 29 40 • Closed Sun • €€€*

9 Fonda de España
Dine on fine Catalan cuisine under a *Modernista* mosaic and dark-wood ceiling by Domènech i Montaner. Try the filet of sole flavoured with orange. ◎ *Hotel España, C/Sant Pau 9–11 • Map L4 • 93 318 17 58 • €€€€*

10 L'Havana
Despite the name, this serves some of the best Catalan cuisine in the city. Try classic dishes such as pigs' trotters, or the fresh fish of the day (the house speciality). ◎ *C/Lleó 1 • Map K2 • Closed Sun eve, Mon • €€*

For tips on dining and standard opening hours See p138

87

Left **Palau Nacional** Right **Estadi Olimpic**

Montjuïc

NAMED THE "JEWISH MOUNTAIN", *after an important Jewish cemetery that existed here in the Middle Ages, this sizeable and mountainous park rises 213 m (700 ft) above the port. The park itself was first landscaped for the 1929 International Exhibition, when the elegant Palau Nacional and the strikingly modern Mies van der Rohe Pavilion were also built. During the following decade, the area fell into general disuse and soon became synonymous with decline. Together with the grim shadow cast over the hill by the castle, which for years acted as a slaughterhouse for Franco's firing squads, it is little short of miraculous that Montjuïc is now one of Barcelona's biggest tourist draws. However, as the main site for the 1992 Olympics, held on its southern slopes, Montjuïc was given a comprehensive face-lift and the area was transformed into a beautiful green oasis, with two fabulous art museums and a host of stunning sports facilities.*

Statue, Castell de Montjuïc

All these elements are interconnected by a network of exterior escalators and interlaced with quiet, shady gardens, which offer dazzling views over Barcelona and a welcome respite from the bustle of the city.

🔟 Sights

1. Palau Nacional & Museu Nacional d'Art de Catalunya
2. Fundació Joan Miró
3. Font Màgica
4. Castell de Montjuïc & Museu del Cómic y la Ilustración
5. Estadi Olímpic
6. Teatre Grec
7. Palau Sant Jordi
8. Pavelló Mies van der Rohe
9. Poble Espanyol
10. Caixa Fòrum

For more on Barcelona's history See pp30–31

Fountains, Palau Nacional

1 Palau Nacional & Museu Nacional d'Art de Catalunya

The Palau Nacional is home to the Museu Nacional d'Art de Catalunya which exhibits Catalonia's historic art collections. Boasting one of Europe's finest displays of Romanesque art, the museum includes a series of breathtaking, 12th-century frescoes, rescued from Catalan Pyrenean churches and painstakingly reassembled in a series of galleries here. *See pp18–19.*

2 Fundació Joan Miró

One of Catalonia's most representative painters, Joan Miró (1893–1983), donated many of the 11,000 works held by the museum. Housed in a stark, white building designed by his friend, architect Josep Lluís Sert, the collection – the world's most complete array of Miro's work – was recently extended to include 25 new pieces by him. *See pp22–3.*

3 Font Màgica

Below the cascades and fountains that splash down from the regal Palau Nacional is the Magic Fountain, designed by Carles Buigas for the International Exhibition of 1929. As darkness descends, countless jets of water are choreographed in a mesmerizing sound and light show. When the water meets in a single jet it can soar to 15m (50ft). The extravagant finale is often accompanied by a recording of Freddie Mercury and Montserrat Caballé singing the anthem *Barcelona* as the fountain fades from pink to green and back to white before silently and gracefully disappearing. ✆ *Av de la Reina Maria Cristina • Map B4 • May–Sep: every 30 minutes 9:30–11:30pm Thu–Sun; Oct–Apr: every 30 minutes 7–8:30pm Fri & Sat • Free • DA*

Castell de Montjuïc

4 Castell de Montjuïc & Museo del Cómic y la Ilustración

Dominating Montjuïc's hill, this Baroque-style castle was a prison and torture centre for political prisoners for many years. Today the castle houses the Museo del Cómic y la Ilustración, detailing the development of Spanish comics. There are lovely views of the port below, and beautiful gardens to explore. ✆ *C/Castell • Map B6 • Castell: open Apr–Oct: 9:30am–8pm Tue–Sun; Nov–Mar: 9:30am–5pm Tue–Fri, 9:30am–7pm Sat–Sun • Museum: Open 10am–7pm (5pm in winter) Tue–Sun • Adm to museum & castle*

5 Estadi Olímpic

The Olympic Stadium was first built for the 1936 Workers' Olympics, which were cancelled with the outbreak of the Spanish Civil War *(see p31)*. Today, the original Neo-Classical façade is still in place, though the stadium was entirely rebuilt for the 1992 Olympic Games *(see p31)*. It is home to Espanyol football team *(see p61)*. The Galeria Olímpica holds mementos illustrating the importance of the games for Barcelona. ✆ *Av de l'Estadi • Map B5 • Open May–Sep: 10am–8pm daily; Oct–Apr 10am–6pm daily • Free • DA*

6 Teatre Grec

This beautiful, open-air amphitheatre *(see p60)* was inspired by the Classical ideas of what was known as *Noucentisme*. This late 19th-century architectural movement was a reaction to the overly-decorative nature of *Modernisme*. With its leafy, green backdrop and beautiful gardens, there are few places more enchanting than this to watch *Swan Lake* or listen to some jazz. The theatre is used for shows during the summertime Festival del Grec *(see p66)*, when it also becomes home to a luxurious outdoor restaurant. ✆ *Pg Santa Madrona • Map C4 • 10am–dusk • Free (when there are no shows)*

7 Palau Sant Jordi

The star of all the Olympic installations is this steel-and-glass indoor stadium *(see p66)* designed by Japanese architect Arata Isozaki. Holding around 17,000 people, the stadium is the home of the city's basketball team *(see p61)*. The esplanade – a surreal forest of concrete and metal pillars – was designed by Aiko Isozaki, Arata's wife. Further down the hill are the indoor and outdoor Bernat Picornell Olympic pools *(see p60)*; both open to the public. ✆ *Av de l'Estadi • Map A4 • Open 10am–6pm (to 8pm May–Sep) Sat & Sun • Free • DA*

Palau Sant Jordi

8 Pavelló Mies van der Rohe

You might wonder exactly what this box-like pavilion of stone, marble, onyx and glass is doing bang in the middle of Montjuïc's monumental architecture. Years ahead of its time, this surprisingly rationalist gem represents Germany's contribution to the 1929 Exhibition. Built by Ludwig Mies van der Rohe (1886–1969), the elegant pavilion was soon demolished, only to be reconstructed in 1986. Inside, the elegant sculpture *Morning* by Georg Kolbe

Barcelona Chairs, Pavelló Mies van der Rohe

You can board the Montjuïc Bus Turístic (see p133), which ferries visitors up the hill from Plaça d'Espanya and back (April to October).

Poble Espanyol

(1877–1947) is reflected in a small lake. ✎ *Av Marquès de Comillas • Map B4 • Open 10am–8pm daily • Adm*

Poble Espanyol

9 This Spanish *poble* (village) has been recreated from a hotch-potch of scaled-down famous buildings and streets from around Spain. Although a bit tacky, it has become a centre for arts and crafts, including an impressive glass-blowers' workshop. There are restaurants and cafés aplenty, and a couple of trendy nightclubs *(see p95)*. ✎ *Av Marquès de Comillas • Map A3 • Open 9am–8pm Mon, 9am–2pm Tue–Thu, 9am–4am Fri, 9am–5pm Sat, 9am–midnight Sun • Adm*

Caixa Forum

10 The Fundació La Caixa's impressive collection of contemporary art is housed in a former textile factory, designed by *Modernista* architect Puig i Cadafalch. The collection began in 1985 and assembles some 800 works by Spanish and foreign artists, which are shown in rotation along with temporary international exhibitions. ✎ *Av Marquès de Comillas • Map B3 • Open 10am–8pm Tue–Sun • Free • DA*

A Day in Montjuïc

Morning

🕐 To get to the **Fundació Joan Miró** *(see pp22–3)* before the crowds and with energy to spare, hop on the funicular from Paral·lel metro station. From here it is a short walk to the museum, where you'll need an hour and a half to absorb the impressive collection of Miró paintings, sketches and sculptures. When you've had your fill of contemporary art, refuel with a *cafè amb llet (see p43)* on the restaurant terrace before backtracking along Av de Miramar and jumping on the cable car up to **Castell de Montjuïc** *(see p89)*. Wander the castle gardens and look out over the city and the bustling docks. Return to Av de Miramar by cable car and follow the signs to the **Palau Nacional** *(see p89)*, where you can lunch on typical Catalan cuisine with a modern twist in the grandiose Oval Room *(see p93)*.

Afternoon

Afterwards, spend an hour perusing the **MNAC's** *(see pp18–19)* extraordinary Romanesque art collection. When you exit, turn right and then follow the signs to the Olympic complex. The **Estadi Olímpic** is worth a look, but the silver-domed **Palau Sant Jordi** steals the limelight. Nearby, at Bernat Picornell, spend the late afternoon cooling down with a dip in the fantastic open-air pool. If it's summer, there may even be a film showing. From here it is just a short stroll to the **Poble Espanyol** where you can settle in at a terrace bar in Plaça de Mayor and sip a *cuba libre* as night descends.

GASPAR · BALTASAR · MELCHIOR

Left **Jardins Mossèn Jacint Verdaguer** Right **Castell Jardins**

Parks & Gardens

1 Jardins Mossèn Costa i Llobera
These are among Europe's most important cactus gardens. They are particularly impressive as the sun sets, when surreal and shapes and shadows emerge. ✎ *Map C5*

2 Jardí Botànic
These wild gardens offer splendid vistas and hundreds of examples of typical Mediterranean vegetation. ✎ *Map A4 • Open Feb, Mar, Oct: 10am–6pm daily; Apr, May, Sep: 10am–7pm daily; Jun–Aug: 10am–8pm daily; Nov–Jan: 10am–5pm daily • Adm; free last Sun of month*

3 Jardins Mossèn Cinto Verdaguer
The best time to visit these wonderfully elegant gardens is in spring when the plants are in blossom and the colours and aromas are in full force. ✎ *Map C5*

4 Jardins del Castell
Cannons among the rose bushes, and pathways along the walls of a flower-filled moat, are the highlights of these gardens, which ring the castle. ✎ *Map B5*

5 Jardins del Teatre Grec
Reminiscent of the Hanging Gardens of Babylon, this gracious oasis surrounding the Greek amphitheatre is officially known as La Rosadela. ✎ *Map C4*

6 Jardins de Miramar
Opposite the Miramar, these gardens are scattered with stairways leading to enchanting leafy groves with vistas. ✎ *Map C5*

7 Jardins Laribal
This multi-level park hides a small *Modernista* house, by Puig i Cadafalch, and the Font del Gat – a drinking fountain, which has inspired many local songs. ✎ *Map B4*

8 Jardins de Joan Maragall
An avenue lined with sculptures by Frederic Marès and Ernest Maragall is the main delight here. The garden also has the last of the city's *ginjoler* trees. ✎ *Map B4 • Open 10am–3pm Sat & Sun*

9 Muntanya de Montjuïc
A multitude of secret paths leads through wild gardens on Montjuïc's south side, the only part of the mountain that remains untamed. ✎ *Map A5*

10 El Mirador del Llobregat
A viewing area with small gardens nearby, this is the only place in the city where you can see the plains of the Llobregat stretching below. ✎ *Map A3 • DA*

Unless otherwise stated, parks & gardens are usually open 10am-dusk daily.

Price Categories

For a three-course meal for one with half a bottle of wine (or equivalent meal), taxes and extra charges.

€	under €15
€€	€15–25
€€€	€25–35
€€€€	€35–€45
€€€€€	over €45

Interior, Font de Prades

TOP 10 Restaurants, Cafés, Bars & Clubs

1 Oleum
Dine on refined Mediterranean cuisine under the dome of the Palau Nacional and enjoy amazing views across the city. ◈ Palau Nacional • Map B4 • 93 289 06 79 • closed Mon, eves • DA • €€€

2 Cañota
Cañota's superb, traditional, and supremely economical cooking includes excellent game dishes. This place lives up to its phenomenal reputation. ◈ C/Lleida 7 • Map C4 • 93 325 91 71 • DA • €€€€

3 Fundació Joan Miró Restaurant
A great terrace, views of Miró's sculptures, plus well-presented modern food with an Italian accent. ◈ Parc de Montjuïc • Map B5 • 93 329 07 68 • Closed eve • DA • €€

4 Rias de Galicia
A giant aquarium is full of lobster, crabs and more, all waiting to be plucked out and served up sizzling on a plate. ◈ C/Lleida 9 • Map C4 • 93 424 81 52 • €€€€€

5 Cala Santa Maria
A bit off the beaten track, but worth hunting out, this authentic Spanish eatery offers an excellent selection of tapas. ◈ C/Guadiana 12 • Map B2 • 93 421 87 05 • Closed lunch & Mon • €€

6 El Lliure
The Lliure theatre has a good-value café with an adjoining restaurant. In summer there are tables on the terrace. ◈ Passeig Santa Madrona 40-46 • Map B4 • Closed Mon eve, Sat lunch, Sun • €€€

7 La Terrrazza
Techno music rules at one of Barcelona's most popular nightclubs, housed in a Balearic-style mansion inside the Poble Espanyol. ◈ Poble Espanyol • Map A3 • Closed Sun, mid-Oct–mid-Jun • Adm

8 Font de Prades
By far the best food in the Poble Espanyol. ◈ Poble Espanyol • Map A3 • 93 426 75 19 • Closed Mon, three weeks Jan • €€€

9 Restaurant Forestier
Located in the AC Miramar, this elegant restaurant has wonderful views over the harbour and city. ◈ Pl. Carlos Ibáñez, 3 • Map C5 • 93 281 16 00 • €€€€

10 Quimet & Quimet
This tiny bodega has standing room only, but serves tasty tapas and wonderful wines. ◈ C/Poeta Cabanyes • Map C4 • 93 442 31 42 • Closed Sat eve, Sun, Aug • €

Left **L'Aquàrium** Right **Swing Bridge, between La Rambla & Moll D'Espanya**

Port Vell, Barceloneta & Port Olímpic

THE HEADY ALLURE OF THE MEDITERRANEAN *permeates Barcelona, and a dip into its azure waters is only a few metro stops (or a brisk walk) away. Barcelona's beaches were once hidden behind an industrial wasteland, but things changed radically in preparation for the 1992 Olympics. The rallying cry was to create a new Barcelona* oberta al mar *(open to the sea); the result is phenomenal, as is the presence of large crowds seeking sun and sea. Tons of sand were transported to create miles of silky beaches from the fisherman's quarter of Barceloneta to Port Olímpic and beyond. Palm trees were planted, water cleanliness standards implemented and, this being design-obsessed Barcelona, numerous contemporary sculptures erected. The city's first two skyscrapers, the Torre Mapfre office building and the five-star Hotel Arts (see p143), punctuate the port's skyline, while the nearby Port Olímpic throbs with the highest concentration of bars and clubs in the city.*

Barceloneta beach

🔟 Sights & Attractions

1. Beaches
2. Museu d'Història de Catalunya
3. Rambla de Mar
4. L'Aquàrium
5. Barceloneta
6. Boat & Cable Car Trips
7. Pailebot Santa Eulàlia
8. Submarine Ictíneo II
9. El Centre de la Vila-Port Olímpic
10. World Trade Center

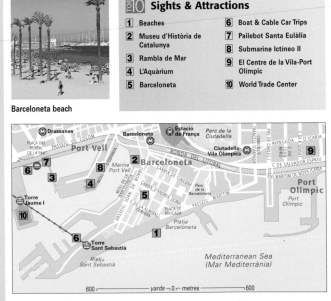

Take a boat tour of the port area **See p133**

1 Beaches

Fancy a splash in the Mediterranean? Trot down to the end of La Rambla, wander along the palm tree-lined Moll de la Fusta, down restaurant-packed Passeig Joan de Borbó, et voilà, the sea beckons. Over four km (2.5 miles) of blue flag beaches stretch north from Barceloneta to Port Olímpic and beyond. Facilities are top-notch, including showers, deck chairs, beach volleyball courts and lifeguards. Convenience, however, means crowds, so finding a spot among the masses of oiled bodies can be a challenge, particularly in the summer. ✪ Map E6

2 Museu d'Història de Catalunya

Housed in the Palau de Mar, a renovated portside warehouse, this museum offers a broad, interactive exploration of Catalonia's history since prehistoric times. Kids *(see p63)* especially will have a ball with the engaging exhibits, such as a Civil War-era bunker and a recreated Catalan bar from the 1960s with an ancient *futbolín* (table football) game. ✪ Pl Pau Vila 3, Palau de Mar • Map N6 • Open 10am–7pm Tue–Sat (until 8pm Wed), 10am–2:30pm Sun • Adm €3, free first Sun of month • DA

3 Rambla de Mar

Saunter along the Rambla de Mar, a floating wooden pier that leads to Maremagnum, a flashy mall that has many shops, restaurants and bars. Nearby the giant IMAX® cinema shows 3-D films on megascreens generally on nature-, adventure-

Museu d'Història de Catalunya

and sports-related topics. ✪ Moll d'Espanya • Map E5 ✪ Maremagnum: shops open 10am–10pm daily; restaurants until 1am daily; bars and clubs until 4:30am daily ✪ IMAX: shows from noon–11:30pm daily • Adm • DA

4 L'Aquàrium

Come face to face with the marine world of the Mediterranean at Barcelona's impressive aquarium, the largest in Europe. The highlight is the 80-m (262-ft) long underwater tunnel, which has a moving walkway that transports visitors through the deep blue unknown, while sharks glide menacingly close. A huge hit with the kids is the new Explora! floor, with interactive exhibits that allow you to explore the ecosystems of the Mediterranean. ✪ Moll d'Espanya • Map E6 • Open Jul–Aug: 9:30am–11pm daily; Sep–Jun: 9:30am–9pm Mon–Fri (to 9:30pm Sat–Sun) • Adm

Yachts, Port Olímpic

 The rooftop café at the Museu d'Història de Catalunya has sweeping views of the city, the port area & Montjuïc.

5 Barceloneta

A portside warren of narrow streets, small squares and ancient bars, this traditional neighbourhood of *pescadors* (fishermen) and *mariners* (sailors) seems worlds apart from the megamalls and disco lights of nearby Port Olímpic. A refreshing foray through this tight-knit community yields a glimpse into

Yachts & skyscrapers, Port Olímpic

the way Barcelona was 150 years ago. Older couples still pull chiars out onto the street to gossip and watch the world go by, and small seafood restaurants serve a *menú del dia* of whatever's fresh off the boat. Running the length of Barceloneta's western edge is Passeig Joan de Borbó, which is lined with restaurants serving *mariscs* (shellfish) and paellas. ✪ *Map F5*

6 Boat & Cable Car Trips

See Barcelona's port activity from a different perspective, either from the air or the sea. The *telefèric* cable cars offer

Street scene, Barceloneta

sweeping bird's-eye views of Barcelona and its coast, while the old-fashioned Les Golondrines boats and the Orsom Catamaran sweep you around the port area. ✪ *Telefèric, from Torre Jaume I & Torre San Sebastià • Map D6 & E6 • Adm ✪ Les Golondrines, Portal de la Pau • Map E5 • roughly 30 mins from 11:30am • 93 442 31 06 • Adm ✪ Orsom Catamaran, Portal de la Pau • Map E5 • Call 93 441 05 37 for times • Adm • DA*

7 Pailebot Santa Eulàlia

Bobbing in the water at the Moll de la Fusta (Timber Quay) is this renovated, three-mast schooner, originally christened *Carmen Flores*. It first set sail from Spain in 1918. On journeys to Cuba, the ship used to transport textiles and salt, and return with tobacco, coffee, cereals and wood. In 1997, the Museu Marítim *(see p81)* bought and restored the ship as part of an ongoing project to create a collection of seaworthy historical Catalan vessels. ✪ *Moll de la Fusta • Map L6 • Open noon–7pm Tue–Sun (from 10am Sat & Sun; to 5:30pm in winter) • Adm*

8 Submarine Ictíneo II

In 1859, Catalan Narcís Monturiol invented one of the world's first submarines, a replica of which stands on the Moll d'Espanya. Hard to believe, but in an earlier version of this wooden, fish-shaped submarine, powered by two internal steam engines, Monturiol made a number of successful underwater journeys.

He invented the submarine as a means of gathering coral; later, he tried to sell it to the army. However, he finally sold his invention in parts and died penniless. ◎ *Moll d'Espanya • Map E5*

El Centre de la Vila-Port Olímpic

This large shopping complex offers a slew of shops, cafés and fast food restaurants. Best of all, it houses the cinemas of the Icària Yelmo Cineplex *(see p67)*, one of the largest cinemas in town to show VO (non-dubbed) films. ◎ *Salvador Espriu 61 • Map H5 • Mall shops open 10am–10pm Mon–Sat*

Pailebot Santa Eulàlia

World Trade Center

This massive, circular structure is home to offices, convention halls, a five-star hotel and the top-notch restaurant Ruccula *(see p101)*. There are also several gift shops, including Galería Surrealista, featuring souvenirs inspired by Dalí and other Surrealists. In the central courtyard is a "rhythmic" fountain that spurts out streams of water at differing velocities. Nearby, you can board cable cars and soak up splendid views from the top of Torre Jaume I. ◎ *Moll de Barcelona • Map D6 • DA*

Exploring the Port

Morning

🕐 Begin your port *passeig* (stroll) with a visit to the **Museu Marítim** *(see p81),* where you can see Barcelona's status as one of the most active ports in the Mediterranean. From here, head towards the Monument a Colom *(see p12)*, and stroll the Moll de la Fusta to admire the **Pailebot Santa Eulàlia**, which has been immaculately restored by the museum. Saunter down the **Rambla de Mar** *(see p97)*, an undulating wooden drawbridge that leads to the glitzy Maremagnum mega-mall. At the start of the pier, embark on the **Orsom Catamaran**, where you can grab a drink and snack and soak up the rays and the port skyline, while sprawled out on a net just inches above the water. Back on land, about 90 minutes later, stroll down the Moll d'Espanya and turn towards the traditional fisherman's quarter of **Barceloneta**, an atmospheric pocket of narrow streets and timeworn bars. Get a real taste of old-style Barcelona at the boisterous tapas bar, **El Vaso de Oro** (C/Balboa 6). Wedge yourself in at the bar and savour some tasty seafood morsels.

Afternoon

Revived, head to Pg Joan de Borbó and make for the beach. Douse yourself in the Med, then siesta in the afternoon sun. Pick yourself up with sangria at the beachside **Salamanca Chiringuito** (at the end of Pg Joan de Borbó), where you can bury your feet in the sand and watch the waves lap on the shore as the sun dips into the horizon.

You can't miss Frank Gehry's massive, glistening Peix sculpture on Passeig Marítim **See p41**

Left **Club Catwalk** Right **Razzmatazz**

Bars & Beach Clubs

Club Catwalk
One of the hottest clubs in town, this has two floors: one for the bar and chilling out, and the other for dancing to music that is strictly electronic and house. ✆ *Ramón Trías Fargas 2–4 • Map G6 • Closed Mon–Wed • DA • Adm*

CDLC
Right by the beach, with a terrace on which to relax, this is a restaurant that becomes a club after dinner. Guest DJs feature every week. ✆ *Passeig Marítim de la Barceloneta 32 • Map G6*

Bar Jai Ca
The TV blares and kids race around in this relaxed neighbourhood favourite. Delicious tapas are on offer. ✆ *C/ Ginebra 13 • Map F5 • 93 319 50 02*

Kennedy Irish Sailing Club
When you tire of dance music, try this open-air Irish bar with live rock and pop bands every night and sport on big TVs. ✆ *Moll Mistral 26–27 • Map G5 • Closed Mon*

Arola
A luxurious, summer-only poolside bar at the plush Hotel Arts, the Arola has huge white beds covered with silk cushions, DJ sessions, and a range of perfectly mixed cocktails. ✆ *C/ Marina 19–21 • Map G5 • 93 483 80 90*

Le Kasbah
With Arabic decoration, soft lights and house music, this bar in the Palau del Mar building provides a city oasis. ✆ *Plaça de Pau Vila 1 • Map F6 • Closed Mon*

Nova Mar Bella beach bars
Head to one of the *xiringuitos* (beach bars) on Barcelona's newest beach and enjoy the DJ sessions. ✆ *Platja Nova Mar Bella*

Suite Royale
This lounge bar overlooking Barcelona's port has sleek, minimalist interiors and attracts a hip, young crowd. ✆ *Passeig Joan de Borbó 54 • Map F6 • 93 225 00 54*

Shôko
A Japanese restaurant during the day, this club by the beach provides all kinds of music in a great setting. ✆ *Passeig Marítim de la Barceloneta 36 • Map E6 • Closed Mon–Tue*

Razzmatazz
Concerts – from rock to jazz – feature several nights a week at this trendy club. On Fridays and Saturdays, Razz Club is alternative. The Loft next door (run by the same people) plays electronica and techno. ✆ *C/Almogàvers 122 (The Loft: C/Pamplona 88) • Map H4 • Razz Club and Loft closed Sun–Thu*

For Barcelona's best nightlife **See pp46–7**

Price Categories

For a three-course meal for one with half a bottle of wine (or equivalent meal), taxes and extra charges.	€ under €15
	€€ €15–25
	€€€ €25–35
	€€€€ €35–€45
	€€€€€ over €45

Agua

🔟 Restaurants & Tapas Bars

1 Set Portes
Founded in 1836, this large institution serves some of the finest Catalan cuisine in the city, including paellas. ◈ Pg Isabel II 14 • Map N5 • 93 319 30 33 • DA • €€€€€

2 Agua
The spacious terrace at this restaurant boasts views of the sea. Superb seafood and Mediterranean fare feature on the menu. ◈ Pg Marítim 30 • Map G6 • 93 225 12 72 • DA • €€€€

3 Can Manel la Puda
The oldest restaurant on this strip serves Catalan cuisine, specializing in catch-of-the-day dishes. ◈ Pg Joan de Borbó 60–61 • Map F6 • 93 221 50 13 • Closed Mon • €€€

4 Somorrostro
This chic restaurant serves a daily changing menu prepared with fresh ingredients. Warm ambience and decor. ◈ Sant Carles 11 • Map F6 • 93 225 00 10 • Closed lunch (except Sun), Tue, three weeks Jan • €€€

5 Kaiku
Decorated with fishing prints and nets, Kaiku is known for its tasty seafood, particularly the arros del xef (chef's rice). Book early for a table on the terrace. ◈ Plaça del Mar 1 • Map E6 • 93 221 90 82 • Closed eve, Mon • €€€

6 Reial Club Marítim Restaurant
The yacht club's restaurant offers views of the harbour and a top-notch seafood menu. ◈ Moll d'Espanya • Map E6 • 93 221 62 56 • Closed Sun eve • €€€€€

7 Can Ganassa
An old-style, family-run tapas bar that has been serving fresh seafood tapas to locals for decades. ◈ Pl de la Barceloneta 4–6 • Map F6 • 93 225 19 97 • €

8 Merendero de la Mari
Located in the grounds of the Palau del Mar building, this restaurant serves seafood and some of the best paellas in the area. ◈ Plaça Pau Vila, 1 • Map F6 • 93 221 31 41 • €€€€

9 Suquet de l'Almirall
This family-run gem serves excellent arroz de barca (rice in broth, with seafood) and suquet (seafood and potato stew). ◈ Pg Joan de Borbó 63 • Map F6 • 93 221 62 33 • Closed Sun eve, Mon, three weeks Aug • DA • €€€€€

10 Lluçanès
Located in Barceloneta's revamped municipal market, award-winning Lluçanès offers exquisite Catalan cuisine in contemporary surroundings. ◈ Plaça de la Font • Map F6 • 93 224 25 25 • €€€€

Unless otherwise stated, all restaurants accept credit cards.
For tips on dining and standard opening hours See p138

101

Left **Fountain, Rambla de Catalunya** Right *Modernista* hotel entrance

Eixample

I F THE OLD TOWN IS THE HEART *of Barcelona and the green mountains of Tibidabo and Montjuïc the lungs, the Eixample is the city's nervous system – its economic and commercial core. The area began to take shape in 1860 when the city was permitted to expand beyond the medieval walls (see p30). Its design, based on plans by Catalan engineer Ildefons Cerdà, comprises hundreds of symmetrical grid-like squares. Construction continued into the 20th century at a time when Barcelona's elite was patronizing the city's most daring architects. Modernisme was flourishing and the area became home to the cream of Barcelona's Modernista architecture, with myriad elegant façades and balconies. Today, a wealth of enchanting cafés, funky design shops, gourmet restaurants and hip bars and clubs draws the professional crowd, which has adopted the neighbourhood as its own.*

Spires, Sagrada Família

Sights

1 Sagrada Família
2 La Pedrera
3 Mansana de la Discòrdia
4 Hospital de la Santa Creu i de Sant Pau
5 Fundació Tàpies
6 Palau Macaya
7 Fundació Francisco Godia
8 Rambla de Catalunya
9 Universitat de Barcelona
10 Museu Egipci

For more on Modernista *architecture* **See pp32–3**

1 Sagrada Família
Gaudí's wizardry culminated in this enchanting, wild, unconventional temple, which dominates the city skyline (see pp8–10).

2 La Pedrera
A daring, surreal fantasyland, and Gaudí's most remarkable civic work (see pp20–21).

3 Mansana de la Discòrdia
At the heart of the city's *Quadrat d'Or* (Golden Square) lies this stunning block of houses. Literally "the block of discord", the Mansana de la Discòrdia is so-called because of the dramatic contrast of its three flagship buildings. Built between 1900 and 1907 by the three *Modernista* greats, rival architects Gaudí, Domènech i Montaner and Puig i Cadafalch, the buildings were commissioned by competing bourgeois families. Domènech is represented by the ornate Casa Lleó Morera (see p33); Puig makes his mark with the Gothic-inspired Casa Amatller (see p33); and Gaudí flaunts his architectural prowess with Casa Batlló (see p33). All boast superb interiors – sadly closed to the public – with the exception of Casa Batlló. The lesser-known houses at Nos. 37 and 39 add to the overall splendour of the block.

Windows, Casa Battló, Mansana de la Discòrdia

The Perfume Museum at No. 39 is heaven for scent-lovers (see p41). ◈ Pg de Gràcia 35–45 • Map E2

4 Hospital de la Santa Creu i de Sant Pau
It's almost worth feigning illness to be admitted to this fully functioning hospital, which was built in two stages from 1905 by Domènech i Montaner and his son. A tribute to *Modernisme* – and Domènech's answer to Gaudí's Sagrada Família – the sumptuous design comprises eight pavilions and various other buildings linked by underground tunnels. The pavilions, each different, recall the history of Catalonia with murals, mosaics and sculptures. Interlacing the buildings are gardens creating beautiful outdoor oases, where patients can recuperate. The courtyards and gardens are open to visitors. ◈ C/Sant Antoni Maria Claret 167 • Map H1

Left **Hospital de la Santa Creu i de Sant Pau** Right **Casa Lléo Morera, Mansana de la Discòrdia**

Courtyard, Palau Macaya

Fundació Tàpies

Paintings and sculptures by Antoni Tàpies (b. 1923), Catalonia's foremost living artist, are housed in this early *Modernista* building *(see p32)*. For a glimpse of what awaits inside, look up: crowning the museum is the artist's eye-catching wire sculpture *Cloud & Chair* (1990). The collection of over 300 pieces covers Tàpies' whole range of work, including impressive abstract pieces such as *Grey Ochre on Brown* (1962). Temporary exhibitions are also held here, with past shows by Mario Herz, Hans Hacke and Craigie Horsfield. *C/Aragó 255 • Map E2 • Open 10am–8pm Tue–Sun • Adm • DA • Free under 16*

Palau Macaya

Designed by Puig i Cadafalch (1901), this palace is a fine example of the Neo-Gothic style in *Modernista* architecture. A magical, white façade is broken up by engravings and two towers. Of note are the decorative sculptures by *Modernista* sculptor Eusebi Arnau. The palace belongs to the Centre Cultural de la Caixa and, unfortunately, is closed at the moment; it is, however, worth a visit to see the outside alone. *Pg Sant Joan 108 • Map F2*

Ildefons Cerdà

Ildefons Cerdà's design for the new city, comprising a uniform grid of square blocks, received backing in 1859. Reflecting Cerdà's utopian socialist ideals, each block was to have a garden-like courtyard, surrounded by uniform flats. Real estate vultures soon intervened and the court-yards were converted into warehouses and factories. Today these green spaces are gradually being reinstated.

Fundació Francisco Godia

Although Francisco Godia (1921–90) was best known for his prowess behind the wheel – notably as an F1 racing driver – his passions extended to the art world. His once private collection now forms this museum and encompasses a range of art from medieval times to the 20th-century: from Jaume Huguet's altarpiece *St Mary Magdalene* (c. 1445) to a range of Spanish ceramics and works by 17th-century fresco-painter Luca Giordano. *C/Valencia 284 • Map E2 • Open 10am–2pm, 4–7pm Mon & Wed–Sat, 10am–2pm Sun • Adm*

Cloud & Chair sculpture, Fundació Tàpies

Rambla de Catalunya

8 This elegant extension of the better-known Rambla is a more up-market version. Lined with trees that form a leafy green tunnel in summer, it boasts scores of pretty façades and shops, including the *Modernista* Farmàcia Bolos (No. 77). The avenue teems with terrace bars and cafés, which are ideal for people-watching. *See also p50.* ✎ *Map E2*

Interior courtyard, Universitat de Barcelona

Universitat de Barcelona

9 Until 1958, this was the only university in Barcelona – today it is one of six. The graceful building (1861–1889) occupies two blocks of the Eixample and has a distinct air of academia. The interior gardens with their fountains and patios make for a cool, shady hideaway on hot afternoons. ✎ *Pl de la Universitat • Map E3*

Museu Egipci

10 Spain's most important Egyptology museum houses more than 350 exhibits from over 3,000 years of Ancient Egypt. Exhibits include terracotta figures, human and animal mummies, and a bust of the lion goddess Sekhmet (700–300 BC). ✎ *C/Valencia 284 • Map E2 • Open 10am–8pm Mon–Sat, 10am–2pm Sun • Adm*

The Modernista Route

Morning

🕐 Pop into the decrepit chess bar El Pato Loco (cnr Diputació & Aribau) to get a sepia picture of Barcelona that hasn't changed for a century. Wake up with a *cafè solo* and watch the old men playing speed-chess, then stroll around the gardens of the **Universitat**. Head east along Gran Via past the elegant Palace Barcelona Hotel *(see p143)* and right down C/Bruc for your first real taste of Catalan Art Nouveau, with Gaudí's **Casa Calvet** *(see p107)* on C/Casp. Turn right onto C/Casp and walk three blocks west to the majestic Pg de Gràcia; then go right again three blocks to the impressive buildings known as the **Mansana de la Discòrdia** *(see p103)* and the **Perfume Museum** *(see p41)*. Sniff around **Regia** perfume shop *(see p106)* before continuing north to marvel at Gaudí's **La Pedrera** *(see pp20–21)*. Feeling peckish? Stop at **Tragaluz** on Ptge de la Concepció *(see p109)*. The set menu is an economical way to experience this glitterati hang-out.

Afternoon

After lunch, head north on Pg de Gràcia, turn right along Diagonal, taking in the fairy-tale **Casa de les Punxes** at No. 416 *(see p33)*. Walk along Diagonal, making a detour left at Pg Sant Joan to see **Palau Macaya** at No. 108. Then stroll along C/Mallorca to the **Sagrada Família** *(see pp8–11)*. Here you can take in the Nativity Façade and rest weary legs in the Plaça de Gaudí before climbing the bell towers for a breathtaking view of the city.

Left **Light, Dos i Una** Centre **Shoppers, Passeig de Gràcia** Right **Furniture, Vinçon**

Design Shops

1 Vinçon
The cream of the crop in Spanish design with out-of-this-world designs for the most everyday objects. Furniture is displayed in a 1900 upper-class apartment. Breathtaking.
◎ *Pg de Gràcia 96 • Map E2*

2 Favorita
Superb design shop in *Modernista* Casa Thomas, selling the best in Catalan furniture. Worth a visit to see the exhibition furniture by the likes of Gaudí and Dalí. ◎ *C/Mallorca 291 • Map F2 • Closed three weeks Aug*

3 Regia
The biggest perfume shop in the city has over one thousand scents, including all the leading brands and other surprises. Also home to the Perfume Museum *(see p41).* ◎ *Pg de Gràcia 39 • Map E2*

4 Dos i Una
A designer gift shop with a steel-tiled floor and a psychedelic colour scheme. Concentrates on selling "made in Barcelona" items, which make for unusual souvenirs. ◎ *C/Rosselló 275 • Map E2*

5 Muxart
Excellent and arty shoe shop for men, women and kids in a country famed for its leather.
◎ *C/Rosselló 230 • Map E2*

6 Biosca & Botey
Exceptionally elegant shop selling all kinds of lamps, from Art-Nouveau mushrooms to ultra-modern steel shades. ◎ *Rambla de Catalunya 125 • Map E2 • DA*

7 Pilma
Breathtaking designer shop selling quality modern furniture and interior accessories by big names, as well as cuttting-edge creations by Catalan designers.
◎ *Av Diagonal 403 • Map E1*

8 D Barcelona
An eclectic range of gadgets and gifts in a shop that doubles as an exhibition space for up-and-coming designers and more established artists.
◎ *Av Diagonal 367 • Map F2*

9 Kowasa
A specialist photography bookshop with over 7,000 titles, including foreign magazines. The ambience is friendly and intimate and browsing is encouraged.
◎ *C/Mallorca 235 • Map E2 • DA*

10 Sadur
The owner designs and sells her own leather accessories: wallets, bags and a few gifts. Classy designs are well made and well priced. ◎ *C/Bruc 150 • Map F2*

For tips on shopping and standard opening hours **See p139**

Left **Lika Lounge** Right **OmmSessions Club**

TOP 10 After-Dark Venues

La Fira
Decked out in vintage fairground memorabilia, this striking bar rates high on novelty factor. Order a *cuba libre* while swaying in a swing. Lively atmosphere, unique setting. ◎ *C/Provença 171 • Map D2 • Closed Mon • Adm*

Lika Lounge
This New York-style cocktail bar boasts an ice bar and the best martinis in town. One of the city's hippest nightspots, it hosts DJ sessions with a different theme each night. ◎ *Passatge de Domingo 3 • Map E2*

Dry Martini
A classic and elegant venue where extraordinarily professional barmen are ready to prepare your favourite cocktail. Quiet jazz sounds play in the background. ◎ *C/Aribau 162 • Map D2*

OmmSessions Club
Located in possibly the most fashionable address in town, the OmmSessions Club attracts a young, international crowd. ◎ *C/Rosselló 265 • Map E2*

Velvet
Large, popular and populist disco bar with lavish decor, luxury fittings and music ranging from Elvis to Abba. ◎ *C/Balmes 161 • Map E2 • Adm*

Luz de Gas
A classic late-night watering hole, this half concert hall, half bar has live music nightly – from blues to jazz and soul. ◎ *C/Muntaner 246 • Map D1 • DA*

Ideal
Luxurious cocktail lounge opened by legendary barman José María Gotarda in the 1950s and now run by his son. More than 80 varieties of whisky. ◎ *C/Aribau 89 • Map D2 • Closed Sun*

City Hall
This popular club has two dance floors. Club nights cover a range of music styles, from electro pop to drum 'n' bass. ◎ *Rambla de Catalunya 2-4 • Map E3*

Dietrich Gay Teatro Café
A trendy gay club with a mixed door policy and a beautiful internal garden. It plays house and garage, and holds shows by singers, trapeze artists and acrobats. ◎ *Consell de Cent 255 • Map D3*

Les Gens que j'Aime
The ideal place to have a drink while enjoying soft music, after walking around Paseo de Gràcia and Rambla Catalunya. ◎ *Valencia 286 • Map E2 • Open 6pm–2:30am daily (3am weekends)*

For Barcelona's best nightlife **See pp46–7**

Left **Laie Llibreria Cafè** Right **Casa Alfonso**

Cafés

1 Laie Llibreria Cafè
A cultural meeting place with a lively atmosphere, airy terrace and foreign newspapers. There's an excellent set lunch and live jazz (on Thursdays). ◈ *C/Pau Claris 85 • Map E3 • Closed Sun & Mon eve*

2 Cafè del Centre
Said to be the oldest café in the Eixample, with dark wooden interiors that have not changed for a century. An unpretentious spot for a quiet coffee. ◈ *C/Girona 69 • Map F3 • Closed after 9pm*

3 Casa Alfonso
This classy café has been in business since 1929. Arguably the best *pernil* (serrano ham) in the city. ◈ *C/Roger de Llúria 6 • Map F3 • Closed Sun*

4 Cacao Sampaka
An infinite array of chocolate, including innovative combinations such as chocolate with Parmesan cheese or olive oil. ◈ *C/Consell de Cent 292 • Map E3 • Closed Sun, mornings in Aug*

5 Mauri
One of the best pastry shops in town. Enjoy a hot drink with an elaborate dessert in *Modernista* surroundings. ◈ *Rambla Catalunya 102 • Map E2 • Closed Sun eve*

6 Bar Paris
Chaotic and lively, with a sunny terrace, Bar Paris attracts a student crowd. Open 24 hours a day, seven days a week, it's ideal for clubbers not ready to go home. ◈ *C/Paris 187 • Map D1*

7 Palace Barcelona
This elegant *Modernista* hotel is the perfect place for breakfast in the conservatory or afternoon tea in the Grand Hall. It's thoroughly luxurious, but pricey. ◈ *Gran Via de les Cortes Catalanes 668 • Map F3 • DA*

8 Bauma
A mixed crowd drifts in to read the paper or smoke a Havana cigar with a post-lunch *carajillo* (coffee and cognac). ◈ *C/Roger de Llúria 124 • Map F2 • Closed Sat • DA*

9 Mantequería Ravell
A deli-style shop offering incredible breakfasts, including eggs with foie gras, at a huge communal table. Wine and traditional hams and cheeses are also available. ◈ *C/Aragó 313 • Map F2 • Closed Mon & Sat after 6pm, Tue & Wed after 9pm, Sun*

10 Tragarrapid
This newly opened spot is one of the most chic cafés in town. Up-market tapas and coffee served with style. ◈ *Ptge de la Concepció 5 • Map E2*

For tips on dining and standard opening hours **See p138**

Price Categories

For a three-course meal for one with half a bottle of wine (or equivalent meal), taxes and extra charges.

€	under €15
€€	€15–25
€€€	€25–35
€€€€	€35–45
€€€€€	over €45

Casa Calvet

🔟 Restaurants & Tapas Bars

1 Tragaluz
Popular with the fashionable crowd, this design-conscious, three-floored restaurant serves imaginative Mediterranean cuisine. ® *Ptge de la Concepció 5 • Map E2 • 93 487 01 96 • €€€€€*

2 La Semproniana
Set in an old printworks, this place serves food that's a cross between Catalan and nouvelle cuisine – with a sense of playfulness. Try the black pudding lasagne. ® *C/Rosselló 148 • Map E2 • 93 453 18 20 • Closed Sun • €€€€ • DA*

3 Cinc Sentits
Indulge the five senses (*cinc sentits* in Catalan) at this stylish restaurant, where diners are wowed with modern interpretations of classic Catalan cuisine. ® *C/Aribau 53 • Map D2 • 93 323 94 90 • Closed Mon eve, Sun • €€€€*

4 L'Olivé
An unassuming, family-style restaurant with excellent, well-priced regional cuisine. Reputedly the best place to eat that Catalan speciality pig's trotter. The broad bean salad with mint is recommended. ® *C/Balmes 47 • Map E3 • 93 452 19 90 • Closed Sun eve • €€€€€*

5 Noti
Apart from the superb French-Mediterranean cuisine and stylish decor, Noti also has an adjoining cocktail bar. ® *C/Roger de Lluria 35–37 • Map F3 • 93 342 66 73 • Closed Sat lunch, Sun • DA • €€€€*

6 Casa Calvet
Splurge on Catalan food with a modern twist in these impressive Gaudí-designed dining rooms. ® *C/Casp 48 • Map F3 • 93 412 40 12 • Closed Sun • €€€€€ • DA*

7 Moo
Run by the Roca brothers, Moo serves creative Catalan recipes prepared with the finest local ingredients. ® *C/Rosselló 265 • Map E2 • 93 445 40 00 • €€€€ • DA*

8 Inopia
Tucked away in a residential neighbourhood, Inopia serves traditional tapas. ® *C/Tamarit 104 • Map C3 • 93 424 52 31 • Closed Tue–Fri lunch, Sun, Mon • €€ • DA*

9 Cervecería Catalana
Just a few steps from Rambla de Catalunya, with some of the best tapas in town and a variety of beers. ® *C/Mallorca 236 • Map E2 • 93 216 03 68 • €€€ • DA*

10 Parco Meralgo
This bright, modern tapas bar has a gourmet menu based on recipes from around the country. ® *C/Muntaner 171 • Map D1 • 93 430 90 27 • €€*

Unless otherwise stated, all restaurants accept credit cards. For tips on dining and standard opening hours **See p138**

Left **Cloister, Monestir de Pedralbes** Right **Exterior, Monestir de Pedralbes**

Gràcia, Tibidabo & Zona Alta

THE ZONA ALTA *(Uptown) is an area covering several neighbourhoods that, as the name suggests, are in the hilly part of the city. From the moneyed streets of Pedralbes and Tibidabo to bohemian Gràcia, this entire northern area of the city offers stunning views and regal attractions. But what really sets this area apart from the rest of the city is its 15 parks; the best are Gaudí's stunning and imaginative Parc Güell, and the colossal natural park of Collserolla, which spreads out like green baize over Tibidabo mountain. Gràcia stands out as the city's most cosmopolitan neighbourhood. Its strong political tradition and gypsy community have long drawn artists and writers to the labyrinthine streets, and it is now home to scores of innovative boutiques, bars and squares, which teem with life most nights of the week.*

Parc d'Atraccions del Tibidabo

🔟 Sights & Attractions

1. Parc d'Atraccions del Tibidabo
2. Monestir de Pedralbes
3. Torre de Collserola
4. Museu del FC Barcelona & Camp Nou Stadium
5. Palau Reial de Pedralbes
6. Park Güell
7. Temple Expiatori del Sagrat Cor
8. Parc de Collserola
9. Tramvia Blau
10. Jardins del Laberint d'Horta

The best way to visit this area is on the Bus Turístic **See p133**

1 Parc d'Atraccions del Tibidabo

Take the 100-year-old funicular up to the top of Tibidabo's 517-m (1,695-ft) mountain to visit this traditional amusement park, which first opened in 1908. Although there are a couple of stomach-churning, white-knuckle rides, the real attractions are the quaint, old-fashioned ones, including a beautifully conserved carousel and a Ferris wheel. Here also is the Museu dels Autòmates *(see p41)*, with automatons, mechanical models and a scale model of the park. ✆ Pl de Tibidabo • Map B1 • Opening times vary, call 93 211 79 42 for details • www.tibidabo.es • Adm • DA

2 Monestir de Pedralbes

Named after the Latin *petras albas*, which means white stones, this outstandingly beautiful Gothic monastery was founded by Queen Elisenda de Montcada de Pinós in the early 14th century. Her alabaster tomb lies in the wall between the church and the particularly impressive three-storey Gothic cloister. An interesting glimpse of medieval life is provided by the furnished kitchens, cells, infirmary and refectory, all of which are well preserved. ✆ C/Baixada Monestir 9 • Map A1 • Open 10am–2pm Tue–Sun • Adm; free 1st Sun of the month • DA

3 Torre de Collserola

This slender telecommunications tower was designed by British architect Norman Foster. The needle-like upper structure

Torre de Collserola

rests on a concrete pillar and is anchored by 12 huge steel cables. Rising to a height of 560 m (1836 ft) above sea level, the top is reached by a glass-fronted elevator. On a clear day, you can see Montserrat and the Pyrenees. ✆ Parc de Collserola • Map B1 • Open 11am–2pm, 3:30–6pm Wed–Sun; 11am–6pm Sat–Sun (to 7pm Apr–Sep) • Adm • DA

4 Museu del FC Barcelona & Camp Nou Stadium

Barcelona's most visited museum is a must for fans of the beautiful game. With football memorabilia of every conceivable kind, you can learn all about the club's history. Work donated by some of Catalonia's leading artists is also on display. Admission includes access to Barca's 120,000-seater stadium, an impressive monument to the city's love-affair with the game. ✆ Entrance 9 Stadium, Av Arístides Maillol • Map A2 • Open 10am–6:30pm Mon–Sat (to 8pm Apr–Oct), 10am–2:30pm Sun • Adm

Camp Nou Stadium

Gràcia

Until the end of the 19th century, Gràcia was a fiercely proud independent city. Despite locals' protests, it became part of Barcelona proper in 1898, but has always maintained a sense of separatism and has been a hotbed of political activity. It is now home to a booming cottage industry nurtured by a growing band of artisans. Don't miss the barrio's annual fiesta (see p65) in the second week of August.

Palau Reial de Pedralbes

The former main residence of Count Eusebi Güell was donated by the count to the Spanish royal family in 1919. Open to the public since 1937, this majestic palace now houses the Museu de Ceràmica and the Museu de les Arts Decoratives. The former has a fine collection of Catalan and Moorish ceramics, including works by Miró and Picasso; the latter has period furniture, plus a number of artifacts dating from the Middle Ages to the present day. The magnificent gardens include a fountain designed by Gaudí and some pleasant strolls. ⚘ Av Diagonal 686 • Map A2 • Museums open 10am–6pm Tue–Sat, 10am–3pm Sun • Adm (free 1st Sun of the month) • DA

View, Temple Expiatori del Sagrat Cor

Parc Güell

Declared a UNESCO World Heritage Site in 1984, this heady brew of architectural wizardry includes *trencadís* tiling, a serpentine bench, fairy-tale pavilions, Gothic archways, and the columned Sala Hipóstila (originally intended as a market hall). In true Gaudí style, playfulness and symbolism pervade every aspect of the park. The Casa-Museu Gaudí, where Gaudí lived for 20 years, is dedicated to the architect's life. ⚘ C/d'Olot • Map B2 • Open 10am–dusk daily • Free ⚘ Casa-Museu Gaudí • Map B2 • Open Oct–Mar: 10am–5:45pm; Apr–Sep: 10am–7:45pm • Adm €4

Museu de Ceràmica, Palau Reial

Temple Expiatori del Sagrat Cor

Visible from almost anywhere in Barcelona, the Temple of the Sacred Heart was built by Enric Sagnier between 1902 and 1911. It has a dramatic sculpture of Jesus and an elaborately decorated door that verges on the psychedelic. Take the elevator up the main tower, or climb the steps to the outside terrace for breathtaking views. ⚘ Pl del Tibidabo • Map B1 • Open 10am–8pm daily (Elevator open 10:30am–2pm & 3–7pm daily) • Adm

Parc de Collserola

Beyond the peaks of Tibidabo mountain, this 6,500-ha (16,000-acre) natural park of wild forest

Parc del Laberint d'Horta

and winding paths is an oasis of calm. It is great for hiking and biking *(see p59)*, with sign-posted paths and nature trails. ⊗ *Info point: C/Església 92 • Map B1*

9 Tramvia Blau

The city's blue trams, with their old-fashioned, wooden interiors are attractions in themselves. The route, from the FGC station to Plaça Doctor Andreu, passes many *Modernista* mansions to the top of Avinguda Tibidabo. ⊗ *Av Tibidabo • Map B1 • Trams run 10am–8pm (Oct–May 6pm) daily (mid-Sep–late June Sat, Sun & bank hols only) • Adm*

10 Parc del Laberint d'Horta

In 1802, the Marquès d'Alfarràs hosted a huge party in these wonderful Neo-Classical gardens to celebrate the visit of Carles IV. Designed by Italian architect Domenico Bagotti, they incorporate a lake, a waterfall, canals and a recently restored cypress-tree maze. ⊗ *C/German Desvalls • Map C1 • Open 10am–dusk daily • Free (Wed & Sun), Adm (all other days)*

Museu de les Arts Decoratives, Palau Reial

Exploring the Heights

Morning

⏱ Taking the northern route of the Bus Turístic *(see p133)* is the easiest way to negotiate the vast northern area of the city; it also gives discounts on entrance to major sights en route. Start off at Plaça de Catalunya (tickets can be bought on board) and sit on the top deck for a good view of the *Modernista* magic along Pg de Gràcia. Make the whimsical **Parc Güell** your first stop and spend the morning ambling around Gaudí's otherworldly park. Get back on the bus and continue north to the southern end of Av Tibidabo. Walk about 500 m (1600 ft) up Av Tibidabo and stop off for a leisurely lunch in the garden of the palatial **El Asador d'Aranda** *(see p117)*.

Afternoon

After you've had your fill of fine Castilian cuisine, continue strolling up Av Tibidabo to Plaça Doctor Andreu where you can hop on the steep funicular train to go higher still to Plaça de Tibidabo. Pop into the **Parc d'Atraccions** *(see p111)* for a ride on the dod-gems or the Ferris wheel. Then head to the landmark **Torre de Collserola** *(see p111)*, where a glass elevator whisks you up to an observation deck for spectacular views. Return to Plaça Doctor Andreu on the funicular and treat yourself to a *granissat (see p43)* in one of the terrace bars. Then go down Av Tibidabo on the charming **Tramvia Blau** and catch the Bus Turístic back to the city centre.

Left **Món de Mones** Right **El Piano**

TOP 10 Gràcia Boutiques

1 Naftalina
Of all the cottage industry boutiques in Gràcia, Naftalina has the most stylish interior – befitting the equally stylish, hand-made designer clothes. Chic, elegant, understated women's wear with an emphasis on textured fabrics.
◇ C/La Perla 33

2 Ninas
Nina, an American designer, sells simple, modern women's clothes made from fine fabrics. The shop is housed in a gorgeous *Modernista* building which was once a butcher's, and has a work-shop at the back.◇ C/Verdi 39

3 Llena eres de Gràcia
For gorgeous women's fashions, accessories and evening wear at surprisingly reasonable prices, try this colourful boutique. The clothes are very wearable but most have a quirky twist.
◇ C/Ros de Olano 52

4 José Rivero
José provides his own original in-house creations for men and women; he also sells crafted accessories, including handbags, by young local designers. ◇ C/Astúries 43

5 Multiart
This fabric workshop sells colourful, hand-printed textiles, bedlinen, and clothes for men and women. It also runs educational dress-making workshops.
◇ C/Sant Joaquim 23

6 Món de Mones
For colourful jewellery and accessories, try the 'World of Monkeys' (*món de mones* in Catalan) near the Plaça del Sol. The designer, Teresa Roig, uses a variety of materials from glass to felt to create her original designs. ◇ C/Xiquets de Valls 9

7 Camiseria Pons
One of the oldest shops in this area, this men's specialist shop sells shirts by top Spanish and international designers, including Ralph Lauren. ◇ Gran de Gràcia 49

8 Mushi Mushi
From hard-to-find, small labels to the best international collections, this pretty little boutique stocks a fine selection of women's fashion. It also offers a small range of shoes, bags and accessories. ◇ Plaça Rius i Taulet 5

9 El Piano
El Piano sells elegant and stylish women's clothes with a retro flair made by Catalan designer Tina García. It also stocks clothes by other independent designers. ◇ C/Verdi 20 bis

10 Zucca
One of three branches in Barcelona, Zucca offers a superb range of ultra-stylish fashion accessories. The stock includes plastic flowers for your hair and stick-on navel rings.
◇ C/Torrent de l'Olla 175

Most of Gràcia's small boutiques accept commissions.

Left **Sign, Cafè Salambo** Right **Tea urns, Teteria Jazmin**

🔟 Gràcia Cafés

1 Cafè del Sol
This café-bar is a cut above the others in the lively, bohemian Plaça del Sol. The atmosphere buzzes, the conversation inspires and the excellent coffee keeps on coming. 🕸 *Pl del Sol 16 • DA*

2 Cafè Salambó
Scrumptious sandwiches and a tasty range of salads are the draw at this beautiful, wooden, trendy bar-cum-café. There are pool tables upstairs. 🕸 *C/Torrijos 51 • DA*

3 Teteria Jazmín
An aromatic café that serves hundreds of different teas; the most unusual is the mint tea served with pine-kernels. Typical Morrocan dishes (*tagines* and couscous) are also available. 🕸 *C/Maspons 11 • Closed Mon, Tue, two weeks Sep*

4 La Cafetera
Of all the cafés on Plaça de la Virreina, this one, with its outdoor terrace and tiny patio full of potted plants, is easily the most pleasant for a quiet and leisurely morning coffee and a sandwich. 🕸 *Pl de la Virreina*

5 Aroma
It's always a pleasure to smell the coffee being freshly ground at this cream-walled and wood-beamed café. Hundreds of coffees to choose from, with takeaway packets available. 🕸 *Travessera de Gràcia 151 • DA*

6 Vreneli
The cosy Plaça de Rius i Taulet boasts four café terraces to choose from. Vreneli is the most interesting one, with a mixture of Mexican, Swiss and Spanish fare. No alcohol is served. 🕸 *Pl Rius i Taulet 8 • Closed Mon • DA*

7 Blues Cafè
The walls at this dusky, atmospheric café-bar are plastered with black-and-white photos of John Lee Hooker and Leadbelly, among others. The music, electric or acoustic, is always the blues. 🕸 *C/Perla 35*

8 Cafè del Teatre
This is an ideal place to find a young, friendly crowd and good conversation. The only connection with the theatre here seems to be the velvet curtains on the sign over the door of this scruffy, but busy, café. 🕸 *C/Torrijos 41*

9 Cafè de Gràcia
This airy and spacious café, with salmon walls and mirrors, is an ideal spot for a quick coffee away from the crowds. Service is speedy and a touch more formal than most places in Gràcia. 🕸 *C/Gran de Gràcia 34*

10 Sureny
A new addition to this square, Sureny is simple but stylish, with a tantalizing selection of tapas and plenty of wines available by the glass. 🕸 *Pl Revolució 17 • Closed Mon • DA*

Left **Mirasol** Right **Gràcia Nightlife, Plaça del Sol**

TOP10 Hip Drinking Spots

1 Mirasol
Possibly Gràcia's most classic bar, the atmospheric Mirasol has been a bohemian hang-out for decades. In summer, there's outdoor seating on the *plaça*. ◈ *Pl del Sol 3 • Closed Sun • DA*

2 Universal Café
Open until 5:30am, Universal Café is a late-night, two-level bar with a spacious, airy interior. The image-concious crowd comes to flirt and dance to house (upstairs) and acid jazz (below). There are also occasional live bands. ◈ *C/Marià Cubí 182 • Closed Sun • Occasional adm*

3 Mirablau
A slightly older, well-heeled set, who adhere to the smart dress code, come to this club-bar for cocktails and amazing views of the city. ◈ *Pl Dr Andreu*

4 Elephant
Lavish, stylish and totally unique, Elephant is one of the best clubs in the city for a fun night out. In summer, you can lounge in the garden on huge, white beds. ◈ *Passeig dels Til.lers 1*

5 Casa Quimet
The "Guitar House" is always crowded and noisy. If you can play, join the enthusiasts and would-be flamenco players who pick guitars off the wall and have an impromptu jam session. Wonderful. ◈ *C/Rambla de Prat 9 • Closed Mon–Wed & Feb & Aug*

6 Sala BeCool
A favourite in the chic Sant Gervasi neighbourhood, Sala BeCool offers a wide-ranging programme of DJ sessions, club nights and live gigs. ◈ *Plaça Joan Llongueras 5 • Map C1*

7 Otto Zutz
Barcelona's media crowd flocks to this New-York-style club to chatter in the corners upstairs and shoot pool downstairs. The huge dance floors throb with house music. ◈ *C/Lincoln 15 • Closed Sun–Mon • Adm*

8 Mond Bar
The comfortable sofas, low lights and innovative music policy (pop, lounge and trip-hop) make this one of the coolest hang-outs in the city. Some of Barcelona's best DJs play here. ◈ *Pl del Sol 21*

9 Heliogàbal
This cult, live music venue is best on Thursday or Sunday nights when you can hear anything from an indie band to a poetry slam. Prices are very reasonable too. ◈ *C/Ramón y Cajal 80 • Map F1*

10 Bikini
Opening from midnight onwards, this huge venue has three spaces, which offer dance and Latin music and a cocktail lounge. Regular live music includes some of the best up-and-coming acts in Europe. ◈ *C/Deu i Mata 105 • Closed Mon • Adm • DA*

Normal closing times for bars is 2:30am, 3am weekends. Clubs open until 4:30/6am. For more on Barcelona's nightlife See pp46–7

Price Categories

For a three-course meal for one with half a bottle of wine (or equivalent meal), taxes and extra charges.

€	under 15
€€	15–25
€€€	25–35
€€€€	35–45
€€€€€	over 45

Interior, Flash Flash

TOP 10 Restaurants & Tapas Bars

1 El Asador d'Aranda
Housed in the magnificent *Modernista* Casa Roviralta, this restaurant is a magnet for business-folk. Order the delicious lamb roasted in an oak-burning oven and dine in the beautiful garden. ◈ *Av Tibidabo 31 • 93 417 01 15 • Closed Sun dinner • €€€€*

2 Bar-Restaurante Can Tomàs
This tapas bar, in the Sarrià neighbourhood, is an institution. It has the well-deserved reputation of making some of the best tapas in town. Particularly recommended are the *patates braves.* ◈ *C/ Major de Sarrià 49 • 93 203 10 77 • Closed Wed • No credit cards • €€*

3 Hofmann
Run by the talented chef Mey Hofmann, this restaurant serves some seriously delicious Catalan cuisine. Save room for the desserts. ◈ *C/La Granada del Penedès 14–16 • 93 218 71 65 • DA • €€€€*

4 Neichel
Top-class in every way, Neichel lures a moneyed clientele with *nouvelle cuisine* and a luscious interior. Reserve in advance. ◈ *C/Beltrán i Rózpide 1 • 93 203 84 08 • Closed Sun & Mon • €€€€€*

5 Taverna El Glop
This tavern-like local eatery serves traditional Catalan food. Its *calçots* (chargrilled, gigantic spring onions served with spicy romesco sauce) are legendary. ◈ *C/St Lluis 24 • 93 213 70 58 • DA • €€*

6 Àbac
At the foot of Tibidabo mountain, Àbac offers French-Mediterranean cuisine prepared by award-winning chef, Xavier Pellicer. ◈ *Avinguda Tibidabo 1 • 93 319 66 00 • Closed lunch Sun, Mon, Fri lunch • DA • €€€€*

7 Flash Flash
Truites (omelettes) rule here, from the classic (Spanish) to the inventive (garlic and asparagus). The owners claim to have used five million eggs in just over 30 years. ◈ *C/Granada de Penedès 25 • 93 237 09 90 • DA • €€€*

8 La Balsa
In the quiet Bonanova district, La Balsa is a beautiful spot, with two garden terraces. Fine Basque, Catalan and Mediterranean dishes are on the menu. ◈ *C/Infanta Isabel 4 • 93 211 50 48 • Closed Sun dinner, Mon lunch & lunch in Aug • €€€€€*

9 Tram Tram
Housed in a handsome old town house, this restaurant serves, innovative, contemporary Catalan cuisine. ◈ *C/Major de Sarria 121 • 93 204 85 18 • Closed Sat lunch, Sun, Mon, fortnight in Aug • €€€€*

10 Botafumeiro
The fish tanks at this sea-food restaurant are teeming with crabs and lobster destined for plates. Try the tender *pulpo Gallego* (Galician octopus). Reservations are essential. ◈ *C/Gran de Gràcia 81 • 93 218 42 30 • DA • €€€€€*

 Unless otherwise stated, all restaurants accept credit cards. For more on dining and standard opening hours See p138

Left **Monestir de Santes Creus** Right **Cadaqués**

Beyond Barcelona

STEEPED IN TRADITION, *with its own language and an enormous sense of pride in its separate identity, Catalonia is immensely rich in both cultural heritage and physical geography. It is no exaggeration to say that Catalonia really does have everything. To the north are the 3,000-m (9840-ft) peaks of the Pyrenees. The coastline is dotted with hundreds of beautiful sandy beaches and intimate rocky coves with crystal-clear waters. These staggering natural treasures are complemented by a wealth of fabulous churches and monasteries, many set in stunning, isolated mountain scenery. For the gourmet, the regional cuisine is particularly rewarding, while the locally-produced cava easily holds its own against its French champagne counterparts.*

Teatre-Museu Dalí

TOP 10 Sights & Attractions

1. Montserrat
2. Teatre-Museu Dalí, Figueres
3. Vall de Núria
4. Alt Penèdes
5. Begur & Around
6. Tarragona
7. Girona
8. Empúries
9. Port Aventura
10. Costa Daurada & Sitges

*For tips on getting around Catalonia **See p132***

Montserrat

The dramatic mount of Montserrat, with its remote Benedictine monastery (dating from 1025), is a religious symbol and a place of pilgrimage for the Catalan people. The Basilica houses a statue of Catalonia's patron virgin, La Moreneta, also know as the "Black Virgin". Some legends date the statue to AD 50, but research

Basilica, Monestir de Montserrat

suggests it was carved in the 12th century. The monastery itself was largely destroyed in 1811 during the War of Independence, and rebuilt some 30 years later. Montserrat forms part of a ridge of mountains that rise suddenly from the plains. Take the funicular to the mountain's unspoilt peaks, where paths run alongside spectacular gorges to numerous hermitages. ◈ *Tourist Info: Pl de la Creu • 93 877 77 77*

Teatre-Museu Dalí, Figueres

Salvador Dalí was born in the town of Figueres in 1904. Paying tribute to the artist is the fantastic Teatre-Museu Dalí, which is full of his eccentric works. Housed in a former theatre, the country's second-most-visited museum (after the Prado in Madrid) provides a unique insight into the artist's extraordinary creations, from *La Cesta de Pan* (1926) to *El Torero Alucinogeno* (1970). Twenty minutes' drive away, near the beach town of Cadaqués, the Dalí connection continues. Here you can visit the Casa-Museu Salvador Dalí, the artist's summer house for nearly 60 years until his death in 1989.

◈ *Pl Gala-Salvador Dalí, Figueres • 972 67 75 00 • Open Mar–Jun, Oct: 9:30am–6pm Tue–Sun; Jul–Sep: 9am–8pm daily; Nov–Feb: 10:30am–6pm Tue–Sun • Adm* ◈ *Casa-Museu Salvador Dalí, Port Lligat • 972 25 10 15 • Closed early Jan to mid-Mar • Guided visits only, Tue–Sun (15 Jun–15 Sep daily) by reservation • Adm*

Vall de Núria

This enchanting Pyrenean hideaway, surrounded by crests reaching as high as 3,000-m (9,840-ft), is a ski resort in winter and a green, peaceful oasis attracting hikers and nature-lovers in summer. The mountain resort centres on a tiny religious sanctuary and has a youth hostel and apartments for rent. The valley is only accessible via a silent cog railway, which trundles above the clouds through breathtaking mountain scenery. ◈ *Tourist Info: Railway Station, Vall de Núria • 97 273 20 20 • Rack railway train from Ribes de Freser, 10 km N Ripoll*

Rainy Taxi, Teatre-Museu Dalí

Anywhere in Catalonia can be reached by car from Barcelona in less than three hours.

4 Alt Penedès

Catalonia's most famous wine region is the *cava*-producing area of the Penedès. The *cava* brands of Cordoníu and Freixenet have become household names worldwide. Many of the area's wineries and bodegas are open to the public. One of the most spectacular is the Cordoníu bodega, housed in a *Modernista* building designed by Puig i Cadafalch, with a phenomenal 26 km (16 miles) of cellars on five floors. ◈ *Tourist Info: C/Cort 14, Vilafranca del Penedès • 93 818 12 54 • The tourist office has details on all winery visits in the region, including the Cordoníu winery*

Riu Onyar, Girona

5 Begur & Around

The elegant hilltop town of Begur, with its ruined 14th-century castle, looks down on the nature reserve of Aiguamolla and some of the prettiest coves on the Costa Brava. The town's population quadruples in summer as visitors make this their base for exploring nearby beaches and small, isolated coves. Many of the area's beaches stage jazz concerts throughout the summer. This is perhaps the best stretch of coastline in Catalonia. ◈ *Tourist Info: Av Onze de Setembre 5 • 972 62 45 20*

Codorníu *cava*

6 Tarragona

Entering the city of Tarragona, past the oil refineries and its huge industrial port, it's hard to envisage the astounding archaeological treasures that await. Once the capital of Roman Catalonia, the city's main attractions today are from this era. Highlights include an impressive amphitheatre and the well-kept Roman walls that lead past the Museu Nacional Arqueològic and the Torre de Pilatos, a tower where Christians were supposedly imprisoned before being thrown to the lions. Also in Tarragona is the Catedral de Santa Tecla *(see p124)*. ◈ *Tourist Info: C/Fortuny 4 • 977 23 34 15*

7 Girona

Said to have the highest living standards in Catalonia, Girona is a pleasant town surrounded by lush green hills. Hidden away in the old town, the atmospheric Jewish quarter (known as El Call) is one of the best-preserved medieval enclaves in Europe. Girona's cathedral is a must *(see p124)*. ◈ *Tourist Info: Rambla de la Llibertat 1 • 972 22 65 75*

8 Empúries

After Tarragona, Empúries is Catalonia's second most important Roman site. Occupying an impressive position by the sea, it includes more than 40 hectares (99 acres) scattered with Greek and Roman ruins, the highlights of which are the remains of a market street, various temples and part of a Roman amphitheatre. Coupled with lovely nearby beaches, it's an ideal spot for those looking to mix a bit of history with a dip in the sea. ✪ *Empúries • 972 77 02 08 • Open Jun–Sep: 10am–8pm daily; Oct–May: 10am–6pm daily • Adm*

Port Aventura
Universal Studios' theme park is divided up into five areas: China, Far West, Mediterranean, Polynesia and Mexico, each offering rides and attractions. Thrill-junkies will appreciate one of Europe's biggest roller coasters, Dragon Kahn (China). There are also shows, and the entire experience is like being on a film set. ✪ *Av Pere Molas, Vila-seca, Tarragona • 902 20 22 20 • Open mid-Mar–Oct daily, call for seasonal hours • Adm • DA*

Costa Daurada & Sitges
With its wide sandy beaches and shallow waters, the Costa Daurada differs from the northern Catalonian coastline. The sleepy town of Torredembarra is a pleasant and rarely busy family resort, but the jewel in the crown is undoubtedly Sitges. It's the summer home to Barcelona's chic crowd, as well as being a popular gay resort *(see p49)*. All this gives it a cosmopolitan, frenetic feel, but the town never reaches the tacky excesses of some of the Costa Brava's resorts. ✪ *Tourist Info: C/Sínia Morera • 902 10 34 28*

Waterfront, Sitges

A Scenic Drive

Morning
From Barcelona take the AP7 motorway until exit 4, then take the C260 to Cadaqués. The journey should take about two and a half hours in all. Just before dropping down to the town, stop at the viewpoint and take in the azure coastline and the whitewashed houses of this former fishing village. Once in **Cadaqués**, now one of Catalonia's trendiest beach towns, wander the quaint boutique-filled streets. After a splash in the sea and a coffee on one of the chic terrace cafés, take the road leaving Port Lligat and head for the **Cap de Creus** *(see p125)* lighthouse. Drive through the desolately beautiful landscape of this rocky headland before doubling back and heading off to Port de la Selva. The road twists and winds interminably, but the picture-perfect scenery will leave you speechless.

Afternoon
Stop in the tiny, mountain-enclosed Port de la Selva for an excellent seafood lunch at the Cala Herminda. Then drive to the neighbouring village of Selva del Mar with its tiny river and have a post-prandial coffee on the terrace of the Bar Stop before continuing up to the **Monestir Sant Pere de Rodes** *(see p124)*. You'll be tempted to stop several times on the way up to take in the views. Don't, because the best is to be had from the monastery, which offers an incredible sweeping vista of the whole area. There are plenty of well-signposted walks around the mountain top here and it is worth staying put to see the sun set slowly over the bay.

Beyond Barcelona

Following pages **Inner Courtyard, Monestir de Montserrat**

Left **Chapterhouse detail, Monestir de Santes Creus** Right **Monestir de Poblet**

Churches & Monasteries

1 Monestir de Montserrat
Catalonia's holiest place is the region's most visited monastery. It boasts some Romanesque art and a statue of the "Black Virgin" *(see p119)*. ✪ *Montserrat • 93 877 77 77 • Adm • DA to Basilica*

2 Monestir de Poblet
This busy, working monastery contains the Gothic Capella de Sant Jordi, a Romanesque church, and the Porta Daurada, a doorway that was gilded for Felipe II's visit in 1564. ✪ *off N240, 10 km W of Montblanc • 97 787 02 54 • Adm*

3 Monestir de Ripoll
The west portal of this monastery (879) has reputedly the finest Romanesque carvings in Spain. Of the original buildings, only the doorway and cloister remain. ✪ *Ripoll • 972 70 23 51 • Adm*

4 Monestir de Santes Creus
The cloister at this Gothic treasure (1150) is notable for the beautifully sculpted capitals by English artist Reinard Funoll. ✪ *Santes Creus, 25 km NW of Montblanc • 977 63 83 29 • Closed Mon • Adm • Tue free*

5 Monestir de Sant Pere de Rodes
The dilapidated charm of this UNESCO World Heritage Site may have dwindled since its face-lift, but nothing detracts from the views it offers over Cap de Creus and Port de la Selva. ✪ *22 km E of Figueres • 972 38 75 59 • Closed Mon • Adm*

6 Sant Climent i Santa Maria de Taüll
These two churches are perfect examples of the Romanesque churches that pepper the Pyrenees. Dating from 1123, most of the original frescoes are now in the MNAC in Barcelona *(see pp18–19)*. ✪ *138 km N of Lleida • 973 69 40 00*

7 Catedral de La Seu d'Urgell
Dating from around 1040, this cathedral is one of the most elegant in Catalonia. ✪ *La Seu d'Urgell • 973 35 32 42 • Free • DA*

8 Catedral de Santa Maria
This cathedral is remarkable for possessing the widest Gothic nave anywhere in Europe and the second widest of any type after the Basilica in the Vatican. ✪ *Old Town, Girona • 972 21 58 14 • Adm • Sun free*

9 Catedral de Santa Tecla
At 104-m (340-ft) long, Tarragona's cathedral is the largest in the region. Its architecture is a mixture of Gothic and Romanesque, and it is crowned by a huge octagonal bell tower. ✪ *Old Town, Tarragona • 977 23 86 85 • Closed Sun except for 11am mass • Adm*

10 Sant Joan de les Abadesses
This pretty French Romanesque-style monastery in the Pyrenees harbours a prestigious collection of Romanesque sculpture. ✪ *Sant Joan de les Abadesses • 972 72 05 99 • www.santjoandelesabadesses.com • Adm*

Usual opening hours for monasteries and churches are 10am–1pm & 3–7pm Mon–Sat, 10am–1pm Sun. Call to confirm seasonal times.

Parc Natural de la Zona Volcànica de la Garrotxa

⏰10 National Parks & Nature Reserves

1 Parc Nacional d'Aigüestortes i Estany de Sant Maurici

The magnificent peaks of Catalonia's only national park are accessible from the resort of Espot. You'll find ponds and lakes 2,000 m (6,560 ft) up. ☜ *148 km N of Lleida*

2 Delta de l'Ebre

This giant delta is a patchwork of paddy fields. The wide expanse of the River Ebre is a nature reserve for migratory birds and has scores of bird-watching stations. ☜ *28 km SE of Tortosa*

3 Parc Natural de la Zona Volcànica de la Garrotxa

It is 10,000 years since La Garrotxa last erupted and the volcanoes are long since extinct. The largest crater is the Santa Margalida, at 500 m (1,640 ft) wide. It is magical here in spring when thousands of butterflies emerge. ☜ *40 km NW of Girona*

4 Cap de Creus

As the Pyrenees tumble into the Mediterranean, they create a rocky headland, which juts out 10 km (6.25 miles). It forms Catalonia's most easterly point and offers spectacular views of the craggy coastline. ☜ *36 km E of Figueres*

5 Parc Natural del Cadí-Moixeró

Covered in a carpet of conifers and oaks, this mountain range has surprisingly lush vegetation. Several peaks are over 2,000 m (6,560 ft) high. ☜ *20 km E of La Seu d'Urgell*

6 Parc Natural del Montseny

Forming Catalonia's most accessible natural park, these woodland hills are well-equipped for walkers and mountain bikers, with a huge network of trails. Climb the well-signposted and popular Turó de l'Home, which is the highest peak. ☜ *48 km NW of Barcelona*

7 Massis de Pedraforca

A nature reserve surrounds this huge outcrop of mountains, a favourite of rock climbers with peaks rising to 2,500 m (8,200 ft). ☜ *64 km N of Manresa*

8 Serra de l'Albera

On the eastern part of the border between Spain and France, the tree-covered slopes of Albera are speckled with interesting ruins. ☜ *15 km N of Figueres*

9 Parc Natural dels Aiguamolls de l'Empordà

This nature reserve hides bird-watching towers. Those in the Laguna de Vilalt and La Bassa de Gall Mari allow bird-lovers to observe herons, moorhens and other bird species nesting in spring. ☜ *15 km E of Figueres*

10 Parc Natural de Sant Llorenç del Munt

Surrounded by industry and within easy reach of Barcelona, this is a surprisingly untamed park inhabited by large numbers of wild boar. Walk up Cerro de la Mola to see the Romanesque monastery. ☜ *12 km E of Manresa*

Rafting, La Noguera Pallaresa

Outdoor Activities

1 Rafting & Kayaking
One of Europe's best rivers for white-water sports is La Noguera Pallaresa in the Pyrenees. Late spring is the best time to go, as the mountain snow thaws. ॐ *Yeti Emotions: • Llavorsí, 14 km N of Sort • 973 62 22 01 • www.yetiemotions.com*

2 Scuba Diving
The beautiful Reserva Natural de les Illes Medes, with its thousands of species and coral reefs, is a haven for divers. Glass-bottomed boats cater to non-divers. ॐ *López Bender, Port Alegre 1, Ampuriabrava • 972 45 02 41 • www.lopez-bender-sub.com*

3 Watersports & Sailing
Good sailing can be found in Sitges, along with yachts for rent, classes for the novice, canoeing and windsurfing. ॐ *Club de Mar Sitges, Pg Marítim, Sitges • 93 894 09 05 • www.clubdemardesitges.com*

4 Skiing
La Molina is the most accessible ski-resort from Barcelona, but Baqueira-Beret is where the jet-set goes. Both offer all levels of skiing (including off-piste) from December. ॐ *La Molina, 25 km S of Puigcerdà • 972 89 20 31 • www.lamolina.com Baqueira-Beret, 14 km E of Vielha • 973 63 90 00 (snow reports: 973 63 90 25) • www.baqueira.es*

5 Golf
The Costa Brava is one of Europe's top golf destinations; the best courses are around Platja d'Aro. ॐ *Santa Cristina d'Aro • 972 83 71 50 ॐ Platja d'Aro • 972 82 69 00*

6 Horse Riding
Montseny national park *(see p125)* is ideal for horse riding, with a number of centres. ॐ *Can Marc, 6 km W of Sant Celoni • 938 48 27 13*

7 Ballooning
A balloon journey over the volcanic area of Osona is an unbeatable way to get a bird's-eye view of Catalonia. ॐ *Baló Tour, Vic • 93 414 47 74 • www.balotour.com*

8 Boat trips
Take a picturesque cruise from Calella and Blanes to Tossa de Mar, stopping at the old town and the castle of Tossa de Mar. ॐ *Dofi Jet Boats, Blanes • 972 35 20 21 www.dofijetboats.com • boats every hour daily from Blanes (twice daily from Calella) • Closed Nov–Feb*

9 Windsurfing, Rowing & Golf
Used for rowing competitions in the 1992 Olympics, the huge Canal Olímpic is now a leisure complex offering a host of activities. ॐ *Canal Olímpic • Av Canal Olímpic, Castelldefels • 93 636 28 96*

10 Foraging for Mushrooms
From late September to late October, thousands of Catalans flock to the hills in search of the highly prized *rovelló*. There are also poisonous varieties, so amateurs should get a guide through the Diputació de Barcelona.

Diputació de Barcelona has information on activities in Catalonia, from gastro tours to guided walks. Check www.turismetotal.org

Price Categories

For a three-course meal for one with half a bottle of wine (or equivalent meal), taxes and extra charges.

€	under €15
€€	€15–25
€€€	€25–35
€€€€	€35–45
€€€€€	over €45

Anchovy tapas, El Pescadors

Places to Eat

1 El Bulli

A once-in-a-lifetime experience. Extraordinary creations by the three-Michelin-star chef Ferran Adria such as wild mushrooms in test tubes. Book months in advance (via their website). ◉ Cala de Montjoi, Roses • 972 150 457 • Closed Oct–Mar • www.elbulli.com • €€€€€

2 El Racó de Can Fabes

The traditional French-Catalan food at this three-Michelin-star country-house restaurant includes duck in blood with cep mushrooms. ◉ Sant Joan 6, Sant Celoni, Montseny • 93 867 28 51 • Closed Sun eve & Mon • €€€€€

3 La Torre del Remei

A Modernista palace provides an elegant setting for wonderfully presented Catalan food. The game dishes are sublime. ◉ Camí Reial, Bolvir, Cerdanya, 3 km SW of Puigcerdà • 972 14 01 82 • DA • €€€€€

4 El Mirador de les Caves

This restaurant is set in a castle overlooking Catalonia's wine country. Traditional cuisine is complemented by bottles of local wine and cava. ◉ Els Casots, 4 km S of Sant Sadurní d'Anoia • 93 899 31 78 • Closed Sun eve & Mon eve • €€€€€

5 Fonda Europa

Established over 150 years ago, Fonda Europa was the first in a line of successful Catalan restaurants. Ample portions include pig's trotters. ◉ Anselm Clavé 1, Granollers • 93 870 0312 • DA • €€€

6 Mare Nostrum

The seafood at this family restaurant, with its splendid terrace, includes typical paella and sípia a la planxa (grilled cuttlefish). ◉ Pg de la Ribera 60, Sitges • 938 94 33 93 • Closed Wed, & 15 Dec–1 Feb • DA • €€€€

7 Carme Ruscalleda Sant Pau

Carme Ruscalleda is considered to be one of the finest chefs in Spain. For an unforgettable dining experience, head to the pretty, seaside village of Sant Pol de Mar, where her restaurant offers sublime Catalan cuisine. ◉ C/Nou 10, Sant Pol de Mar • 93 760 06 62 • Closed Sun, Mon, Thu lunch • €€€€€

8 Els Pescadors

"The Fishermen", a traditional Empordà-style restaurant, offers local specialities, including an array of blue fish dishes. ◉ Port d'en Perris 3, l'Escala • 972 77 07 28 • Closed Sun eve (winter), Thu & Nov • €€€€€

9 El Celler de Can Roca

The Roca brothers provide exciting, contemporary Catalan cuisine that is complemented by an exceptional wine list. ◉ C/Can Sunyer 46, Girona • 972 22 21 57 • €€€€

10 Boix

Foodies come to Boix (in Cadí-Moixeró natural park) for country cooking including crabs' legs, lobster and many meat dishes. ◉ N-260 Lleida-Puigcerdà, Km 204, Martinet • 973 51 50 50 • Closed Sun eve & Mon • DA • €€€

Unless otherwise stated, all restaurants accept credit cards.
For more on dining and standard opening hours See p138

127

STREETSMART

Tips on Getting To
Barcelona
130

Tips on Getting Around
Barcelona

131

Ways to Explore
Catalonia
132

Tours & Trips
133

Sources of Information
134

Communication Tips
135

Security & Health Tips
136

Banking & Money Tips
137

Eating & Drinking Tips
138

Shopping Tips
139

Budget Tips
140

Things to Avoid
141

Accommodation Tips
142

Places to Stay
143–149

BARCELONA'S TOP 10

Left **Airport sign** Right **Iberia logo**

Tips on Getting To Barcelona

By Air
British Airways, Iberia and easyJet offer direct flights from the UK to Barcelona. From the US, Delta and Continental fly direct from the east coast, but flights from the west coast usually involve one stopover. Qantas flies from Australia and New Zealand to Barcelona via a series of stopovers.
Ⓢ *British Airways: 90 211 13 33 • www.britishairways.com* Ⓢ *Iberia: 90 240 05 00 • www.iberia.es* Ⓢ *easyJet: 90 229 99 92 • www.easyjet.com* Ⓢ *Delta: 90 111 69 46 • www.delta.com* Ⓢ *Continental: 90 096 12 66 • www.continental.com*

Barcelona Airport
Prat de Llobregat airport's two adjoining terminals are 12 km (7 miles) from the city centre. Ⓢ *90 240 47 04 • www.aena.es*

From the Airport
One of the most convenient ways from the airport to the city centre is by Aerobús, which depart every 6 minutes from 6am to 1am, and make various stops, terminating at Plaça de Catalunya. RENFE trains leave the airport every 30 minutes, stopping at Estació de Sants, Passeig de Gràcia and Estació de França; all link up with the metro. A taxi from the airport into the city centre costs €20–€25.
Ⓢ *Aerobús: 93 415 60 20* Ⓢ *RENFE: 90 224 02 02*

By Train
Trains run throughout Spain and Europe from Estació de Sants and Estació de França. Both stations have lockers, ATMs and bureaux de change. RENFE is Spain's national train company.
Ⓢ *Estació de França: • Av Marqués de l'Argentera • Map Q5* Ⓢ *Estació de Sants: • Pl dels Països Catalans • Off map* Ⓢ *RENFE: 90 224 02 02 (24 hours) • www.renfe.es*

By Bus
Both Eurolines and Linebús serve Barcelona from numerous European cities, including Rome, Paris and London. Buses usually operate from Barcelona's main bus station, Estació del Nord, and also from Estació de Sants. Ⓢ *Estació del Nord: • C/Ali Bei 80 • Map R2 • 90 226 06 06 • www.barcelonanord.com* Ⓢ *Eurolines: 90 240 50 40* Ⓢ *Linebús: 90 233 55 33*

By Car
Barcelona is linked to the rest of Spain and Europe by *autopistes* (toll highways) and toll-free roads. The tolled AP7 runs between Barcelona and the border of France.

Domestic travel
The city is connected to the rest of Spain by train, bus and plane. Iberia and its low-cost airline, Clickair, fly to and from many domestic destinations and offer a shuttle

service between Madrid and Barcelona with up to 30 flights a day. Spanair, Vueling and Air Europa serve Barcelona from the rest of Spain. RENFE and several bus companies link Barcelona to most of Spain's major cities.
Ⓢ *Spanair: 90 213 14 15 • www.spanair.es* Ⓢ *Air Europa: 90 240 15 01 • www.aireuropa.com* Ⓢ *Vueling: 90 233 39 33 www.vueling.com*

Cheap Travel
Book long before your departure date to cut costs. If you're flexible and open to stopovers, you're likely to find better deals. The internet is great for cheap fares (try www.travelocity.com or www.cheaptickets.com). Many airlines offer discounts if you buy online.

Planning
Citizens from the US, Canada, the UK, Ireland, Australia and New Zealand need a valid passport. For non-EU citizens, a visa is required if you intend to stay in Spain for longer than three months. If you're taking any kind of medication, bring your prescription.

When to Visit
If you're in search of sun, visit Barcelona during the blazing months of July or August. To avoid the crowds, however, the best time is before or after the peak summer months, in May or October.

Left **Metro sign** Centre **Barcelona taxi** Right **Tram**

Tips on Getting Around Barcelona

1 Metro
Barcelona's five-line metro system is convenient, fast, easy to use and extensive. The metro stays open all night on Saturdays. ✆ 93 318 70 74 • www.tmb.net • Open 5am–midnight Mon–Thu, 5am–2am Fri–Sat, 5am Sat–midnight Sun

2 FGC
The FGC (Ferrocarrils de la Generalitat de Catalunya) is the city's commuter rail system, serving northern and eastern Barcelona. The FGC shares several key stations with the metro, including Plaça de Catalunya and Plaça d'Espanya, and has the same prices and similar hours. ✆ 93 205 15 15 • www.fgc.es • Open 5am–midnight Mon–Thu, 5am–2am Fri–Sat, 6am–midnight Sun

3 Bus
Barcelona's bus system covers the entire city. Bus stops are clearly marked and buses have their destinations on the front. For information on routes and schedules call 010 or pick up a bus guide from tourist offices. ✆ 93 318 70 74 • www.tmb.net • 6am–10pm daily

4 Nightbus
There are about 17 Nitbús (nightbus) routes across the city, many of which pass through Plaça de Catalunya. ✆ 93 318 70 74 • www.tmb.net

5 Tickets & Passes
A single fare on the metro, FGC, bus or nightbus costs €1.35. The T-10 personal ticket costs €7.40 and permits 10 journeys on metro, FGC and bus, providing the total journey is completed within 1 hour 15 minutes. One-, two-, three-, four- and five-day passes are also available, which provide unlimited travel on public transport. Tickets are available from attendants and machines at all metro stations.

6 Taxi
Hail a yellow-and-black taxi on any major street in town; a green light on the roof indicates that one is free. For two or more passengers, taxis are almost as cheap as the metro for short hops. A minimum fare applies. ✆ Taxi Radio: 93 303 30 33 ✆ Barna Taxi: 93 357 77 55

7 On Foot
Barcelona is extremely compact and most areas are best negotiated on foot, especially the old town and Gràcia, where a leisurely stroll is the only way to soak up the architectural and cultural riches. Barcelona's waterfront, from the Port Vell to the Port Olímpic, is also made for walking. See pp58–9.

8 By Bicycle
Pedalling around the port, Barri Gòtic or Parc de la Ciutadella is a refreshing alternative to walking. There are over 70 km (43 miles) of bike lanes throughout the city, outlined on maps available from the tourist office and bike rental shops. Bikes are available to rent daily from Budget Bikes or CicloBus. ✆ Budget Bikes: 93 304 18 85 ✆ CicloBus: 93 285 38 32

9 Transport for the Disabled
The airport bus is accessible to wheelchair users as are Lines 1 and 2 of the metro, some city buses, a few FGC stations and all nightbuses. Taxi Amic has cars and vans dedicated to wheelchair users – give advance notice. For information on transport for the disabled, call Informació Transport Adaptat. For details about specific routes, call 010 or check the TMB website. ✆ Taxi Amic: 93 420 80 88 • Informació Transport Adaptat: 93 486 07 52 ✆ TMB: 93 318 70 74 • www.tmb.es

10 Getting Around in a Wheelchair
Barcelona's Institut Municipal de Persones amb Disminució (see p134) has developed a detailed computer database that charts all the streets accessible to wheelchair users. Call 010, give your departure point and destination, and they'll advise you of a route and places accessible en route.

Left **RENFE train ticket** Centre **Road sign** Right **RENFE sign**

🔟 Ways to Explore Catalonia

By Train
RENFE operates lines out of Barcelona in all directions, making it easy to escape the city. Most regional trains leave from Estació de Sants (see p130) and Estació Passeig de Gràcia. Call the RENFE information line for destinations and schedules. Ⓢ Estació Passeig de Gràcia • Pg de Gràcia • Map E2 Ⓢ RENFE • 902 24 02 02

By Bus
Numerous regional bus companies operate all over Catalonia. Most depart from Estació del Nord – call the station for more information. Ⓢ Estació del Nord: C/Ali Bei 80 • Map R2 • 90 226 06 06 • www.barcelona-nord.com

By Car
A car is essential if you wish to explore off the beaten track, particularly in the Pyrenees and the Catalonian heartland. There are many car rental companies, including all the big names (Avis, Budget, Hertz), all of which have offices at the airport. Prices range from €240–420 for a medium-sized car for a week. To rent a car, you should be over 25, and have a valid driver's licence, a credit card and a passport. Booking your rental car from abroad or on-line is often cheaper. Ⓢ Avis: 90 218 08 54 • www.avis.com Ⓢ Budget: 93 298 36 00 • www.budget.com

Ⓢ Hertz: 91 372 93 00 • www.hertz.com

By Bike
Mountain bikers will find a wealth of rugged terrain in the Pyrenees. The Turisme de Catalunya has maps and brochures as well as a good website showing regional bike routes. Club Element leads mountain-bike tours through the lush Cerdanya Valley and along the Costa Brava. Ⓢ Club Element • Pl Lesseps 33 • 90 219 04 15

Sea Cruises
"Sightsea" off the Costa Brava aboard glass-bottomed boats and other sea cruisers. L'Aventura del Nautilus conducts coastal sea cruises from L'Estartit to the Medes Islands off the Costa Brava. Excursiones Marítimas plies the Mediterranean from Calella and Blanes to Tossa de Mar, stopping at lovely coves along the way. Ⓢ L'Aventura del Nautilus: L'Estartit, 100km N of Barcelona • 972 75 14 89 Ⓢ Dofi Jet Boats: Calella, 40km N of Barcelona; Blanes, 60 km N of Barcelona • 972 35 20 21

Bus Tours
Discover Catalonia on organized bus tours, which include trips to the Monestir de Montserrat, Girona, the Teatre-Museu Dalí in Figueres and the Costa Brava. Also offered is a one-day tour that visit Montserrat and Barcelona's Modernista

marvels. Bus tours are organized by Julià and Pullmantur. Ⓢ Julià Tours: Ronda Universitat 5 • 93 317 64 54 Ⓢ Pullmantur: Gran Via de les Corts Catalanes 645 • 93 317 12 97 • www.pullmantur-spain.com

Main Roads
The new numbers for many roads in Catalonia that were issued in 2001 are now all that appear on signs. The old names have been phased out.

Avoiding Traffic
The best time to get out of town is in the late morning. Avoid long holiday weekends (pont) and Friday evenings, when traffic is always heavy. Since most Spanish take their holidays in August, motorways are particularly busy around this period.

Tips for Families
RENFE offers a 40 per cent discount for children aged four to 11. Enquire when booking tickets.

Turisme de Catalunya
This well-stocked tourist office offers plenty of material on Catalonia, from maps to information on outdoor sports and festival listings. Changing exhibits on the region are also on display. Ⓢ Palau Robert, Pg de Gràcia 105 • Map E2 • 012 • www.gencat.es/probert • Open 10am–7pm Mon–Sat, 10am–2:30pm Sun

Left **Tren Turístic** Right **Bus Turístic, Plaça de Catalunya**

🔟 Tours & Trips

1 Bus Tours
The open-topped Bus Turístic is a grand way to experience the city's sights and sounds. The red route explores northern Barcelona; the blue route takes in the southern area. You can hop on and off as many times as you like. Discounts to sights and shops are included. ✪ *Depart from Pl de Catalunya • Every 5–25 mins 9am–7pm (8pm Apr–Oct) daily • Purchase on the bus, at tourist offices and at Estació de Sants*

2 Walking Tours
The tourist office *(see p134)* organizes reasonably priced guided walks from the main office in Plaça de Catalunya – they explore the Roman and medieval history of the Barri Gòtic *(see p134)*. The Travel Bar *(see p134)* also conducts lively walking tours.

3 La Ruta Modernista
The Modernisme Route guidebook contains several itineraries, a map and discount vouchers for all admission fees. For the guide, tours and information, visit the Centre del Modernisme at the Tourist Information Office in Plaça Catalunya. ✪ *010 • www.rutadel modernisme.com*

4 Boat Tours
See the city from the sea on one of Las Golondrines' sightseeing boats. Trips lasting 35 minutes depart every half-hour; longer tours are available on a catamaran with an underwater view. The Voyages Orsom sailing catamaran departs from Portal de la Pau for a glide through the port. ✪ *Las Golondrines: Portal de la Pau • 93 442 31 06 • www.lasgolondrinas.com* ✪ *Orsom Catamaran: Portal de la Pau • 93 441 05 37 • www.barcelonaorsom.com*

5 Cable Cars
Cable cars *(telefèric)* depart from Montjuïc (Miramar station), Torre de Jaume I and Torre de Sant Sebastià, yielding stunning views of the city. ✪ *93 441 48 20*

6 Night Kayaking
Kayak under the stars off Barcelona's shores on a summer's night – with a beer and *pica pica* (snack) en route. Nàutica Base arranges various outdoor water activities and provides all the necessary equipment and insurance. After kayaking, go back to base for a barbecue, cocktails and ambient, DJ-spun music. ✪ *Base Nàutica Municipal, Platja Mar Bella • 93 221 04 32 • Jun–Sep: 9pm Thu–Sat*

7 Coach & Car Tours
See Barcelona's major sights and neighbourhoods on a guided coach tour organized by Julià or Pullmantur Tours. Also offered are night-time tours (Thu–Sat), with a stop for tapas followed by a flamenco or other music show. Live Barcelona organizes group guided tours in a Mercedes van (for up to seven people). ✪ *Julià Tours • 93 317 64 54* ✪ *Pullmantur • 93 318 02 41 • www.pullmantur-spain. com* ✪ *Live Barcelona Car Tours • 93 632 72 59 • www.livebarcelona.com*

8 Bike Tours
Whiz about the old town and the Parc de la Ciutadella on group bike tours organized by bike rental shops. Un Cotxe Menys ("One Car Less"). Barcelona by Bike also runs bike tours in English. ✪ *Un Cotxe Menys (Bike-tours Barcelona), C/Espartería 3 • 93 268 21 05 • www. biketoursbarcelona.com* ✪ *Barcelona by Bike: 93 268 81 07 • Open all year • www.barcelonabybike.com*

9 Horse-drawn Carriages
It may be a tourist trap, but riding up La Rambla on a horse and carriage can raise a smile, especially for kids. ✪ *Depart from Pl de Portal de la Pau • 93 421 15 49*

10 Tren Turístic
Explore Montjuïc on this sightseeing open-top bus, which departs from Plaça d'Espanya and climbs past all the main sights. Get on and off as you wish. ✪ *93 415 60 20 • Open Apr–Oct*

Left **Tourist information sign** Centre **Newsstand on La Rambla** Right **Magazines**

10 Sources of Information

1 Tourist Information

Multilingual staff give out free maps and information at Barcelona's main tourist office on Plaça de Catalunya. They also have a hotel booking service, a bureau de change, internet access and a souvenir shop. Other offices are located in Estació de Sants and on Plaça de Sant Jaume. For information on the rest of Catalonia, visit the Turisme de Catalunya *(see p132)*. For information over the phone on everything from museum opening hours to bus routes, call 010 or the Turisme de Barcelona's information line. ◉ *Turisme de Barcelona, Pl de Catalunya 1 • Map M1 • www.barcelonaturisme. com • 93 285 38 34 • Open 9am–9pm daily*

2 Information Officers

In summer red-jacketed tourist information officers roam the city's busiest areas giving out maps and advice. There are also information points in Las Ramblas, Estació del Nord and Plaça Espanya.

3 Magazines

The weekly *Guía del Ocio* covers the city's nightlife (music, theatre, dance and film), has extensive restaurant listings and is available from all newsstands. *Barcelona Metropolitan* (free) is the city's leading English-language monthly magazine, featuring

culture, the arts and restaurant and nightlife listings. *Time Out* is another English-language monthly. *b-guided* gives the latest on trendy places to shop, eat and drink – in English and Spanish.

4 Consulates

Various nations have consulates in Barcelona. ◉ *UK: Av Diagonal 477 • 93 366 62 00* ◉ *US: Pg Reina Elisenda 23 • 93 280 22 27* ◉ *Australia: Pl Gala Placidia 1–3, 1st floor • 93 490 90 13* ◉ *New Zealand: Travessera de Gràcia 64 • 93 209 03 99* ◉ *Canada: C/Elisenda de Pinós 10 • 93 204 27 00* ◉ *Ireland: Gran Via Carles III 94 • 93 491 50 21*

5 Institut de Cultura de Barcelona

Get the lowdown on cultural and arts events among others, from the Institut de Cultura in the Palau de la Virreina *(see p13)*. ◉ *La Rambla 99 • 93 316 10 00 • Open 11am–8pm Mon–Sat, 11am–2:30pm Sun*

6 Websites

Numerous websites cover Barcelona, including the official tourist office site (www.barcelona turisme.com). The in-depth www.bcn.es is another excellent source. The website of Turisme de Catalunya (www.gencat.es/ probert) has extensive coverage of Catalonia.

7 TravelBar

This friendly bar, with internet access and

amiable staff, is a good source of information. The bar hosts guided walking *(see p133)* and bike tours, "intercambio" nights to practise your Spanish, and a popular bar crawl to the best bars of the old town. ◉ *C/Boqueria 27 • 93 342 52 52*

8 University Bulletins

If you're after cheap, short-term accommodation or if you're looking to practise your Spanish, peruse the university notice boards posted around the building's cloisters. ◉ *Gran Via de les Corts Catalanes • 93 403 54 17*

9 Libraries & British Institute

The city's main library is the Biblioteca de Catalunya; bring your passport to apply for a one-day pass. The Institut Britànic houses a library of English books and newspapers. ◉ *Biblioteca de Catalunya: C/Hospital 56 Institut Britànic: C/Amigó 83 • Closed Aug*

10 Disabled Travellers

Disabled access in Barcelona is limited – especially in old buildings. The Institut Municipal de Persones amb Disminució provides a list of places with wheelchair access and gives advice on getting around. ◉ *Av Diagonal 233 • 93 413 27 75*

Left **Postage stamp** Centre **Telephone** Right **Mailbox**

TOP 10 Communication Tips

Public Phones

There are public phones (*cabines*) throughout the city. Use coins or a phonecard.

Phonecards

Purchase a phonecard from a newsstand, phone centre or tobacco shop (*estanc*). The Telefónica phonecard comes in denominations of €6 and €12. Other phonecards (BT, Fortune) for international calls are also available and tend to offer cheaper calls.

Long-Distance Calls

To make an international call, dial 00 followed by the country code (UK: 44; US/Canada: 1; Australia: 61; New Zealand: 64), the area code and the phone number. To call Spain from abroad, dial the international access code then 34 for Spain plus the full phone number. To make a collect call, or to pay by credit card or your calling card, dial the international operator (9009900) plus the country code. For operator assistance in making international calls from Spain, dial 1008 for EU countries and 1005 for all others. For international information and directory enquiries, dial 11825.

Local & Regional Calls

The cost of a local call from a phone booth to a land line is generally about 20 cents. Barcelona phone numbers all begin with the code 93; the rest of Catalonia is divided up into the provinces of Lleida (973), Girona (972) and Tarragona (977). For operator assistance, dial 11818.

Phone Centres

Phone centres (*locutoris*) provide a more comfortable – and usually cheaper – alternative to public pay phones. Phones are hooked up to a digital display showing the cost, which is paid at the end. Note that the more central the location, the more expensive the call. Prices do not vary dramatically, but Telecomunicaciones del Caribe offers some of the best prices in the city centre. ❧ *Telecomunicaciones del Caribe: C/Xuclà 16 • Open 10am–10pm daily*

Post

Post offices (*correus*) are usually open 8:30am–8:30pm Mon–Fri and 9:30am–1pm Sat, though hours may vary slightly. Barcelona's main post office is open longer hours. It also offers a range of services, including fax and express mail services (*urgente*). The city's mailboxes are bright yellow, generally with one slot for *ciutat* (city) and one for *altres destinacions* (other destinations). ❧ *Main Post Office: Pl Antoni López • Open 8:30am–10pm Mon–Sat, noon–10pm Sun*

Poste Restante

You can receive mail at any post office, but it's safest to have it sent to the main one. Bring your passport (or a copy of it) to collect mail. ❧ *Address letters to: Lista de Correos, 08070, Barcelona, Spain*

Internet Access

Internet centres are dotted all over Barcelona, many around Plaça de Catalunya and La Rambla. Most are open until 11pm, sometimes midnight. For 24-hour internet access, head to Workcenter and for good deals, opt for easyInternetCafé (until 2am). ❧ *Workcentor: C/ Roger de Lluria 2; Diagonal 439 ❧ easyInternetCafé: La Rambla 31; Ronda Universitat 17 ❧ People @ Web: C/Provença 367 • 93 207 01 97*

Courier Services

Courier services will pick up a package and deliver it anywhere in the world, usually within 1–5 days. ❧ *Federal Express: 902 10 08 71 ❧ UPS: 902 88 88 20 ❧ DHL Worldwide Express: 902 12 24 24*

Fax

You can send and receive faxes at most post offices. Many internet centres also offer fax services, at lower prices.

Left **Guardia Urbana** Centre **Pharmacy shop front** Right **Pharmacy sign**

Security & Health Tips

1 Emergencies
The national emergency number is 112, through which you can contact the *policia* (police), *bombers* (firemen) and *ambulància* (ambulance).

2 Police
Dial 091 to call the national police (Policia Nacional), and 092 for the local police (Guàrdia Urbana). The Turisme Atenció centre, run by the Guàrdia Urbana and Turisme de Barcelona, provides advice and help to visitors who have been victims of crime. ✪ *Turisme Atenció • La Rambla 43 • 93 344 13 00 • Open 24 hours*

3 Personal Security
Although petty crime is rife, more serious incidences of violence are rare. Thieves occasionally carry knives – if threatened, hand over your belongings immediately.

4 Valuables
Leave all your valuables, including your passport, behind in a hotel safety deposit box. Take as little cash as possible and carry what you do have in a money belt hidden under clothes. Carry wallets in front pockets and ensure bags are strapped across your front. On the beach and in cafés and restaurants, always keep your belongings on your lap or tied to your person. Also be cautious of any odd or

unnecessary human contact, verbal or physical, whether it's a tap on the shoulder or someone spilling their drink at your table. Thieves often work in twos, so while one is catching your attention, the other is swiping your wallet.

5 Hospitals
Hospital de la Creu Roja de Barcelona, Hospital de la Santa Creu i de Sant Pau *(see p103)* and Hospital Clinic all have 24-hour emergency rooms (called *urgències*). For an ambulance, dial 061. ✪ *Hospital de la Creu Roja de Barcelona: C/Dos de Maig 301 • 93 433 15 51* ✪ *Hospital de la Santa Creu i de Sant Pau: C/Mas Casanovas, 90 • 93 291 90 00* ✪ *Hospital Clinic: C/Villaroel 170 • 93 227 54 00*

6 Doctors & Clinics
The tourist office can provide information on English-speaking doctors. There are many walk-in clinics in the city, including the Creu Blanca near Plaça de Catalunya, where there is no need to make an appointment. There is also a 24-hour clinic at Paseo Reina Elisenda de Montcada, 17. ✪ *Creu Blanca: C/Pelai 40 • 93 412 12 12 • Open 8:30am–2pm, 4–8pm Mon–Sat*

7 Health Insurance
EU citizens can receive free medical care with a European health insurance card,

which must be obtained before travelling. Non-EU citizens are strongly advised to take out medical cover.

8 Dental Treatment
Dental care is not covered by the EU health service. There are numerous dental clinics in Barcelona where you can walk in and get a consultation, including the Clínica Dental Barcelona, where dentists are generally on duty 9am–midnight daily. ✪ *Clínica Dental Barcelona: Pg de Gràcia 97 • 93 487 83 29*

9 Pharmacies
Pharmacies *(farmàcies)* are marked by a large green or red cross, usually in neon. All chemists have trained pharmacists who can offer advice (places on and around La Rambla usually have a pharmacist who speaks English). Regular hours are generally 10am–10pm. One pharmacy per neighbour-hood is open all night from 9pm until 9am on a rotating basis, (information is listed on the front door of each). A number of places, particularly on La Rambla, stay open 24 hours a day.

10 Drinking Water
Spain's tap water is perfectly safe to drink. Most visitors, however, generally prefer to drink bottled water.

Left **Caixa de Catalunya logo** Right **Twenty-euro note**

Banking & Money Tips

The Euro
Since 1 January 2002, the official currency of Spain, and much of Europe, has been the Euro. For general information on the Euro check the European Union website.
⊛ *europa.eu.int/euro*

Banks
Banks are generally open 8am–2pm on weekdays. Some are open 4–8pm on Thursdays and 8am–2pm on Saturdays, except from July to September. Banks tend to offer better exchange and commission rates than bureaux de change, although rates do vary from bank to bank. There's a Caixa de Catalunya exchange in Plaça de Catalunya, next to the tourist office, which stays open until 9pm. Numerous small bank branches exchange money in Estació de Sants train station and the airport; these are open from 7 or 8am to 10pm daily.

Changing Money
Avoid changing money at bureaux de change in tourist areas as commission rates tend to be high or exchange rates poor. On the whole, banks offer better deals, but bureaux de change have the advantage of longer opening hours. Some, particularly those on La Rambla, are open until midnight.

ATMs
ATMs (cash machines) provide the easiest way to access money and are a good way to beat commission charges. Surcharges depend on your bank. Relying on ATMs also means that you can take out money in smaller denominations and avoid carrying large amounts of cash. Before travelling, check with your bank that your PIN number works with foreign ATMs. Nearly all take VISA or MasterCard (Access) cards.

Traveller's Cheques
Buy traveller's cheques in Euros. All banks cash traveller's cheques, as do larger stores. Always carry the cheque numbers separately from the cheques. American Express traveller's cheques can be cashed free of charge at the American Express office and at any Banco Central Hispano; a passport is required.
⊛ *American Express: La Rambla 74 • 91 393 82 16 • 9am–9pm Mon–Sat*

Credit Cards
Visa and MasterCard are readily accepted in all but budget hotels, restaurants and shops. American Express can generally be used in hotels, but less often in restaurants and shops. Diner's Card is accepted in about 50 per cent of restaurants. Credit card cash advances are available from any bank (or ATM if you have a PIN number). Note that the transaction fee for cash advances on credit cards can be high.

Emergency Numbers
If your credit card is lost or stolen, call the police and your credit card company. Most credit cards have a number to call collect from abroad, which is provided at the time of issue. ⊛ *Visa: 900 991 216* ⊛ *MasterCard: 900 97 12 31* ⊛ *American Express: 900 99 44 26*

Online Banking
The quickest and cheapest way to keep track of your bank account and credit card bills is by checking them online. It's best to set up your online account before travelling.

Emergency Cash
It is advisable to carry some emergency cash hidden inside your luggage, separate from your wallet.

Tipping
Tipping is not the norm in Spain. In restaurants, most diners usually tip about five per cent of the bill. If you're eating a light meal, round up the bill to the nearest 50 cents. Taxi drivers are usually tipped five per cent and hotel porters about 50 cents per bag.

Left **Coffee and croissant** Right **Terrace café, Barri Gòtic**

Eating & Drinking Tips

Opening Hours
The Spanish eat much later than much of Europe; lunch starts around 2 or 3pm, with dinner any time after 9pm. Restaurants are usually open 1:30–4pm and 8:30–midnight. Many are closed one day of the week and during the month of August. Cafés and bars are open from around 7:30am, closing around 2am. It is difficult to get a drink or bite to eat after 4am.

The Menu
Multilingual menus are increasingly the norm. Many restaurants offer their best deal for lunch from Monday to Friday, so do as the Spaniards do and fill up from the *menú del día* between 1:30 and 4pm. The fixed-price menu of the day usually includes three courses, wine and water.

Catalan Cuisine
Catalan cuisine is characterized by the meeting of *mar i muntanya* (surf and turf), and signature dishes include *llagosta i pollastre* (lobster and chicken). Side dish mainstays are *samfaina* (aubergine/eggplant, grilled peppers, tomatoes and onion in olive oil and garlic) and *escalivada* (sweet peppers, onion and garlic). Other Catalan favourites are *botifarra amb mongetes* (Catalan sausage with white beans) and *pa amb tomàquet* (bread

smeared with tomato and drizzled with olive oil). If innards are your thing, ask for *call* (tripe). For dessert, enjoy *crema catalana*, a custard topped with caramelized sugar.

Seafood & Paella
For prime seafood, head for the sea. Along Passeig Joan de Borbó in Barceloneta is a string of restaurants, many specializing in seafood and paellas. Seafood restaurants also abound in the Port Olímpic, where you can feast on fresh-off-the-boat fish and seafood on open-air terraces. Fresh seafood is served year-round, but the traditional day for paella is Thursday.

Vegetarian
Barcelona has a handful of vegetarian eateries. Carrer Pintor Fortuny, in El Raval, has a couple of options, including Biocenter (at number 25), with its all-you-can-eat salad bar. Vegetarians can also feast almost anywhere on an array of tapas, including *patates braves* (spicy potatoes) and *truita de patates* (potato omelette). If you eat fish, then you'll be spoiled for choice.

Seasonal Specialities
From the end of the year until mid-Spring, try the Catalan speciality of *calçots*, sweet grilled scallions usually in a *romesco* sauce (spicy tomato sauce). Another autumn

favourite are *bolets* (mushrooms), usually lightly grilled and served with a sprinkling of olive oil.

Etiquette
Some restrictions for smoking in bars or restaurants apply from January 2006. Dress codes rarely apply.

Tipping
Tipping is not expected in most establishments, so it's up to your own preference and how you rate the service. If leaving a tip, five per cent is usually acceptable. In upscale restaurants, however, a tip of 10 per cent is the norm. Catalans occasionally tip at the bar, perhaps leaving the small change from their drinks bill.

Children
The Spanish are relaxed about bringing children to restaurants and bars. Though kids' menus are rare, restaurants are often willing to serve half portions on request.

Disabled Access
All new restaurants must be wheelchair accessible by law, which includes access from the street to the dining room and at least one accessible bathroom. Contact the Institut Municipal de Persones amb Disminució *(see p134)* for a list of accessible restaurants. And always call ahead to double check.

For Barcelona's best restaurants & tapas bars **See pp44–5**

Left **Shopper, Pg de Gràcia** Centre **Shoe shop, C/Portaferrissa** Right **Clothes boutique, Gràcia**

Shopping Tips

Opening Hours
Most stores are open 10am to 2pm and 4:30pm to 8pm Monday to Saturday. Department stores and other large shops don't close at lunch time.

Sales
Barcelona's big sales *(rebaixes)* come twice a year, from 1 July to the end of August and from 7 January until the end of February.

Reclaiming VAT
Non-EU citizens can claim an IVA (VAT) refund on most purchases over €90 when they leave Spain. Shops displaying the tax-free logo will provide a tax-refundable receipt, which you present before checking-in on departure. IVA (VAT) of 16 per cent (7 per cent on food) is included in the advertised price. IVA for hotels is 7 per cent, which is not always included in the price.

Leather
Leather items are a good buy in Spain and are of high quality. There are good shoe stores on Carrer Portal de l'Àngel, Carrer Pelai, Rambla de Catalunya and Passeig de Gràcia. Loewe and Kastoria sell quality leather goods. ◉ *Loewe: Pg de Gràcia 35* ◉ *Kastoria: Av de la Catedral 6–8*

Antiques
Antiques aficionados will be richly rewarded with a stroll along Carrer Banys Nous and Carrer de la Palla in the Barri Gòtic. For more antique finds, head to the Bulevard dels Antiquaris *(see p50)* on Passeig de Gràcia, home to over 60 antiques and arts shops. The antique markets, including the Mercat dels Antiquaris *(see p53)* and the Port Vell antique market, at weekends (10am–8pm), are also worth a browse.

Clothing
High-end clothing stores dot Passeig de Gràcia and Avinguda Diagonal. For trendier gear, head to Carrer Portaferrissa and Carrer Pelai. Spain's success story is the wildly popular men's and women's contemporary clothing chain Zara, which is all over town (and all over Europe). Another universal favourite is Mango, targeted towards younger women, which also has branches all over the city. If you're looking to buy local, there are a number of top-end Catalan designers, including Antonio Miró. ◉ *Zara: Pg de Gràcia 16* ◉ *Mango: Pg de Gràcia 65* ◉ *Antonio Miró: C/Consell de Cent 349*

Sizes
Clothing sizes tend to be small in Spain. Size conversions for women's clothing are: US/UK 6/8 is 36; 8/10 is 38; 10/12 is 40; 12/14 is 42; 14/16 is 44. For men's clothing, the conversions are: US & UK 36 is 46; 38 is 48; 40 is 50; 42 is 52.

Music
FNAC has a vast music selection, as does the department store El Corte Inglés. Equally popular among locals are the small eclectic music shops along Carrer Tallers *(see p82)*. Also worth a look are the CD and vinyl music shops on nearby Carrer Riera Baixa *(see p82)*. ◉ *FNAC: El Triangle, Pl de Catalunya 4* ◉ *El Corte Inglés: Portal de l'Àngel 19–21*

Late-night Shops
Vip's is an all-purpose drugstore-bookstore-café, where you can buy books, gifts, beer, wine and snacks. Open Cor sells everything from fresh flowers to wrapping paper, beer and wine. ◉ *Vip's: Av. Diagonal, 3 • Open until 3am daily* ◉ *Open Cor: Ronda de Sant Pere 33 and Gran de Gràcia, 29 • Open until 2am daily*

Department Stores
Barcelona's leading department store is El Corte Inglés, which has branches across the city. You can find seemingly everything under one roof, including a supermarket and a gourmet food shop. ◉ *El Corte Inglés: several locations, including Pl de Catalunya 14, Av Diagonal 471–473 & Av Diagonal 617–619*

For Barcelona's best shopping areas **See pp50–51**

Left **Shop sale sign** Centre **Five-euro note** Right **Menú del Día**

Barcelona on a Budget

1 Sightseeing Passes

The Barcelona Card offers up to 50 per cent off the city's main attractions, plus free travel on buses and the metro. It's available for two to five days at all tourist offices and El Corte Inglés department stores. The Articket, which costs €20 and is valid for six months, provides free entry to seven art museums, including MNAC (see pp18–19), MACBA (see pp28–9) and the Fundació Joan Miró (see pp22–3). The tourist office on Plaça de Catalunya (see p134) sells it, as do the museums themselves.

2 Museums

Many museums offer free entry on the first Sunday of the month, including the Museu Picasso (see pp24–5) and MNAC (see pp18–19). The tourist office has a list of all the free museum days. Most museums also offer a 30–50 per cent discount – or free admission – for people over 65.

3 Public Transport

The T-10 ticket permits 10 rides on metro, FGC and buses, but only lasts for 1 hour 15 minutes. Alternatively, you can purchase a two-, three-, four- or five-day pass, which provides unlimited travel on the same services. See p131.

4 Concerts & Opera

Enjoy rock-bottom prices for concerts and the opera (Sep–Jul) by buying seats with partial views – or no view at all. The Gran Teatre del Liceu (see p66) sells cheap tickets for opera and classical recitals. The Palau de la Música Catalana (see pp26–7) has reduced price early-evening weekend shows twice a month. For general information on cultural events – and special deals – call or visit the Institut de Cultura in the Palau de la Virreina (see p13). ✆ Gran Teatre del Liceu ticket office: 93 485 99 00 Institut de Cultura: 93 301 77 75

5 Eating

The most economical way to get a bite to eat is to pick up picnic goodies at one of the city's food markets (see pp52–3). The menú del dia (fixed lunch menu) offered from Monday to Friday at many restaurants is often very reasonable. Dining on the terrace can be more pricey than eating inside, where sitting at the bar is usually the cheapest option.

6 Fast Food

Bypass McDonald's and Burger King and sample Spain's cheaper fast food equivalents. Pans & Company and Bocatta are found all over town; both offer cheap meals, particularly if you eat between 10am and noon, and 4 and 7pm.

7 Drinking

Start out the night in your hotel with a bottle of Spanish wine from the supermarket. Then head to the Barri Gòtic or El Raval where there are plenty of cheap dive bars. Order a canya (tap beer) or a Spanish bottled beer, Estrella or San Miguel, which are usually cheaper than imported beers.

8 Hotels

Visit Barcelona during the low season, from October to April, and you'll find cheaper hotel deals (and air fares). Enquire about special deals when booking a room – many places don't volunteer information on reductions unless specifically asked.

9 Hotel Bars

You don't have to stay at the ritzy hotels to enjoy their luxurious environs. Most of the bars and cafés at the five-star hotels are open to the general public. Try the Hotel Arts (see p143), near the Port Olímpic, where you can sip a cocktail to the rippling tunes of classical piano.

10 Cinemas

Go to the cinema (see p67) on el dia del espectador (often Monday or Wednesday) or for a matinée (usually before 2:30pm), when tickets are cheaper.

Left **Overpriced eatery, La Rambla** Right **Traffic jam**

Things to Avoid

1 Dangerous Areas

Beware of under-populated alleys and streets in the old town after dark, particularly in the Barri Gòtic and El Raval. These attract thieves who tend to operate in groups. Prime pickpocketing times are between 9pm and midnight, when most locals are eating dinner and only visitors are out on the streets. The early hours (3–6am), after the bars and clubs close, are also popular with thieves.

2 Overpriced Leather Shops

Avoid the pricey leather shops clustered on and around La Rambla. The leather is often poor quality and prices are high. Stop off at the tourist office for a list of approved leather shops, or head for established stores (see pp50–51).

3 La Rambla Scams

Don't get sidetracked by the raucous "find the hidden ball" games on La Rambla. Usually played on makeshift tables, presided over by a skilled, nimble-fingered trickster, it appears at first glance to be a lively game of chance. In reality, it's a confidence trick. The lively folk who cheer you on are all accomplices who are in on the act. Though you may win the first few rounds, you'll soon start to lose, and you'll walk away with a much lighter

wallet. Also to be avoided are the gypsies who try to sell you flowers and often pick your pocket at the same time!

4 Overpriced Eats

Rip-off, touristy terrace restaurants line La Rambla. Most of these paella and tapas eateries cater solely to tourists, charging sky-high prices for mediocre meals. The side streets off La Rambla offer better food at more reasonable prices.

5 Crowds

Miss the crowds and interminably long queues at the city's most popular sights by visiting first thing in the morning when the sights open or towards the end of the day, an hour or two before closing time. To avoid the hordes on the beaches in summer go on weekday afternoons.

6 Money Exchange

Steer clear of the bureaux de change on La Rambla, Plaça de Catalunya and near major tourist sights. They usually charge much higher commission than banks. If they advertise no commission, exchange rates are generally poor.

7 Looking Like a Tourist

Avoid attracting attention to yourself as a tourist. Keep cameras hidden, try not to display large banknotes and don't wear

valuable jewellery. When consulting a guidebook or map, keep a vigilant eye on your belongings.

8 Traffic

Avoid city traffic congestion by driving around late morning (10am–1pm) or late afternoon (5–7pm). Most office workers have a lunch break between 2pm and 4pm, which means that the roads are packed during this period. Similarly, avoid leaving town on Friday evenings, particularly during the summer. The best time to head out of the city is mid- to late-morning after 10am.

9 August

During the month of August, many Barcelona establishments shut down altogether, the locals disappear on holiday and the city fills with visitors. With so many restaurants, bars, shops and even some sights closed, not to mention the distinct lack of local life, August in Barcelona has its drawbacks. Always call first to check on opening times during this period.

10 Monday Sightseeing

Many of the top museums are closed on Mondays, including the Museu Picasso (see pp24–5) and the MNAC (see pp18–19). So always double-check opening times on this day.

Left **Room, Hotel Mesón Castilla** Right **Suite, Hotel Claris**

🔟 Accommodation Tips

Book Ahead
If visiting Barcelona in the high season (Mar–Sep), book ahead as the city's hotels, *pensions* and *hostals* (smaller, more basic guesthouses rated at one to three stars) usually fill to capacity. When reserving a room, ask about special deals as many hotels have these, especially in the low season (Oct–Mar).

Where to Find Budget Beds
There are scores of cheap *pensions* and *hostals* on La Rambla and its sidestreets in the Barri Gòtic and El Raval. Plaça Reial also has a cluster of budget accommodation options.

Pensions & Hostals
Room size (and comfort level) in *pensions* and *hostals* varies widely, but in the accredited budget places (the tourist office has a list of these), you'll find clean rooms and good security. Rooms come either *amb bany* (with a bath) or *sense bany* (without a bath); most have a washbasin.

Getting the Room you Want
Hotels and *hostals* give the best rooms to those who ask for them – so always inquire. Most *hostals*, particularly in the old town, have some rooms with lovely wrought-iron balconies,

which can make all the difference to a small room. Ask for *una habitació exterior amb vistes* (a room with a view) or *amb balcó* (with balcony). If you're a light sleeper, opt for a *una habitació interior* (interior room).

Single Travellers
Single rooms at *hostals* and *pensions* are few and far between, but hotels are legally obliged to let double rooms to single occupants at a fixed price. All rates must be posted at reception or in the rooms.

Families
Many hotels offer discounts for children under 12 when they share their parents' room on a temporary bed.

Security
If you're going to be staying at youth hostels and campsites, carry a chain and padlock to tie your luggage to something sturdy. Always leave your valuables in a safe or locked box, which most places have.

Hotel Booking Service & Websites
The tourist office *(see p132)* in Plaça de Catalunya has a hotel booking service, which is useful if you arrive in high season without a reservation. It offers bookings in hotels of all categories, but most often in three-star hotels and above. A

deposit is payable on reservation. The tourist office also produces a list of the best *pensions* and *hostals* for budget travellers. On the web, try www.barcelonahotels.es and www.barcelona turisme.com.

Cases de Pagès
Discover rural Catalonia by staying at *Cases de Pagès* (country or farm houses), which offer B&B-style lodgings. They vary widely, from small, rural homes with a handful of rooms to luxurious, palace-sized farmhouses. The high-end *Cases de Pagès* are called *Gîtes*. Stop by the Turisme de Catalunya office *(see p132)* for a free list of the *Gîtes de Catalunya* and (to buy) the *Cases de Pagès* book, which has detailed listings and pictures of all such houses. This information is also accessible through its website (www.gencat.es/probert).

Refugis
Throughout the Pyrenees and other mountainous areas, you'll find *refugis* (basic mountain hostels for hikers and bikers). They offer simple, cheap accommodation, usually bunk beds in a dorm room. In the summer months, *refugis* fill up quickly, so book in advance. Ask at tourist offices for a list of local ones; or stop by Turisme de Catalunya *(see p132).*

Visitors seeking long-term accommodation, beware of agencies that charge for accommodation lists; they are invariably a scam.

Price Categories

For a standard, double room per night (with breakfast if included), taxes and extra charges.

€	Under €60
€€	€60–120
€€€	€120–180
€€€€	€180–240
€€€€€	Over €240

Exterior, Hotel Claris

10 Luxury Hotels

1 Hotel Arts
Barcelona's grande dame five-star hotel is mere steps from the sea, with ample, sumptuous rooms and top-notch eating places. The first-floor, outdoor pool has stunning views. ❧ C/Marina 19–21 • Map G5 • 93 221 10 00 • www.hotelartsbarcelona. com • DA • €€€€€

2 Hotel Claris
This exquisite, 19th-century Eixample palace was once home to the counts of Vedruna. Inside, you'll find a small museum of pre-Colombian art, part of the owner's collection, some of which also decorates the suites. Guests get free admission to the nearby Museu Egipci (see p105), run by the hotel owner. ❧ C/Pau Claris 150 • Map E2 • 93 487 62 62 • www.derby hotels.es • DA • €€€€€

3 Hotel Palace Barcelona
This deluxe hotel, is an emblem of tradition and style, with great service. The famous Restaurant Caelis, offers an innovative gourmet menu. Some parts of the hotel will be under renovation until mid-2009. ❧ Gran Via de les Corts Catalanes, 668 • Map F3 • 93 510 11 30 • www.hotelpalacebarce lona.com • DA • €€€€€

4 Hotel Majestic
Stately decor and faultless service are the hallmarks of this aptly named hotel. Exit through the heavy brass-and-glass doors and you're mere steps from the Eixample's *Modernista* gems. The rooftop swimming pool has views of the Sagrada Família and the Barcelona cityscape. ❧ Pg de Gràcia 68 • Map E2 • 93 488 17 17 • www.hotelmajestic.es • DA • €€€€€

5 Hotel Omm
Designed by award-winning Catalan architect Juli Capella, this is one of the hottest hotels in the city. There is an excellent restaurant and bar (see p107), a great spa and stunning views from the rooftop deck and pool. ❧ C/Rosselló 265 • Map E2 • 93 445 40 00 • www. hotelomm.es • €€€€€

6 Prestige Passeig de Gràcia
The fashionable Prestige is a relatively small hotel (just 45 rooms), which prides itself on the excellence of its 'Ask Me' concierge service. Located on the Passeig de Gràcia, there are plenty of shops, bars and restaurants nearby. ❧ Passeig de Gràcia 62 • Map E3 • 93 272 41 80 • www.prestige hotels.com • €€€€€

7 Granados 83
Rooms at this designer hotel are decorated with African zebrawood, chocolate brown leather and original pieces of Buddhist and Hindu art. Suites have private terraces overlooking a plunge pool. There is a restaurant, and a pretty rooftop pool with a very fashionable bar. ❧ C/Enric Granados 83 • Map E2 • 93 492 96 70 • www. derbyhotels.es • €€€€

8 Casa Camper
Dating from the 19th-century, this hotel oozes with innovative yet comfortable design touches. Big rooms, roof-terrace, extraordinary vertical garden and a free 24-hour bar. ❧ Elisabets 11 • Map L2 • 93 342 62 80 • www.casacamper.com • DA • €€€€€

9 Hotel Rey Juan Carlos I
This massive complex includes a vast private garden and a conference hall for up to 2,500 people. The spacious rooms are sumptuously decorated in a contemporary style. The top floors offer unobstructed views of the city and mountains. ❧ Av Diagonal 661–671 • Off map • 93 364 40 40 • www.hrjuan carlos.com • DA • €€€€€

10 Grand Hotel Central
This large, elegant hotel has a great location close to the Gothic Quarter and Born. But the real draw is the stunning rooftop pool which has spectacular views over the whole city. ❧ Via Laietana 30 • Map E4 • 93 295 79 00 • www.grandhotelcentral. com • €€€€€

Left **Salon, Hotel Mesón Castilla** Right **Swimming Pool, Hotel Ducs de Bergara**

Historical Hotels

Hotel Mesón Castilla

A historical gem in the heart of El Raval, this family-run hotel is housed in an early-1900s mansion. A home-turned-hotel, it shines under the loving care of its management. From the opulent first-floor salon to the lovely rooms – each with antique furniture – this hotel offers a chance to step back in time. Enjoy breakfast on the outdoor patio. ✆ *C/Valldonzella 5 • Map L1 • 93 318 21 82 • www. mesoncastilla.com • €€€*

Hotel Ducs de Bergara

Housed in a lovely 1898 *Modernista* building, this luxurious hotel has well-appointed rooms. There's a large interior courtyard with a swimming pool. ✆ *C/Bergara 11 • Map L1 • 93 301 51 51 • www. hoteles-catalonia.es • DA • €€€€€*

Gran Hotel La Florida

Set in a Modernista villa in the hills above Barcelona, this luxurious hotel has been beautifully renovated by the finest designers and architects. ✆ *Ctra Vallvidrera al Tibidabo 83-93 • 93 259 30 00 • www. hotellaflorida.com • €€€€€*

Hotel Neri

This 17th-century former palace at the heart of the Barri Gòtic opened in 2003 and offers an exclusive combination of

history, the avant-garde and glamour. There is Internet access in all rooms, a library, solarium and a roof terrace with views to the Cathedral. ✆ *C/Sant Sever 5 • Map M3 • 93 304 06 55 • www. hotelneri.com • €€€€€*

Hotel Oriente

Opened in 1842, this Barri Gòtic institution has hosted its share of luminaries, including many opera greats from the nearby Liceu *(see p12)*. It was built on the site of an old Franciscan monastery and the ballroom was created out of the cloister. The hotel may be showing its age, but for many, its charm lies in the faded grandeur. ✆ *La Rambla 45 • Map L4 • 93 302 25 58 • www.hotelhusaoriente. com • €€€*

1898

A 19th-century tobacco factory houses this chic hotel, which has retained some original fittings and combined them with 21st-century amenities. These include pools, a fitness centre, and a good restaurant. ✆ *La Rambla 109 • Map L2 • 93 552 95 52 • www.barcelonahotel 1898.com • DA • €€€*

Hotel Duquesa de Cardona

Located in a 16th-century building, this recently opened hotel combines the original structure with avant-garde decor and

all the modern facilities. Most rooms have views of Montjuïc Mountain and the Olympic Port. ✆ *Paseo Colón 12 • Map M6 • 93 268 90 90 • www.hduquesade cardona.com • €€€€€*

Hotel Montecarlo

This friendly, family-owned hotel, with a 1930s façade, is particularly eye-catching lit up at night. Rooms are pleasant and bright, and many have balconies overlooking La Rambla. ✆ *La Rambla 124 • Map L2 • 93 412 04 04 • www.montecarlobcn. com • €€€€*

Casa Fuster

Originally designed by Domènech i Muntaner, the Casa Fuster has been involved in a long and expensive restoration. Now open, it is one of the city's most prestigious and luxurious hotels. ✆ *Passeig de Gràcia 132 • Map E1 • 93 255 30 00 • www.hotelcasafuster. com • €€€€€*

Hotel España

Designed by architect Domènech i Montaner in 1899, this hotel is awash with Art Nouveau, including a restaurant rich with floral mosaics *(see p87)*. The rooms, in contrast to the ground-floor splendour, are all modern, if a little frayed around the edges. ✆ *C/Sant Pau 9-11 • Map L4 • 93 318 17 58 • www.hotelespanya. com • DA • €€*

It is always worth checking hotel websites for off-season promotional offers.

Price Categories

For a standard, double room per night (with breakfast if included), taxes and extra charges.

€	under €60
€€	€60–120
€€€	€120–180
€€€€	€180–240
€€€€€	over €240

Exterior, Hotel Colón

🔟 Central Stays

Hotel Colón
A handsome, family-owned Barri Gòtic hotel, the Colón has traditional decor with mirrors and oil paintings throughout. The magnificent views of the Cathedral and Plaça de la Seu from this homely, quaint place, are stunning. ⬡ Av de la Catedral 7 • Map N3 • 93 301 14 04 • www.hotelcolon.es • €€€

Hotel 54 Barceloneta
The seaside neighbourhood of Barceloneta has traditionally had very few hotels. This trendy newcomer fills a welcome gap on two counts – it's perfectly located overlooking the yacht-filled port, and the modest but bright rooms are very reasonable. ⬡ Passeig Joan de Borbó 54 • Map F6 • 93 225 00 54 • www.hotel54barceloneta.com • €€€

AC Miramar
Celebrity architect, Oscar Tusquets, is responsible for designing this spectacular hotel, which enjoys a unique location on Montjuïc hill. The stunning views, over the entire city and out to the sea, are absolutely breathtaking. There are beautiful gardens to relax in, a luxurious spa and an excellent restaurant. ⬡ Plaça Carlos Ibáñez 3 • Map C5 • 93 281 16 00 • www.hotelacmiramar.com • €€€€€

Hotel Banys Orientals
Behind the traditional frontage lies a modern, cosy hotel with free internet access in every room. The Cathedral, Picasso museum and Barceloneta beach are all close by. ⬡ C/Argenteria 37 • Map N4 • 93 268 84 60 • www.hotelbanysorientals.com • €€€

Hotel Avinyó
This ultra-modern hotel is located on one of the hippest shopping streets in the Gothic Quarter. The amenities, which are fantastic for a three-star hotel, include WiFi, plasma screen TVs and a small rooftop pool. ⬡ C/Avinyó 16 • Map M5 • 90 249 54 96 • www.hotelavinyo.com • €€€

Park Hotel
A 1950s design classic with a gorgeous wraparound staircase, the Park Hotel was refurbished in the 1990s by the original architect's son. Rooms are small but comfortably furnished, and some have balconies. It is near the fashionable Born boutiques and clubs. ⬡ Avinguda Marquès de l'Argentera • Map F5 • 93 319 60 00 • www.parkhotelbarcelona.com • €€€

Jazz
The modern Jazz hotel may not be the most stylish option, but it is centrally located and has many amenities including a small rooftop pool. It is great value for money, and the friendly staff are always on-hand to offer help and advice. ⬡ C/Pelai 3 • Map L1 • 93 552 96 96 • www.nnhotels.com • €€€

Petit Palace Opera Garden
This boutique hotel is located in a converted townhouse just off La Rambla. The rooms are decorated with a musical theme inspired by the nearby opera house. The large garden with its candle-lit corners is very romantic. ⬡ C/Boquería 10 • Map L4 • 93 302 00 92 • www.hthoteles.com • €€€

Soho
Top Spanish architect Alfredo Arribas, designed this swanky hotel which opened in 2007. Located in Eixample, it's perfect for shopping, sight-seeing and enjoying the nightlife. ⬡ Gran Vía Corts Catalanes 543 • Map D3 • 93 552 96 10 • www.hotelsohobarcelona.com • €€€€

AB Skipper
Located on the beachfront, AB Skipper has the perfect location for a summer city-break. It has all the facilities you would expect in a five-star hotel. Designed for business travellers, weekend bargains are often available. ⬡ Avenida Litoral 10 • Map G6 • 93 221 65 65 • www.hotelabskipper.com • €€€€

Unless otherwise stated, all hotels accept credit cards, have en-suite bathrooms and air conditioning.

Left **Hostal Jardí** Right **Entrance hall, Hostal Oliva**

Budget Accommodation

1 Hostal Residència Rembrandt

Spic-and-span rooms, some with en-suite bath-rooms, and a friendly, international staff, make for a great, all-round *hostal*. Ask for an exterior room, most of which have wrought-iron balconies that are perfect for checking out the Barri Gòtic action below. Ⓢ *C/Portaferrissa 23* • Map M3 • 93 318 10 11 • www. hostalrembrandt.com • €

2 Hostal Oliva

From the lovely, *Modernista* elevator to the individually wrapped soaps imprinted with the Oliva logo, this cheerful, family-run *hostal* is one of Barcelona's best. The ornate *Modernista* build-ing has bright rooms that are sparklingly clean; some have en-suite bath-rooms. Ⓢ *Pg de Gràcia 32* • Map E3 • 93 488 01 62 • www.lasguias.com/ hostaloliva • No credit cards • €€

3 Hostal Goya

A well-run *hostal* that has been accommodating visitors since 1952. The newly renovated first floor has airy rooms in tan and blonde wood. The charm-ing older floor upstairs is less expensive, with orig-inal tiled floors from the late 1800s. Most rooms have en-suite bathrooms and some have air-condi-tioning. Ⓢ *C/Pau Claris 74* • Map N1 • 93 302 25 65 • www.hostalgoya.com • €€

4 Hostal Fernando

Spotless and bright, this central *hostal* has well-maintained doubles (with or without bath), plus dorm rooms that sleep 4 to 8 people. There are also left-lug-gage lockers. Ⓢ *C/Ferran 31* • Map L4 • 93 301 79 93 • www.hfernando.com • €

5 Market

Close to the *Modernista* market of Sant Antoni, this is a very stylish hotel. The rooms have an oriental feel, with glossy lacquered wood and a red-white-and-black colour theme. Market has a popular restaurant, where break-fast is served. Book well in advance. Ⓢ *Passatge Sant Antoni Abat 10* • Map D3 • 93 325 12 05 • www. markethotel.com.es • €€

6 Hostal Jardí

Get your beauty sleep in the snug heart of the Barri Gòtic at this hotel. Newly renovated rooms, all with en-suite bathrooms, are done up in light wood and cool colours. The bright break-fast room has balconies overlooking the plaça. Ⓢ *Pl Sant Josep Oriol 1* • Map M3 • 93 301 59 00 • €€

7 Hostal Palacios

This delightful *hostal* is located in a *Modernista* mansion, which still has many of its original details like the magnificent, carved wooden doors and the colourful floor tiles. The rooms have contemporary prints and renovated bathrooms. Ⓢ *Rambla de Catalunya 27* • Map E3 • 93 301 30 79 • www.hostalpalacios. com • €€

8 Bonic

A great budget option, this charming hotel has stylish rooms and many thoughtful extras, such as free tea, coffee, muffins, Internet access and dressing gowns. Bath-rooms, however, are shared. Ⓢ *C/Josep Anselm Clavé 9* • Map L6 • 62 605 34 34 • www.bonic-barcelona.com • €€

9 Chic and Basic

This converted 19th-century townhouse is a big hit with fashionistas. Rooms are minimalist white, with contemporary glass and steel bath-rooms, and colourful LED lights that add a kitsch touch. The White Bar is also very popular. Ⓢ *C/Princesa 50* • Map P4 • 93 295 46 52 • www. chicandbasic.com • €€

10 Gat Xino

This is the second *hostal* in the Gat Accom-modation group, and is typical of their signature style: simple, modern design at great prices. It's worth splashing out on the suite, which has its own private terrace. Ⓢ *C/Hospital 149* • Map K3 • 93 324 88 33 • www.gat accommodation.com • €€

Unless otherwise stated, none of these establishments has air-conditioning or en-suite bathrooms.

Price Categories

For a standard, double room per night (with breakfast if included), taxes and extra charges.

€ under €60
€€ €60–120
€€€ €120–180
€€€€ €180–240
€€€€€ over €240

First floor, Gothic Point Youth Hostel

🔟 Hostels and Student Residences

1 Gothic Point Youth Hostel

This bright, well-run, central hostel has dorm rooms sleeping 8 to 16. Breakfast is included in the price, and there's free 24-hour internet access. There is air-conditioning in all rooms. ◎ C/Vigatans 5 • Map N4 • 93 268 78 08 • www.gothicpoint.com • €

2 Ideal Youth Hostel

Situated close to La Rambla, this is a modern hostel with dorms for four, six and eight people, each with balcony, en-suite toilet and shower. It also has single and double rooms. Breakfast is included as is free internet access. There is a self-service laundrette. ◎ C/Unió 12 • Map L4 • 93 342 61 77 • www.idealhostel.com • €

3 Feetup Hostel-Garden House

This friendly hostel is located on the outskirts of the city, near the beautiful Gaudí-designed Park Güell. It's only a 15-minute metro ride into the centre of town. There is a lovely garden and roof terrace, and a relaxed, easygoing vibe. ◎ C/d'Hedilla 58 • 93 427 24 79 • www.feetup hostels.com • €

4 Downtown Paraiso Hostel

Established by four former travellers, this friendly hostel is a hit with young backpackers. It is central, has no curfew, you don't need to rent sheets and blankets, and it offers a range of rooms, with or without bathrooms. ◎ C/Junta de Comerç 13 • Map K4 • 93 302 16 34 • www.down townparaisohostel.com • €

5 Alberg Kabul

Kabul is a favourite with young backpackers, so it's often full (and noisy). Dorm rooms, all with air-conditioning and some with balconies on the Plaça Reial (see p36), sleep 4 to 20 people. There's a laundry, free internet access, lockers and a small cafeteria that serves cheap food during the day. ◎ Pl Reial 17 • Map L4 • 93 318 51 90 • www.kabul.es • €

6 Barcelona Dream

This hostel may not be central, but it is only a 20-minute train ride from the city centre. It is well-priced, close to the beaches, and the rooms accommodate between two and 12 persons. Kitchen and laundry facilities are included. ◎ Ave. Alfonso XIII, Badalona • 93 399 14 20 • www.barcelonadream.net • €€

7 Centric Point Hostel

Housed in a renovated Modernista building, this hostel offers large dorms, as well as single and double rooms with private facilities. There is a common room with a bar, free Internet access and satellite TV. ◎ Passeig de Gràcia 33 • Map E3 • 93 215 65 38 • www.centric pointhostel.com • €

8 Melon District

Part student residence and part-hostel, Melon District has rooms available to rent for short- or long-term stays. The rooms are not large, but they have great facilities. ◎ Avda Paral.lel 101 • Map D4 • 93 217 88 12 • www.melondistrict.com • €

9 Mambo Tango

Toto and Marino, ex-travellers themselves, are behind this warm and welcoming hostel. It has dorms for four, six and eight people, breakfast and sheet-hire are included in the price, and extras include a home cinema. Party animals are actively discouraged, so you can count on a good night's sleep. ◎ C/Poeta Cabanyes 23 • Map C4 • 93 442 51 64 • www.hostelmambotango.com • €

10 Itaca Hostel

Located in the heart of the Gothic Quarter, this is a clean and friendly hostel with space for 30 guests in double rooms (for up to six) and apartments. Bedding and lockers are included in the price and there is WiFi available in the main building. ◎ C/ Ripoll 21 • Map N3 • 93 301 97 51 • www.itacahostel.com • €

Recommend your favourite hotel on traveldk.com

Left **Camping Tamariu** Right **Swimming Pool, Aparthotel Bertran**

Campsites and Aparthotels

1 Camping Roca-Grosa

Situated between the mountains and the sea, this modern campsite has good installations and access to the nearby beach. It also has a large swimming pool, restaurant and bar and is 1 km away from the lively resort of Calella. Bungalows are also available. ✆ Ctra, N-II km 665, Calella • 93 769 12 97 • www.rocagrossa.com • €

2 Camping Sitges

A small and well-kept campsite with swimming pool, supermarket and playground. It is located 2 kms (1 mile) southward from Sitges, and is close to its famous beaches. ✆ Ctra, Comarcal 246, km 38, Sitges • 93 894 10 80 • www.campingsitges.com • Closed mid-Oct–Feb • €

3 Camping Masnou

Located 12 kms (7.5 miles) to the north of Barcelona, this family-owned camp site faces the sea and has a small beach nearby. Facilities include a supermarket, restaurant and bar. ✆ Camil Fabra 33 (N-II, km 663), El Masnou • 93 555 15 03 • Credit cards from €100 • DA • €

4 Camping Tamariu

This well-kept camp site is on the Costa Brava, near the lovely beach town of Tamariu. It is 200 m (656 ft) from the beach and within sauntering distance of the town for bars, restaurants and grocery shops. ✆ Costa Rica 2, near Tamariu, 5 km E of Palafrugell • 97 262 04 22 • www.campingtamariu.com • Closed Oct–Apr • €

5 Camping Playa Sol

Twenty-eight kms (17.5 miles) north of Barcelona is this campsite next to a small beach. It is also close to several larger beaches. The camp site is about 1 km (0.6 mile) from the train station. Bungalows are also available. ✆ Carretera A2, km 650, 8 km E of Mataró • 93 790 47 20 • www.campingplayasol.com • Closed Nov–Mar • DA • €

6 Camping Globo Rojo

Close to the beaches of Canet de Mar and with a swimming pool, tennis court, football pitch as well as all kinds of sporting activities. Great for kids. ✆ Ctra, N-II km 660, 9, Canet de Mar • 93 794 11 43 • www.globo-rojo.com • Closed Oct–mid-Mar • DA • €

7 Citadines

If you're smitten with Barcelona, try an aparthotel for a longer stay. The Citadines aparthotel on La Rambla has well-appointed studios and small apartments with amenities, such as a kitchen (with oven and microwave), iron and a CD stereo. The rooftop solarium, equipped with beach chairs and showers, is just the spot to unwind. ✆ La Rambla 122 • Map L2 • 93 270 11 11 • www.citadines.com • €€€

8 Aparthotel Bertran

This aparthotel has ample studios and apartments (many with balconies), a rooftop terrace with swimming pool, a small gym and 24-hour laundry service. Breakfast is served in your apartment. ✆ C/Bertran 150 • 93 212 75 50 • www.hotelbertran.com • €€€

9 Atenea Aparthotel

Designed with business travellers in mind, this top-notch aparthotel sits near Barcelona's business and financial district around upper Diagonal. Rooms are ample and well-equipped, and there are several conference rooms and a 24-hour laundry service. ✆ C/Joan Güell 207–211 • 93 490 66 40 • www.apart hotelatenea.com • €€€

10 Habit Servei

This agency can help find furnished apartments for both short- and long-term stays. They can also find flat-shares for varying lengths of time. The average cost is around €700 a month ✆ C/Muntaner 200 • Map D2 • 93 240 50 23 • www.habitservei.com

Unless otherwise stated, all campsites are open all year round, though many open only at weekends October–March.

Price Categories

For a standard, double room per night (with breakfast if included), taxes and extra charges.

€	under €60
€€	€60–120
€€€	€120–180
€€€€	€180–240
€€€€€	over €240

Coastline, Costa Brava

Getaways Beyond Barcelona

1 La Torre del Remei
Close to the Pyrenean town of Puigcerdà, this restored 1910 *Modernista* palace, with its series of sumptuous rooms, has an outdoor heated pool and a renowned restaurant. Take your pick of views: impressive mountain peaks or the lush garden.
◈ *Camí Reial, Bolvir, 3 km SW of Puigcerdà • 97 214 01 82 • www.relais chateaux.com • €€€€€*

2 El Hostal de la Gavina
This elegant mansion, set in peaceful grounds, is just 200 m (656 ft) from the beach. The rooms have antique furniture and fixtures, and there's a saltwater pool. The first-rate restaurant serves divine Mediterranean fare.
◈ *Pl de la Rosaleda, 3km S of S'Agaró • 97 232 11 00 • www.lagavina.com • Closed mid-Oct–Easter (except New Year) • €€€€€*

3 Hotel Aiguablava
This coastal institution is perched atop rugged cliffs overlooking the Mediterranean. It is run by the fourth generation of the same family. Many of the rooms – each individually decorated – have splendid vistas of the sea. There's a large outdoor pool and breakfast is included.
◈ *Platja de Fornells, Begur • 97 262 45 62 • www. aiguablava.com • Closed Nov–Feb • €€€*

4 Fonda Biayna
The Fonda Biayna has been in operation since the 1820s. Wood-beamed ceilings and antique furniture imbue it with rustic flair. The inn's most famous guest was Picasso, who arrived here by mule en route to Paris (with paintings in tow). ◈ *C/de Sant Roc 11, Bellver de Cerdanya • 97 351 04 75 • www. fondabiayna.com • €€*

5 Hostal Sa Tuna
Take in the sea views from your terrace at this five-room, family-run hotel on the pretty Platja Sa Tuna. The restaurant serves excellent Catalan cuisine and breakfast is included. ◈ *Pg de Ancora 6, Platja Sa Tuna, 5 km N of Begur • 97 262 21 98 • www.hostalsatuna.com • Closed Oct–Mar • €€€*

6 Mas de Torrent
This beautifully restored 18th-century farmhouse near Pals has antique decor offset by museum-worthy contemporary art. There is an outdoor pool and spa facilities. ◈ *Finca Mas de Torrent, Torrent, 5 km NW of Palafrugell • 90 255 03 21 • www.relaischateaux. com • DA • €€€€€*

7 Parador de Tortosa
Looming over the town of Tortosa is the ancient Arab Castillo de la Zuda, within which this parador is housed. Decor is suitably old-world, with dark-wood furniture and antique fixtures, and the view of countryside and mountains is superb.
◈ *Castillo de la Zuda, Tortosa • 97 744 44 50 • www.parador.es • €€€*

8 Ca L'Aliu
This restored, cosy *casa rural* is in the tiny medieval town of Peratallada. Comfortable rooms all have antique furniture. The amiable owners will lend you bikes. ◈ *C/Roca 6, Peratallada, 12 km NW of Palafrugell • 97 263 40 61 • www.calaliu.com • €€*

9 Royal Tanau
This luxury hotel has chair lifts direct to the slopes of the ski resort Baqueira-Beret (see p120). Cosy cabin-style rooms offer a view of the peaks.
◈ *Ctra/de Beret, Baqueira-Beret, 120 km N of Lleida • 97 364 44 46 • www. meliaroyaltanau.solmelia. com • Closed mid-Apr–Nov • DA • €€€€€*

10 El Paller de Can Viladomat
This 18th-century country house has simple rooms and a small pool. Visitors can only rent the entire property (sleeps up to 12 people) and the minimum stay is one weekend. Breakfast and dinner are included in the price
◈ *Can Viladomat, Navès, 19 km E of Solsona • 97 329 90 26 • www. elpaller.com • No credit cards • €€€€€*

General Index

1898 144

A

Àbac 117
AB Skipper 145
activities 60–1
Aerobús 130
Agut 79
Agut d'Avignon 79
aigua 43
Air Europa 130
Air Shop, The 84
air travel 130
Al Limón Negro 77
Alfarràs, Marques d' 113
Alfons I, King 30
Alfons XIII, King 31
Alt Penedès 120
Amargós, Josep 17
ambulances 136
American football 61
Àntic Hospital de la
   Santa Creu 83
Antinous Llibreria-Cafè 48
Antiquari, L' 73
antiques 139
Antoni de Padua, Sant 39
Aparthotel Bertran 148
aparthotels 148
Aquàrium, L' 62, 97
Arc de Triomf 16
Arca de l'Àvia, L' 75
architecture, Modernista 32–3
Arena Madre 46
Arnau, Eusebi 27, 32, 33, 104
Arola 100
Aroma 115
Arribas, Alfred 46
art festivals 65
art galleries, El Raval 84
Asador d'Aranda, El 44, 113, 117
Atalanta Manufactura 75
Atenea Aparthotel 148
ATMs (cash machines) 137
Auditori de Barcelona 66
August, avoiding 141
Aventura del Nautilus, L' 132
Avinguda Diagonal 51
Avis 132

B

Bacon, Francis 21
Bagotti, Domenico 113
ballooning 126
Balsa, La 117
banking 137
Bar Almirall 86
Bar L'Ascensor 76
Bar Jai Ca 100
Bar Kasparo 42
Bar Lobo 42
Bar Paris 108
Bar Ra 44, 87
Bar Resolis 86
Bar-Restaurante Can Tomàs
   45, 117
Barceló, Miquel 91
Barcelona Airport 130
Barcelona by Bike 133
Barcelona Cathedral
   6, 14–15, 38, 55, 71
Barcelona Dream 147

Barceloneta 98, 99
   see also Port Vell,
   Barceloneta & Port Olímpic
Barri Gòtic & La Ribera 58, 70–9
   best of the rest 74
   cafés & light eats 78
   clubs & music venues 77
   cocktail & conversation
   spots 76
   map 70
   restaurants & tapas bars 79
   shops 75
   sights & attractions 70–73
   walks 73
Barri Xinès 82–3
bars 46–7
   budget travel 131
   Gràcia, Tibidabo & Zona Alta
   116
   Montjuïc 95
   Port Vell, Barceloneta &
   Port Olímpic 100
   El Raval 86
Báscula, La 78
basketball 61
Bassa, Ferrer 38
Bauma 108
beach clubs
   Port Vell, Barceloneta &
   Port Olímpic 100
beaches
   for children 63
   Port Vell, Barceloneta & Port
   Olímpic 49, 57, 97
   Sitges 49
   sunbathing & swimming 60
Beethoven, Ludwig van 27
Begur 120
Betty Ford's 86
Beyond Barcelona
   churches & monasteries 124
   national parks & nature
   reserves 125
   outdoor activities 126
   places to eat 127
   sights & attractions 118–121
Bernat Picornell Olympic pool 60
bicycles 131
   bike rides 58–9
   mountain biking 132
   tours 133
Biking 61
Bikini 116
Biosca & Botey 106
bird stalls 13
Blay, Miquel 32
Blues Cafè 115
Boadas Cocktail Bar 86
boat trips
   beyond Barcelona 126
   les golondrines 54, 63, 133
   Port Vell, Barceloneta &
   Port Olímpic 98
   sea cruises 132
Boix 127
Boliche 67
Bonic 146
Book & Coin Market at Mercat
   de Sant Antoni 52
Borgonya, Joan de 14
Born, El 51, 72
Botafumeiro 117
Bravo, Arranz 28

British Airways 130
British Institute 134
Bruno Quadras Building 13
Bubó 75
Budget (car hire) 132
Budget Bikes 131
budget travel 140
Buigas, Carles 89
Bulevard dels Antiquaris 50
Bulevard Rosa 50
Bulli, El (Roses) 127
bureaux de change 137, 141
buses 131
   in Catalonia 132
   getting to Barcelona 130
   nightbuses 131
   tours 132, 133

C

Ca L'Aliu 149
Ca L'Isidre 87
Caballé, Montserrat 12, 66, 89
cable cars 54, 63, 98, 133
cacaolat 43
Cacao Sampaka 108
Cactus Bar 76
Cadaqués 121
Cafè de l'Acadèmia 79
cafè amb llet 43
Cafè-Bar L'Antiquari 78
Cafè Bliss 42, 78
Café del Born 78
Cafè del Centre 108
Cafè d'Estiu 78
Cafè de Gràcia 115
Cafè de l'Òpera 42
Cafè Salambó 43, 115
Cafè sol 43
Cafè del Sol 115
Cafè del Teatre 115
Café Teatre Llantiol 86
cafés 42–3
   Barri Gòtic & La Ribera 78
   Eixample 108
   Gràcia 115
   Montjuïc 95
Cafetera, La 115
Cal Pep 44, 79
Cala Santa Maria 95
calamars 45
Calder, Alexander
   Font de Mercuri 23
Call, El 74
Cambó Bequest19
Cambó, Francesc 19
Camiseria Pons 114
Camp Nou Stadium 111
Camping Masnou 148
Camping Playa Sol 148
Camping Roca-Grosa 148
Camping Sitges 148
Camping Tamariu 148
campsites 148
Can Ganassa 101
Can Manel la Puda 101
Cañota 95
canya 43
Cap de Creus 121, 125
Capella de Sant Jordi 39
Capella de Sant Miquel 38
Capella de Santa Àgata 38
Carme Ruscalleda Sant Pau 127
Carnaval 64

Carrer del Bisbe 74
Carrer del Correu Vell 74
Carrer Montcada 74
Carrer Nou de la Rambla 82
Carrer Pelai 50
Carrer Petritxol 74
Carrer Portaferrissa 51
Carrer Regomir 74
Carrer de Santa Llúcia 74
Carreras, José 66
Carrers Tallers 82
cars 130, 132
    car tours 133
Casa Alfonso 108
Casa Amatller 33, 103
Casa de l'Ardiaca 15
Casa Batlló 33, 103
Casa Calvet 105, 109
Casa Camper 143
Casa Colomina 75
Coca Fuster 144
Casa Leopoldo 45, 87
Casa Lleó Morera 33, 103
Casa Milà see La Pedrera
Casa-Museu Gaudí 112
Casa de les Punxes 33, 105
Casa Quimet 116
Casa Terrades 33
Casablanca 67
Casarramona 91
Casas, Ramon 17
Cascalls, Jaume 19
Cases de Pagès 142
cash machines 137
Castell de Montjuïc 54, 89, 91
Castelldefels 57
Castells 65
Castell de Montjuïc & Museo
    del Cómic y la Ilustración 89
Catalonia
    cuisine 138
    folk festivals & traditions 64–5
    travel 132
    see Beyond Barcelona
Catalunya Rally 61
Catedral Santa Maria 124
Catedral de Santa Tecla 124
Catedral La Seu d'Urgell 124
Cathedral 6, 14–15, 38, 55, 71
cava 43
Cavalcada del Reis 65
CDLC 100
El Celler de Can Roca 127
Centre d'Art Santa Mònica 13
Centre de Cultura
    Contemporània (CCCB)
    7, 28–9, 40, 81, 83
Centre del Disseny 73
Centre de la Vila-Port Olímpic, El
    99
Centric Point Hostel 147
Cerdà, Ildefons 31, 104
Cereria Subirà 75
Cerveçeria Catalana 109
Chagall, Marc 21
chapels 38–9
    Capella de Sant Benet 15
    Capella de Sant Jordi 39
    Capella de Sant Miquel 38
    Capella de Santa Àgata 38
    Capella de Santa Llúcia 15
    Capella del Santíssim
        Sacrament i Crist de
        Lepant 15
Chic and Basic 146

children
    budget travel 142
    children's attractions 62–3
    in restaurants 138
    travel 132
Chillida 28
Christmas 65
churches 38–9
    Barcelona Cathedral 6,
        14–15, 38, 55, 71
    Barri Gòtic & La Ribera 74
    beyond Barcelona 124
    Església del Betlem 13, 39
    Església al Monestir de
        Pedralbes 38
    Església de Sant Pau del
        Camp 38, 83
    Església de Sant Pere de les
        Puelles 38
    Església de Santa Maria del
        Mar 38, 72
    Església de Santa Maria del
        Pi 38
    Sagrada Família
        6, 8–10, 32, 55, 103, 105
CicloBus 131
cigaló 43
Cinc Sentits 44, 109
cinemas 67, 131
Citadines 148
City Hall 107
Clàssica als Parcs 65
Clavé, Josep Anselm 27
climate 130
clinics 136
clothing
    shops 139
    sizes 139
Club Apolo 67
Club Catwalk 100
Club Element 132
Club Fellini 67
clubs
    Barri Gòtic & La Ribera 77
    beach clubs 100
    Montjuïc 95
    El Raval 86
Club 13 77
coach tours 133
Coastal Bike Ride 59
cocktails
    Barri Gòtic & La Ribera 76
Cocotte 75
Columbus, Christopher 31
    Mirador de Colom 54
    Monument a Colom 12
    Palau Reial 71
Comerç 24 45, 79
communications 135
Como Agua de Mayo 75
Companys, Lluís 31
concerts 131
Conjunt Monumental de la
    Plaça del Rei 71
consulates 134
Continental 130
Corte Inglés, El 55, 139
CosmoCaixa Museu de la
    Ciencia 41
Costa Brava Coastal Path 59
Costa Daurada 121
Cotthem Gallery 84
courier services 135
credit cards 137
crime 136

Cristòfol, Sant 39
croquetes 45
crowds, avoiding 141
cruising, night-time 49
Cursa El Corte Inglés 61
Cursa La Mercè 61
cycling see bicycles

D
D Barcelona 106
Dalí, Salvador 21
    Teatre-Museu Dalí (Figueres)
        119
    World Trade Center 99
Dalmau, Lluis
    Madonna of the Councillors 19
dance 61, 65
Delta 130
Delta de l'Ebre 125
dental treatment 136
department stores 139
design shops
    Eixample 106
    El Raval 84
DHL Worldwide Express 135
Dia de Sant Jordi, El 64
Diagonal Bike Ride 59
dialling codes 135
Dietrich Gay Teatro Café 48, 107
disabled travellers 131
    information 134
    in restaurants 138
    travel 131
Discos Edison's 85
Discos Tesla 85
diving 126
doctors 136
Dofi Jet Boats 132
Domènech i Montaner, Lluís
    Casa Fuster 144
    Casa Lleó Morera 33, 103
    Fundació Tàpies 40
    Hospital de la Santa Creu i de
        Sant Pau 32, 103
    Hotel Espanya 144
    Museu de Zoologia 17
    Palau de la Música Catalana
        26, 27, 32, 66
    Parc de la Ciutadella 16
Dos i Una 106
Downtown Paraiso Hostel 147
drinks 43
Dry Martini 107

E
easyInternetCafé 135
easyJet 130
Ebre, River 125
Ego 84
Eixample 58, 102–9
    after dark venues 107
    cafés 108
    design shops 106
    map 102
    restaurants & tapas bars 109
    sights & attractions 102–106
    walks 105
Elena, Santa 39
Elephant 46, 116
Elisenda, Queen 38, 111
emergencies 136
Empúries 120–1
Encants, Els 52
ensaladilla Russa 45
Escribà Confiteria i Fleca 75

Església de Betlem 13, 39
Església al Monestir de
  Pedralbes 38
Església de Sant Just i Sant
  Pastor 74
Església de Sant Pau del Camp
  38, 83
Església de Sant Pere de les
  Puelles 38
Església de Santa Anna 74
Església de Santa Maria del
  Mar 38, 72
Església de Santa Maria Antiga 38
Església de Santa Maria del Pi 38
Espai Barroc 76
Espai Gaudí 20
Espai Ras 84
Estació de França 130
Estació del Nord 130
Estació Passeig de Gràcia 132
Estació de Sants 130
Estadi Olímpic 90, 91
etiquette, restaurants and bars
  138
Eulàlia, Santa 15, 39
Euro 137
Eurolines 130

F
Fantàstico Club 77
fast food 131
Favorita 106
faxes 135
FC Barcelona basketball 61
FC Barcelona football 61
FC Barcelona hockey 61
Federal Express 135
Feetup Hostel–Garden House
  147
Fellini 77
Felipe II, King 124
Ferdinand, King 31, 71
Fernández, Las 87
Festa del Aquelarre 64
Festa Major de Gràcia 64
Festa de la Patum 64
Festes de la Mercè 64
Festival de Flamenco 65
Festival del Grec 65
Festival de Guitarra 65
Festival Internacional de Jazz 65
Festival de Música 65
Festival de Música Antiga 65
Festival de Músiques del Món
  65
Festival del Sónar 65
festivals 64–5
FGC 131
Filmoteca 67
Fira, La 107
Fira Artesana Plaça del Pi 53
Fira de Numismàtica 53
Fira de Santa Llúcia 52
fire services 136
Flash Flash 117
flower stalls 13
folk festivals & traditions 64–5
Foment de les Arts Decoratives
  (FAD) 81, 83, 84
Fonda Biayna 149
Fonda de España 87
Fonda Europa (Granollers) 127
Font de Canaletes 13
Font Màgica 89
Font de Prades 95
Fontseré, Josep 17

food and drink 138
  budget travel 131
  café drinks 43
  tapas 45
  see also restaurants
football 61
Foster, Norman 111
Franco, General 31
Free Girls 49
frontó 61
fuet 45
Fundació Francisco Godia 104
Fundació Joan Miró 7, 22–3, 40,
  89, 91
  restaurant 95
Fundació Tàpies 40, 104
funfair, Tibidabo 62
Funoll, Reinard 124

G
Galeria dels Àngels 84
galleries see art galleries;
  museums and galleries
gambes al' allet 45
gardens see parks and gardens
Gat Xino 146
Gaudí, Antoni 11, 31, 106, 112
  Casa Batlló 33, 103
  Casa Calvet 105
  Casa-Museu Gaudí 112
  Espai Gaudí 20
  Jardins de Pedralbes 56–7
  Palau Güell 33, 81
  Parc de la Ciutadella 16
  Parc Güell 55, 56, 112, 113
  La Pedrera 7, 20–1, 32, 47,
    103, 105
  Plaça Reial 72
  Sagrada Família 6, 8–10, 32,
    55, 103, 105
gay & lesbian hang-outs 48–9
Gehry, Frank
  Peix 41
Gens que j'Aime, Les 107
GI Joe Surplus 85
Giardano, Luca 104
Gimlet 76
Ginger 76
Girona 120
Glaciar 76
Godia, Francisco 104
golf 60, 126
golondrines, les 54, 63, 133
Gothic Point Youth Hostel 147
Govinda 79
Goya, Francisco de, 19
Gràcia, Tibidabo & Zona Alta 51,
  110–17
  boutiques 114
  cafés 115
  hip drinking spots 116
  map 110
  restaurants & tapas bars 117
  sights & attractions 110–113
  walks 113
Gran Hotel La Florida 144
Gran Teatre del Liceu 12, 66
Granados 83 143
Grand Hotel Central 143
granissat 43
Granja Dulcinea 43
Guantería Alonso 75
Guifre II, Count 38
Guifré the Hairy 31

H
Habit Servei 148
Hacke, Hans 104
Hamilcar Barca 30
Harlem Jazz Club 66, 77
L'Havana 87
health 136
helicopter rides 55
Heliogàbel 116
Hertz 132
Herz, Mario 104
history 30–31
hockey 61
Hofmann 117
HoLaLa 85
Homar, Gaspar 17
horse-drawn carriages 133
horseriding 126
Horsfield, Craigie 104
Hospital de la Santa Creu
  i de Sant Pau 32, 103
hospitals 136
Hostal Fernando 146
Hostal de la Gavina 149
Hostal Goya 146
Hostal Jardí 146
Hostal Oliva 146
Hostal Palacios 146
Hostal Residencia Rembrandt
  146
Hostal Sa Tuna 149
hostals 142
hostels 147
Hotel 54 Barceloneta 145
Hotel Aiguablava 149
Hotel Arts 143
Hotel Avinyó 145
Hotel Banys Orientals 145
Hotel Claris 143
Hotel Colón 143
Hotel Ducs de Bergara 144
Hotel Duquesa de Cardona
  144
Hotel Espanya 144
Hotel Majestic 143
Hotel Mesón Castilla 144
Hotel Montecarlo 144
Hotel Neri 144
Hotel Omm 143
Hotel Oriente 144
Hotel Palace Barcelona 108, 143
Hotel Rey Juan Carlos I 143
Hotel Romàntic 49
hotels 142–9
  aparthotels 148
  bars 131
  beyond Barcelona 149
  booking service 142
  budget accommodation 146
  budget travel 131, 142
  central stays 145
  historical hotels 144
  hostels & student residences
    147
  luxury hotels 143
Huguet, Jaume 19, 71, 104

I
Ideal Youth Hostel 147
Iberia 130
Icària Yelmo Cineplex 67
Ideal 107
Imprevist 87
information officers 134
Inopia 44, 109

Institut de Cultura de Barcelona 134
insurance, health 136
Internet 135
Internet Exchange 135
Isabel, Queen 31, 71
Isozaki, Aiko 90
Isozaki, Arata 90
Itaca Hostel 147

J
Jamboree 47, 77
Jardí, El 43, 87
Jardí Botànic 94
Jardins del Castell 94
Jardins de Joan Maragall 94
Jardins del Laberint d'Horta 56, 62–3
Jardins Laribal 94
Jardins de Miramar 94
Jardins Mossèn Costa i Llobera 94
Jardins Mossèn Cinto Verdaguer 94
Jardins de Pedralbes 56–7
Jardins del Teatre Grec 94
Jaume I the Conqueror 31
Jazz 145
JazzSí Club – Taller de Musics 67
Joan, Sant 39
Jordi, Sant 39
José Rivero 114
Juan, Don of Austria 81
Julià Tours 132, 133

K
Kaiku 44, 101
Karma 77
Kasbah, Le 100
kayaking 126, 133
Kennedy Irish Sailing Club 100
Kolbe, Georg 90–1
Kowasa (Photography) 106

L
Laie Llibreria Cafè 43, 108
Lailo 85
late-night shops 139
leather goods 139, 141
libraries 134
Lichtenstein, Roy
  Cap de Barcelona 41
Lika Lounge 107
Linebús 130
Live Barcelona Car Tours 133
Llena eres de Gràcia 114
Llimona, Josep 17
Lliure, El 95
Lluçanès 101
Llúcia, Santa 39
Llull, Ramon 31
London Bar 83, 86
Loring Art 84
Luz de Gas 107

M
Macià, Francesc 31
Madame Jasmine 42
magazines 134
Magic 77
Magritte, René 23
mail boxes 135
Mama Café 87
Mambo Tango 147
Mansana de la Discòrdia 103, 105

Manteguería Ravell 108
Manual Alpargatera, La 75
Maquinista, La 51
Maragall, Ernest 94
Maragall, Joan 65
Mare Nostrum (Sitges) 127
Marès, Frederic 41, 94
  Museu Frederic Marès 72
Mariscal, Javier 44, 46
María Mulata 76
Market 146
markets 52–3
Marsella 46, 83, 86
Martin's 49
Martorelli, Bernat 15
Mas de Torrent 149
Masnou, El 57
Massis de Pedraforca 125
Mauri 108
Mediterráneo, El 49
Meier, Richard 29
Méliès Cinemes 67
Melon District 147
menus 138
Mercal del Art de la Plaça de Sant Josep Oriol 53
Mercat dels Antiquaris 53
Mercat de la Boqueria 12, 52, 83
Mercat de la Concepció 53
Mercat de les Flors 67
Mercat de Santa Caterina 53
Mercat Sant Antoni 52
Mercury, Freddie 89
Merendero de la Mari 101
Metro 129, 131
Miami 49
Mies & Felj 85
Mies van der Rohe, Ludwig 90
Millet, Lluís 27
Mirablau 116
Mirador de les Caves, El (Sant Sadurní) 127
Mirador de Colom 54
Mirador del Llobregat, El 94
Miramar 145
Mirasol 116
Miró, Joan 22–3, 112
  L'Estel Matinal 22
  Fundació Joan Miró 7, 22–3, 40, 89, 91
  Home i Dona Davant un Munt d'Excrement 23
  Miró Mosaic 13
  Museu d'Art Contemporani 28
  Pagès Català al Cla de Lluna 22
  Parc de Joan Miró 57
  Rialto 145
  Sèrie Barcelona 23
  Tàpis de la Fundació 22
Modernista movement 11, 26
  Modernista buildings 32–3
  La Ruta Modernista 133
monasteries 124
Mond Bar 46, 110
Món De Mones 114
Monestir de Montserrat 124
Monestir de Pedralbes 111
Monestir de Poblet 124
Monestir de Ripoll 124
Monestir Sant Pere de Rodes 121, 124
Monestir de Santes Creus 124
money 137
Montagut, Berenguer de 72

Montjuïc 54, 58–9, 88–95
  cable cars 54, 63
  map 88
  parks & gardens 94
  restaurants, cafés, bars & clubs 95
  sights & attractions 88–91
  walks 91
Montmeló 61
Montserrat 119
Monturiol, Narcis 98–9
Monument a Colom 12
monuments 41
Moo 109
Moog 86
motor racing 61
motorways 132
mountain hostels 142
Mudanzas 76
Multiart 114
Muntanya de Montjuïc 94
musclos o escopinyes 45
museums and galleries 40–41
  budget travel 131
  Monday closing 141
  Casa-Museu Gaudí 112
  Crypt Museum (Sagrada Família) 8
  Espai Gaudí 20
  Fundació Francisco Godia 104
  Fundació Joan Miró 7, 22–3, 40, 89, 91
  Fundació Tàpies 40, 104
  Museo del Cómic y la Ilustración 89
  Museu d'Art Contemporani 7, 28–9, 40, 81
  Museu dels Autòmates 41
  Museu Barbier-Mueller d'Art Precolombí 73
  Museu del Calçat 41
  Museu de Carrosses Fúnebres 41
  Museu de Cera 41
  Museu de la Ciència (CosmoCaixa) 41
  Museu Diocesà 15
  Museu Egipci 105
  Museu de l'Eròtica 41
  Museu del FC Barcelona 40, 111
  Museu Frederic Marès 41, 72
  Museu de Geologia 17
  Museu d'Història de Catalunya 63, 97
  Museu d'Història de la Ciutat (Conjunt Monumental de la Plaça del Rei) 40, 71, 73
  Museu de la Màgia 41
  Museu Marítim 41, 62, 81, 99
  Museu Nacional d'Art de Catalunya (MNAC) 7, 18–19, 40, 89, 91
  Museu del Perfum 41
  Museu Picasso 7, 24–5, 40, 71
  Museu de la Xocolata 41
  Museu de Zoologia 17
  Palau de la Virreina 13
  Teatre-Museu Dalí (Figueres) 119
mushroom picking 126
Mushi Mushi 114
music
  Barri Gòtic & La Ribera 77
  budget travel 131

music (cont.)
  festivals 65
  shops 139
  venues 6 6–7
Muxart 106

N
Naftalina 114
national parks 125
nature reserves 125
Neichel 117
New York 77
night kayaking 133
Nightbus 131
nightlife 46–7
  Eixample 107
Ninas 114
Nitbús (Nightbus) 131
Noti 44, 109
Nova Mar Bella Beach Bars 100

O
Oleum 95
Olivé, L' 109
Olympic Games (1992) 31
OmmSessions Club 107
online banking 137
opening hours
  restaurants 138
  shops 139
opera 131
Orfeó Català 27
Organic 49
Orsom Catamaran 54, 99, 133
orxata 43
Otto Zutz 46, 116
outdoor activities 60–61, 126

P
pa amb tomàquet 45
Pailebot Santa Eulàlia 98, 99
Palau Güell 33, 81
Palau Macaya 104, 105
Palau de la Música Catalana
  7, **26–7**, 32, 66, 71
Palau Nacional 89, 91
Palau Reial 71
Palau Reial de Pedralbes 112
Palau Sant Jordi 66, 90, 91
Palau de la Virreina 13
Paller de Can Viladomat, El 149
Parador de Tortosa 149
Parc d'Atraccions del Tibidabo
  62, 111, 113
Parc Nacional d'Aigüestortes i
  Estany de Sant Maurici 125
Parc Natural dels Aiguamolls de
  L'Empordà 125
Parc Natural del Cadí-Moixeró
  125
Parc Natural del Montseny 125
Parc Natural de Sant Llorenç
  del Munt 125
Parc Natural de la Zona
  Volcànica de la Garrotxa 125
Parc Zoològic 16, 62
Parco Meralgo 109
Park Hotel 145
parks and gardens 56–7
  Castell Jardins 94
  Jardí Botànic 94
  Jardins de Joan Maragall 94
  Jardins del Laberint d'Horta
  50, 02–3
  Jardins Laribal 94

parks and gardens (cont.)
  Jardins de Miramar 94
  Jardins Mossèn Costa i
  Llobera 94
  Jardins Mossèn Jacint
  Verdaguer 94
  Jardins de Pedralbes 56–7
  Jardins del Teatre Grec 94
  El Mirador del Llobregat 94
  Montjuïc 94
  Muntanya de Montjuïc 94
  Parc de Cervantes 56
  Parc de la Ciutadella 6, **16–
  17,** 56
  Parc de Collserola 59, 112–13
  Parc de l'Espanya Industrial 57
  Parc Güell 11, 55, 56, 112, 113
  Parc de Joan Miró 57
  Parc del Laberint d'Horta 113
Parlament de Catalunya 17
Parrots 49
Passeig de Gràcia 50
passes
  sightseeing 140
  travel 131
passports 130
Pavelló Mies van der Rohe 90–1
Pedrera, La 7, **20–1**, 32, 103, 105
Pedrera de Nit, La 47
Peña Ganchegui, Luis 57
pensions 142
People @ Web 135
performing arts 66–7
pernil Serrà 45
Pescadors, Els 127
Petit Palace Opera Garden 145
pharmacies 136
phone centres 135
phonecards 135
phones, public 135
Pia Almoina 5, 73
Piano, El 114
Picasso, Pablo, **24–25** 112
  Arlequín 25
  Autoretrato con peluca 24
  Caballo corneado 25
  Ciencia y Caridad 24
  Margot 25
  Hombre con boina 24
  Hombre sentado 25
  Homenatge a Picasso 17
  El Loco 25
  Las Meninas series 25
  Menu de Els Quatre Gats 25
  Museu Picasso 7, **24–5**, 40, 71
  La Nana 25
pickpockets 136, 141
Pilma 106
pitch-&-putt golf 60
Plaça de Catalunya 36, 50
Plaça Comercial 37
Plaça del Pi 37
Plaça de Ramon Berenguer
  el Gran 74
Plaça del Rei 36, 73
Plaça Reial 36, 72
Plaça de Rius i Taulet 37
Plaça de Sant Felip Neri 74
Plaça de Sant Jaume 36, 71
Plaça de Sant Josep Oriol 37
Plaça de Santa Maria 37
Plaça del Sol 37
Plaça do lo Vila de Madrid 37, 73
Planes, Les 59
Poble Espanyol 91

police 136
pool & billiards 61
Port 58
Port Aventura 121
Port Olímpic *see Port Vell,
  Barceloneta & Port Olímpic*
Port Vell, Barceloneta & Port
  Olímpic 96–101
  bars & beach clubs 100
  map 96
  restaurants & tapas bars 101
  sights & attractions 96–99
  walks 99
Portal de l'Àngel 50
post offices 135
poste restante 135
Prat de Llobregat airport 130
Premià 97
Prestige Passeig de Gràcia 143
Privilege 49
Puig i Cadafalch, Josep 17
  Casa Amatller 33, 103
  Casa de les Punxes 33
  Casarramona 91
  Jardins Laribal 94
  Palau Macaya 104
Pujol, Jordi 31
Pullmantur 132, 133
Punto BCN 49

Q
Quimet & Quimet 95

R
Racó de Can Fabes, El
  (Montseny) 127
rafting 126
rally-driving 61
Rambla, La 6, **12–13,** 63
  scams 141
  walks 58
Rambla de Catalunya 50–1, 105
Rambla de Mar 97, 99
Rambla del Raval, La 82
Ramon Berenguer IV, Count 31
Raval, El 80–7
  bars & clubs 86
  galleries & design shops 84
  good-value eats 87
  map 80
  sights & attractions 80–83
  vintage & second-hand
  shops 85
  walks 83
Razzmatazz 47, 100
RCD Espanyol 61
Recicla Recicla 85
refugis 142
Regia 105, 106
Reial Cercle Artístic 73
Reial Club Marítim Restaurant
  101
Rembrandt 18
Renoir Floridablanca 67
Renoir-Les Corts 67
Residencia La Ciutat 147
Restaurante Castro 48
Restaurant Forestier in Hotel
  Miramar 95
restaurants 44–5, 138
  Barri Gòtic & La Ribera 79
  beyond Barcelona 127
  Eixample 109
  Gràcia, Tibidabo & Zona Alta
  117

restaurants (cont.)
Montjuïc 95
places to avoid 141
Port Vell, Barceloneta & Port
Olímpic 101
El Raval 87
Revólver Records 85
Rex 67
Rias de Galicia 95
Ribera, La see Barri Gòtic & La
Ribera
Riera Baixa 82
Rita, Santa 39
roads 132
Roman Barcelona 73
Roth, Dieter 28
Rothko, Mark 23
rowing 126
Royal Tanau 149
Rubens, Peter Paul 19, 41
Rúccula 101
Ruta Modernista, La 133

S
Sadur 106
Safont, Marc 71
Sagnier, Enric 112
Sagrada Família 6, **8–10**, 32, 55,
103, 105
sailing 126
saints 39
Sala BeCool 47, 116
Salamanca Chiringuito 99
Salero 79
sales 139
sangria 43
Sant Climent i Santa Maria de
Taüll 124
Sant Joan de les Abadesses 124
Sardanes 61, 65
Sauna Galilea 48
Schilling 76
scuba diving 126
sea cruises 132
security 136, 141, 142
Semproniana, La 109
Senyor Parellada 79
Serra de l'Albera 125
Sert, Josep Lluís 23, 89
Set Portes 101
Shôko 100
shopping 50–1, 139
Barri Gòtic & La Ribera 75
Eixample 106
Gràcia 114
El Raval 84–5
Sidecar Factory Club 77
sightseeing passes 140
Silenus 87
single travellers 142
Sitges 121
Carnaval 64
gay hot spots 49
Sitges International Film
Festival 65
skiing 126
Smart & Clean 85
Soho 145
Somorrostro 101
Spanair 130
Spanish Civil War 31
sports 60–1, 126
squares 36–7
Barri Gòtic & La Ribera 74
student residences 147

Subirachs, Josep Maria 8, 10
Submarine Ictíneo II 98–9
Suite Royale 100
sunbathing 60
Suquet de l'Almirall 101
Sureny 115
swimming 60
Swing, L 85

T
tallat 43
Taller de Tapas 79
tapas bars 44–5
Barri Gòtic & La Ribera 79
Eixample 109
Gràcia, Tibidabo & Zona Alta
117
Port Vell, Barceloneta & Port
Olímpic 101
Tàpies, Antoni 91
Fundació Tàpies 32, 40, 104
Homenatge a Picasso 17
A Sudden Awakening 29
Tarragona 120
Taverna El Glop 117
taxis 131
Teatre Grec 66, 90
Teatre-Museu Dalí (Figueres) 119
telephones 135
Temple Expiatori del Sagrat Cor
39, 112
tennis 61
Terrazza, La 46–7, 95
Tetería Jazmín 115
Textil Cafè 42
theatre 65
theft 136, 141
Tibidabo 54, 58, 62
see also Gràcia, Tibidabo &
Zona Alta
Tintoretto 41
tipping 137, 138
Titian 41
Torneo Conde de Godo, El 61
Torre de Collserola 111, 113
Torre del Remei, La (Cerdanya)
127, 149
tourist information 134
tours
bike 133
boat 133
bus 132, 133
car 133
coach 133
walking 133
traffic, avoiding 132, 141
Tragarrapid 108
Trailer 49
trains 130, 131, 132
Tram Tram 117
Tramvia Blau 113
Transformer 84
travel 130–3
TravelBar 134
traveller's cheques 137
Tren Turístic 133
truita de patates 45
Turisme de Barcelona 134
Turisme de Catalunya 132

U
Umbracle 17
UNESCO 112, 124
Universal Café 116
Universitat de Barcelona 105

university bulletins 134
UPS 135

V
Vall de Núria 119
valuables 136
VAT 139
vegetarian food 138
Velázquez, Diego 25, 41
Velvet 107
Venus Delicatessen 78
Verbena de Sant Joan 64
Verdaguer, Jacint 94
Verdi 67
Verdi Park 67
Versió Original (VO) cinemas 67
views 54–5
Vilaseca i Casanoves, Josep 16
Villar, F P de 10
Vinçon 106
vintage & second-hand shops,
El Raval 85
Vinya del Senyor, La 76
Virgin Mercè 39
Virgin of Montserrat 39
Virreina Bar 116
visas 139
volleyball 60
Volta Ciclista de Catalunya, La 61
Vreneli 115
Vueling 130

W
Wagner, Richard 27
walks 58–9, 131
Barri Gòtic & La Ribera 73
Eixample 105
Gràcia, Tibidabo & Zona Alta
113
Montjuïc 91
Port Vell, Barceloneta & Port
Olímpic 99
El Raval 83
tours 133
Warhol, Andy 23
water, drinking 136
watersports 60, 126
weather 130
websites 134
weight lifting 60
wheelchair users
see disabled travellers
windsurfing 126
Workcenter 135
World Trade Center 99

X
Xina A.R.T., La 84
Xampanyet, El 79
Xocoa 78
XXL 49

Z
Zelig 86
Zeltas 48
Zentraus 86
Zona Alta see Gràcia,
Tibidabo & Zona Alta
zoo 16, 62
Zucca 114
Zurbarán, Francisco 18, 19, 41
Zush 28

Acknowledgements

The Authors

AnneLise Sorensen is a travel writer cur-rently based in Barcelona. She has written and edited on numerous magazines and travel guides, covering destinations such as Spain, Denmark, California and Ireland.

Ryan Chandler is a writer and journalist who has been working in Barcelona for over ten years. He currently works as Barcelona correspondent for the Spanish magazine *The Broadsheet*.

Produced by Departure Lounge, London

Editorial Director Ella Milroy
Art Editor Lee Redmond
Editor Clare Tomlinson
Designer Lisa Kosky
DTP Designer Ingrid Vienings
Picture Researcher Monica Allende
Research Assistance Amaia Allende, Ana Virginia Aranha, Diveen Henry
Consultant Brian Catlos
Proofreader Catherine Day
Indexer Hilary Bird
Fact Checkers Paula Canal, Brian Catlos, AnneLise Sorensen

Photographers Joan Farré, Manuel Huguet

Additional photography Max Alexander, Mike Dunning, Heidi Grassley, Alan Keohane, Ella Milroy, Naomi Peck, Paul Young

Illustrators Chris Orr & Associates, Lee Redmond

Maps Martin Darlison, Tom Coulson, Encompass Graphics Ltd

AT DORLING KINDERSLEY
Senior Publishing Manager Louise Bostock Lang
Publishing Manager Kate Poole
Senior Art Editor Marisa Renzullo
Art Director Gillian Allan
Publisher Douglas Amrine
Cartography Co-ordinator Casper Morris
DTP Jason Little, Conrad van Dyk
Production Joanna Bull
Design and Editorial Assistance Mariana Evmolpidou, Anna Freiberger, Juliet Kenny, Caroline Mead, Pete Quinlan, Quadrum Solutions, Mani Ramaswamy, Sylvia Tombesi-Walton, Word On Spain

Picture Credits

Placement Key; t-top;tc-top centre; tr-top right; cla-centre left above; ca-centre above; cra-centre right above; cl-centre left; c-centre; cr-centre right; clb-centre left below; cb-cent-re below; crb-centre right below; bl-below left; bc below centre; br below right.

Works of art have been reproduced with permission of the following copyright holders: *Homea* 1974 Eduardo Arranz Bravo © ADAGP, Paris and DACS, London 2006 28br; *Rainy Taxi* Salvador Dalí © Kingdom of Spain, Gala– Salvador Dalí Foundation, DACS, London 2006 119b.

The publishers would like to thank the following individuals, companies and picture libraries for permission to reproduce their photographs:

AGUA RESTAURANT: 101tl; AISA, Barcelona: 1c, 11c, 30tl, 30tr, 30c, 31bl, 31tr, 31cr, 31br, 118c; ALAMY IMAGES: ICSDB 131tr; Melvyn Longhurst 61bl; BARCELONA TURISME: 61tr; 110c; Espai d'Imatge 64c; 65b; Jordi Trullas 64t; BUBO: 75tr; CAL PEP: 79t; CASA ALFONSO: 108tr; CASA CALVET: 109tl; CINC SENTITS: 44tl; CLUB CATWALK: 100tl; COMERÇ 24: 44tr. DK Images: Ian Aitken 85tl; Steve Gorton 134tr; DANIEL CAMPI: 146tl. EGO GALLERY: 84tl; EL PIANO: 114tr; ELEPHANT CLUB: 46ca, 46tc; FUNDACION JOAN MIRO: Pagès Català al cla de Luna Joan Miró © Sucession Miró/ADAGP, Paris and DACS, London 2006 22bl; Tapis de al Fundacio Joan Miró © Sucession Miró/ADAGP, Paris and DACS, London 2006 22–3c; Home i Dona Davant un Munt d'Excrement Joan Miró © Succession Miró/ADAGP, Paris and DACS, London 2006 23tr; GALERIA DELS ANGELS: 84tl; GETTY IMAGES: Tony Stone/Luc Beziat 48c. HOTEL OMM: 107tr; MANUEL HUGUET: 128–9. IMAGE-STATE: AGE-Fotostock 141tr; Courtesy of CAIXA CATALUNYA: 137tl; JAMBOREE: 47tr, 77tr; LA MANUAL ALPARGATERA: 75tc;

LIKA LOUNGE: 107tl; MON DE MONES: 114tl; MUSEU NACIONAL d'ART DE CATALUNYA: 18b; 19tl; 19tr; 19ca; 19b; 92–93; MUSEU d'ART CONTEMPORANI: 28tl; 28cl; 28–29c MUSEU PICASSO: Hombre con Boina Pablo Picasso © Sucession Picasso/DACS, London 2006 24b; La Espera Pablo Picasso © Sucession Picasso/DACS, London 2006 24–5; El Loco Pablo Picasso © Sucession Picasso/DACS, London 2006 25t; Sketch for Guernica Pablo Picasso © Sucession Picasso/DACS, London 2006 25cr; Las Meninas Pablo Picasso © Sucession Picasso/DACS, London 2006 25b; MIRIAM NEGRE: 44tr; 46bl; 58bl; 114l; 144r; 112b; 113t; 117; 139r; PARC ZOOLOGIC: 16bl; FRANCISCO FERNANDEZ PRIETO: 76tl; 76tr; PRISMA, Barcelona: 66b; 125t; 126t; RAZZMATAZZ: Albert Uriach 47cl; 100tr; RENFE: 132tr; SALA BECOOL: 46bl; SIDECAR FACTORY CLUB: Moises Torne (motobi@terra.es) 77tl; TEXTIL CAFE: 42bl; XOCOA: 78tr; ZELIG: 86tl; ZENTRAUS: 86tr.

All other images are © Dorling Kindersley. For further information see www.dkimages.com.

Special Editions of DK Travel Guides

English-Catalan Phrase Book

In an Emergency

Help!	**Auxili!**	ow-**gzee**-lee
Stop!	**Pareu!**	**pah**-reh-oo
Call a doctor!	**Telefoneu un metge!**	teh-leh-fon-**eh**-oo oon **meh**-djuh
Call an ambulance!	**Telefoneu una ambulància!**	teh-leh-fon-**eh**-oo oo-nah ahm-boo-**lahn**-see-ah
Call the police!	**Telefoneu la policia**	teh-leh-fon-**eh**-oo lah poh-lee-**see**-ah
Call the fire brigade!	**Telefoneu els bombers!**	teh-leh-fon-eh-oo uhlz boom-**behs**
Where is the nearest telephone?	**On és el telèfon més proper?**	**on**-ehs uhl tuh-leh-fon mehs proo-**peh**
Where is the nearest hospital?	**On és l'hospital més proper?**	**on**-ehs looss-pee-tahl mehs proo-**peh**

Communication Essentials

Yes	**Sí**	see
No	**No**	noh
Please	**Si us plau**	sees plah-oo
Thank you	**Gràcies**	**grah**-see-uhs
Excuse me	**Perdoni**	puhr-**thoh**-nee
Hello	**Hola**	**oh**-lah
Goodbye	**Adéu**	ah-they-**oo**
Good night	**Bona nit**	bo-nah **neet**
Morning	**El matí**	uhl muh-**tee**
Afternoon	**La tarda**	lah **tahr**-thuh
Evening	**El vespre**	uhl **vehs**-pruh
Yesterday	**Ahir**	ah-**ee**
Today	**Avui**	uh-voo-ee
Tomorrow	**Demà**	duh-**mah**
Here	**Aquí**	uh-**kee**
There	**Allà**	uh-**lyah**
What?	**Què?**	keh
When?	**Quan?**	kwahn
Why?	**Per què?**	puhr keh
Where?	**On?**	ohn

Useful Phrases

How are you?	**Com està?**	kom uhs-**tah**
Very well, thank you.	**Molt bé, gràcies.**	mol beh **grah**-see-uhs
Pleased to meet you.	**Molt de gust.**	mol duh **goost**
See you soon.	**Fins aviat.**	feenz uhv-**yat**
That's fine.	**Està bé.**	uhs-**tah beh**
Where is/are . ?	**On és/són?**	ohn ehs/sohn
How far is it to.?	**Quants metres/ kilòmetres hi ha d'aquí a …?**	kwahnz meh-truhs/kee-**loh**-muh-truhs yah dah-**kee** uh
Which way to …?	**Per on es va a …?**	puhr **on** uhs **bah** ah
Do you speak English?	**Parla anglès?**	**par**-luh an **glehs**
I don't understand	**No l'entenc.**	noh luhn-**teng**

Useful Words

Could you speak more slowly, please?	**Pot parlar més a poc a poc, si us plau?**	pot par-**lah mehs** pok uh pok sees plah-oo
I'm sorry.	**Ho sento.**	oo **sehn**-too

big	**gran**	gran
small	**petit**	puh-**teet**
hot	**calent**	kah-**len**
cold	**fred**	fred
good	**bo**	boh
bad	**dolent**	doo-**len**
enough	**bastant**	bahs-**tan**
well	**bé**	beh
open	**obert**	oo-**behr**
closed	**tancat**	tan-**kat**
left	**esquerra**	uhs-**kehr**-ruh
right	**dreta**	**dreh**-tuh
straight on	**recte**	**rehk**-tuh
near	**a prop**	uh **prop**
far	**lluny**	**lyoon**yuh
up/over	**a dalt**	uh **dahl**
down/under	**a baix**	uh **bah**-eeshh
early	**aviat**	uhv-**yat**
late	**tard**	**tahrt**
entrance	**entrada**	uhn-**trah**-thuh
exit	**sortida**	soor-tee-thuh
toilet	**lavabos/ serveis**	luh-**vah**-boos sehr-**beh**-ees
more	**més**	mess
less	**menys**	**men**yees

Shopping

How much does this cost?	**Quant costa això?**	kwahn kost ehs-**shoh**
I would like …	**M'agradaria …**	muh-**grah**-thuh-ree-ah
Do you have?	**Tenen?**	**tehn**-un
I'm just looking, thank you	**Només estic mirant, gràcies.**	noo-mess ehs-teek mee-**rahn** grah-see-uhs
Do you take credit cards?	**Accepten targes de crèdit?**	ak-**sehp**-tuhn tahr-**zhuhs** duh **kreh**-deet
What time do you open?	**A quina hora obren?**	ah **keen**-uh **oh**-ruh **oh**-bruhn
What time do you close?	**A quina hora tanquen?**	ah **keen**-uh **oh**-ruh tan-kuhn
This one.	**Aquest**	ah-**ket**
That one.	**Aquell**	ah-**kehl**
expensive	**car**	kahr
cheap	**bé de preu/ barat**	beh thuh **preh**-oo/bah-**rat**
size (clothes)	**talla/mida**	**tah**-lyah/**mee**-thuh
size (shoes)	**número**	**noo**-mehr-oo
white	**blanc**	blang
black	**negre**	**neh**-gruh
red	**vermell**	vuhr-**mel**
yellow	**groc**	grok

	verd	behrt
	blau	**blah**-oo
ue store	antiquari/	an-tee-kwah-ree/
	botiga	boo-**tee**-gah/dan-
..ry	d'antiguitats	tee-ghee-**tats**
	el forn	uhl **forn**
	el banc	uhl **bang**
..store	la llibreria	lah lyee-bruh-**ree**-ah
..ner's	la carnisseria	**lah kahr**-nee-suh-**ree**-uh
..y shop	la pastisseria	lah pahs-tee-suh-**ree**-uh
..mist's	la farmàcia	lah fuhr-**mah**-see-ah
..monger's	la peixateria	lah peh-shuh-tuh-**ree**-uh
..ngrocer's	la fruiteria	lah froo-**ee**-tuh-**ree**-uh
..r's	la botiga de	lah boo-**tee**-guh duh
	queviures	keh-vee-**oo**-ruhs
..dresser's	la perruqueria	lah peh-roo-kuh-**ree**-uh
..ket	el mercat	uhl muhr-**kat**
..sagent's	el quiosc	uhl kee-**ohsk**
	de premsa	duh **prem**-suh
..office	l'oficina de	loo-fee-**see**-nuh
	correus	duh koo-**reh**-oos
..e store	la sabateria	lah sah-bah-tuh-**ree**-uh
..ermarket	el supermercat	uhl soo-puhr-muhr-**kat**
..cconist's	l'estanc	luhs-**tang**
..el agency	l'agència de	la-**jen**-see-uh duh
	viatges	vee-**ad**-juhs

..htseeing

..jallery	la galeria d'art	lah gah-luh-**ree**-yuh **dart**
..iedral	la catedral	lah kuh-tuh-**thrahl**
..ch	l'església	luhz-**gleh**-zee-uh
	la basílica	lah buh-**zee**-lee-kuh
..en	el jardí	uhl zhahr-**dee**
..ry	la biblioteca	lah bee-blee-oo-**teh**-kuh
..eum	el museu	uhl moo-**seh**-oo
..ist infor	l'oficina de	loo-fee-**see**-nuh
..tion office	turisme	thuh too-**reez**-muh
..n hall	l'ajuntament	luh-djoon-tuh-**men**
..ed for	tancat per	tan **kat** puhr
..day	vacances	bah-**kan**-suhs
..station	l'estació	luhs-tah-see-**oh**
	d'autobusos	dow-toh-**boo**-zoos
..vay	l'estació	luhs-tah-see-**oh**
..ion	de tren	thuh **tren**

..ying in a Hotel

| ..you have | ¿Tenen una | **teh**-nuhn **oo**-nuh |
| ..acant | habitació | ah-bee-tuh-see-**oh** |

room?	lliure?	**lyuh**-ruh
double	habitació	ah-bee-tuh-see-**oh**
room with	doble amb	**doh**-bluh am
double bed	llit de	**lyeet** duh
	matrimoni	mah-tree-**moh**-nee
twin room	habitació	ah-bee-tuh-see-**oh**
	amb dos llits/	am **dohs lyeets**/
	amb llits	s am **lyeets** in-thee-
	individual	vee-thoo-**ahls**
single room	habitació	ah-bee-tuh-see-**oh**
	individual	een-dee-vee-thoo-**ahl**
room with	habitació	ah-bee-tuh-see-**oh**
a bath	amb bany	am **bah**nyuh
shower	dutxa	**doo**-chuh
porter	el grum	uhl **groom**
key	la clau	lah **klah**-oo
I have a	Tinc una	**ting oo**-nuh
reservation	habitació	ah-bee-tuh-see-**oh**
	reservada	reh-sehr-**vah**-thah

Eating Out

Have you got a	Tenen	**teh**-nuhn
table for…	taula per…?	**tow**-luh puhr
I would like	Voldria	vool-**dree**-uh
to reserve	reservar	reh-sehr-**vahr**
a table.	una taula.	**oo**-nuh **tow**-luh
The bill.	El compte,	uhl **kohm**-tuh
please	si us plau.	**sees plah**-oo
I am a	Sóc	**sok** buh-zhuh-tuh-
vegetarian	vegetarià/	ree-**ah**
	vegetariana	buh-zhuh-tuh-ree-**ah**-nah
waitress	cambrera	kam-**breh**-ruh
waiter	cambrer	kam-**breh**
menu	la carta	lah **kahr**-tuh
fixed-price	menú del	muh-**noo** thuhl
menu	dia	**dee**-uh
wine list	la carta de	ah **kahr**-tuh thuh
	vins	**veens**
glass of water	un got d'aigua	oon **got dah**-ee-gwah
glass of wine	una copa de vi	**oo**-nuh **ko**-pah thuh **vee**
bottle	una ampolla	**oo**-nuh am-**pol**-yuh
knife	un ganivet	oon gun-ee-**veht**
fork	una forquilla	**oo**-nuh foor-**keel**-yuh
spoon	una cullera	**oo**-nuh kool-**yeh**-ruh
breakfast	l'esmorzar	les-moor-**sah**
lunch	el dinar	uhl dee-**nah**
dinner	el sopar	uhl soo-**pah**
main course	el primer plat	uhl pree-**meh** plat
starters	els entrants	uhlz ehn-**tranz**
dish of the day	el plat del dia	uhl **plat** duhl **dee**-uh
coffee	el cafè	uhl kah-**feh**
rare	poc fet	**pok fet**
medium	al punt	ahl **poon**
well done	molt fet	mol **fet**

Menu Decoder

l'aigua mineral	**lah**-ee-gwuh mee-nuh-**rahl**	mineral water
sense gas/	**sen**-zuh gas/	still
amb gas	am gas	sparkling
al forn	ahl **forn**	baked
l'all	**lahl**yuh	garlic
l'arròs	lahr-**roz**	rice
les botifarres	lahs **boo**-tee-fah-rahs	sausages
la carn	lah **karn**	meat
la ceba	lah **seh** buh	onion
la cervesa	lah-sehr-**ve**-sah	beer
l'embotit	lum-boo-**teet**	cold meat
el filet	uhl fee-**let**	sirloin
el formatge	uhl for-**mah**-djuh	cheese
fregit	freh-**zheet**	fried
la fruita	lah froo-**ee**-tah	fruit
els fruits secs	uhlz froo-**eets** seks	nuts
les gambes	lahs **gam**-bus	prawns
el gelat	uhl djuh-**lat**	ice cream
la llagosta	lah lyah-**gos**-tah	lobster
la llet	lah **lyet**	milk
la llimona	lah lyee-**moh**-nah	lemon
la llimonada	lah lyee-moh-**nah**-tuh	lemonade
la mantega	lah mahn-**teh**-gah	butter
el marisc	uhl muh-**reesk**	seafood
la menestra	lah muh-**nehs**-truh	vegetable stew
l'oli	**loll**-ee	oil
les olives	luhs oo-**lee**-vuhs	olives
l'ou	**loh**-oo	egg
el pa	uhl **pah**	bread
el pastís	uhl pahs-**tees**	pie/cake
les patates	lahs pah-**tah**-tuhs	potatoes
el pebre	uhl **peh**-bruh	pepper
el peix	uhl **pehsh**	fish
el pernil	uhl puhr-**neel**	cured ham
salat serrà	suh-**lat** sehr-**rah**	
el plàtan	uhl **plah**-tun	banana
el pollastre	uhl poo-**lyah**-struh	chicken
la poma	la **poh**-mah	apple
el porc	uhl **pohr**	pork
les postres	lahs **pohs**-truhs	dessert
rostit	rohs-**teet**	roast
la sal	lah **sahl**	salt
la salsa	lah **sahl**-suh	sauce
les salsitxes	lahs sahl-**see**-chuhs	sausages
sec	**sehk**	dry
la sopa	lah **soh**-puh	soup
el sucre	uhl-**soo**-kruh	sugar
la taronja	lah tuh-**rohn**-djuh	orange
el te	uhl **teh**	tea
les torrades	lahs too-**rah**-thuhs	toast
la vedella	lah veh-**theh**-lyuh	beef
el vi blanc	uhl **bee** blang	white wine
el vi negre	uhl **bee** neh-gruh	red wine
el vi rosat	uhl **bee** roo-**zaht**	rosé wine
el vinagre	uhl bee-**nah**-gruh	vinegar
el xai/el be	uhl **shahe**/uhl beh	lamb
la xocolata	lah shoo-koo-**lah**-tuh	chocolate
el xoriç	uhl shoo-**rees**	red sausage

Numbers

0	**zero**	**seh**-roo
1	**un (masc)**	oon
	una (fem)	**oon**-uh
2	**dos (masc)**	**dohs**
	dues (fem)	**doo**-uhs
3	**tres**	**trehs**
4	**quatre**	**kwa**-truh
5	**cinc**	**seeng**
6	**sis**	**sees**
7	**set**	**set**
8	**vuit**	**voo**-eet
9	**nou**	**noh**-oo
10	**deu**	**deh**-oo
11	**onze**	**on**-zuh
12	**dotze**	**doh**-dzuh
13	**tretze**	**treh**-dzuh
14	**catorze**	kah-**tohr**-dzuh
15	**quinze**	**keen**-zuh
16	**setze**	**set**-zuh
17	**disset**	dee-**set**
18	**divuit**	dee-voo-**eet**
19	**dinou**	dee-**noh**-oo
20	**vint**	**been**
21	**vint-i-un**	been-tee-**oon**
22	**vint-i-dos**	been-tee-**doh**s
30	**trenta**	**tren**-tah
31	**trenta-un**	**tren**-tah oon
40	**quaranta**	kwuh-**ran**-tuh
50	**cinquanta**	seen-**kwahn**-tuh
60	**seixanta**	seh-ee-**shan**-tuh
70	**setanta**	seh-**tan**-tah
80	**vuitanta**	voo-ee-**tan**-tah
90	**noranta**	noh-**ran**-tah
100	**cent**	**sen**
101	**cent un**	**sent oon**
102	**cent dos**	**sen dohs**
200	**dos-cents (masc)**	dohs-**sens**
	dues-centes (fem)	**doo**-uhs **sen**-tuhs
300	**tres-cents**	**trehs**-senz
400	**quatre-cents**	**kwah**-truh-**se**nz
500	**cinc-cents**	**seeng**-senz
600	**sis-cents**	**sees**-senz
700	**set-cents**	**set**-senz
800	**vuit-cents**	**voo**-eet-**senz**
900	**nou-cents**	**noh**-oo-**cenz**
1,000	**mil**	**meel**
1,001	**mil un**	**meel oon**

Time

one minute	**un minut**	**oon** mee-**noo**t
one hour	**una hora**	**oo**-nuh **oh**-ru
half an hour	**mitja hora**	**mee**-juh **oh**-r
Monday	**dilluns**	dee-**lyoonz**
Tuesday	**dimarts**	dee-**marts**
Wednesday	**dimecres**	dee-**meh**-kruh
Thursday	**dijous**	dee-**zhuh**-uos
Friday	**divendres**	dee-**ven**-druhs
Saturday	**dissabte**	dee-**sab**-tuh
Sunday	**diumenge**	dee-oo-**men**-j